The
BOOK
LOVER'S
BUCKET LIST

A Tour of Great British Literature

CAROLINE
TAGGART

WRITERS' MUSEUM

The
BOOK
LOVER'S
BUCKET LIST

A Tour of Great British Literature

CAROLINE
TAGGART

First published in 2021 by
The British Library
96 Euston Road
London NW1 2DB

Text © Caroline Taggart 2021
Images © the British Library and other
named copyright holders 2021

British Library Cataloguing-in-Publication Data
A catalogue record is available from the British Library

ISBN 978 0 7123 5324 3

Designed and typeset by Jason Anscomb
Cover artwork by Joanna Lisowiec
Picture research by Sally Nicholls

Printed in the Czech Republic by Finidr

For Julia – what fun!

Contents

FOREWORD

When people think of places to visit in the United Kingdom, certain obvious attractions come to mind: the Tower of London, the Houses of Parliament, Canterbury Cathedral, Stonehenge, the Colleges at Oxford and Cambridge, the Cavern Club in Liverpool, Hadrian's Wall, Edinburgh Castle.

For book lovers, however, an extra layer of Must-Visits bubbles away under that more touristy list. If you pass through London King's Cross railway station, for example, of course you will be keeping one eye out for Platform 9 ¾. If you're in Lyme Regis on the Jurassic Coast, you'll be drawn to the Cobb to jump off Granny's Teeth as Louisa Musgrove fatefully did. On the Yorkshire Moors, you'll strain to hear Heathcliff and Cathy calling to each other above the wind. If you're walking down London's busy Brick Lane, you may peer into the same shop windows as Nazneen.

The UK is a country chock full of such literary landmarks, not only of locations in books we've loved, but sometimes the spaces where they were written: Dickens' desk at Gad's Hill Place; Hardy's at Max Gate; Roald Dahl's lap desk in his shed in Great Missenden; Jane Austen's little table at Chawton House, and her writing desk in the British Library Treasures Gallery too.

Caroline Taggart has pulled together many of these cherished spots into one tantalising book that will inspire readers to seek them out. It is fitting too that it would be the British Library publishing such a guide to locations connected to some of our best-loved authors, many of whose archives the Library looks after for the nation. Reading this book made me want to drop my pen to go and celebrate my fellow authors in the places they knew well. I hope it has the same effect on you too.

Tracy Chevalier
February 2021

INTRODUCTION

'This is a work of fiction. Names, characters, locales are either the products of the author's imagination or used in a fictitious manner. Any resemblance to actual persons, living or dead, or actual events is purely coincidental.'

You'll have often read something like this at the start of a novel. It's an attempt on the author or publisher's part to avoid being sued. There's even a Wikipedia page called 'All Persons Fictitious Disclaimer'. And it probably serves some useful purpose. But the true lover of fiction – or poetry, or drama – reads it and thinks, 'Yeah, right.' Particularly when it comes to the locales.

A lot of the places described in this book are actually the authors' homes – sometimes their birthplaces, sometimes the houses where they did much of their writing. You'll often find that they look just as the author might have left them, even if that was hundreds of years ago. Dedicated custodians of our literary heritage – whether they're concerned with Beatrix Potter in the Lake District or William Shakespeare in Stratford – try to give the impression that the writer in question has just gone out for a walk. Or possibly, in the case of Dylan Thomas in Laugharne, nipped down to the pub. When you visit these places, you can see where the authors lived and worked, marvel at how small and dark the rooms are, and study the huge amount of crossing out that they did on their manuscripts – William Wordsworth and Seamus Heaney being prime examples of writers who agonised so much you wonder how they got anything published at all. Sometimes you can dress up in their clothes, walk round the gardens that inspired them or, in the case of Rudyard Kipling, covet the Rolls-Royce in which he used to drive through the Sussex countryside and (presumably) impress the neighbours.

One of the reasons for visiting a writer's home is, obviously, that you like their work. Sometimes, though, you'll find yourself in the vicinity of the home of someone you've never heard of, or at least not read. That's no excuse for avoiding the place. It would be a shame to miss Horace Walpole's ridiculously over-the-top Gothic villa in Twickenham, or the Georgian house in Olney where William Cowper kept hares in an attempt to alleviate his depression, just because you weren't well up on *The Castle of Otranto* or a mock-heroic poem about a sofa.

Obviously that's all fun and very often informative as well. But then we come back to that disclaimer. Not every writer lived somewhere grand enough to leave to the nation, or that the nation was interested in accepting. So to celebrate them we have to go to their locations, the undeniably real places that inspired their works and that very often feature in them. Yes, of course, you can stand on the Cobb at Lyme Regis and admire the view without thinking of Anne Elliot or Sarah Woodruff, but if you go there having read *Persuasion* or *The French Lieutenant's Woman* (or both) it'll bring both the place and the books alive in a completely new way. Madresfield Court is magnificent in any context, but you'll feel a special tremor of emotion if you imagine it as Brideshead and see it through Charles Ryder's bedazzled eyes. You can walk across Dartmoor for the views or the good of your health, but think what fun it would be to imagine sinking up to your neck in Grimpen Mire and being savaged by a gigantic hound.

Well, okay, perhaps that's going too far. Let's not be silly. Instead, let's get a bus through Zadie Smith's North London and be on the lookout for:

> **Bank of Iraq, Bank of Egypt, Bank of Libya. Empty cabs on account of the sunshine.**
> **Boomboxes just because. Lone Italian, loafers, lost, looking for Mayfair.**

Or spend an afternoon at Colliers Wood Nature Reserve in Nottinghamshire and look at the lake 'all grey and visionary, stretching into the moist, translucent vista of trees and meadow' that D. H. Lawrence described in *Women in Love*. Let's come back to London and try to push a trolley through the wall of Platform 9¾ at King's Cross Station. That *really* would be meaningless in a world that didn't include Harry Potter.

So that's what this book is about. Read something – a novel, a play, a poem – and go and visit a place associated with it; go somewhere with literary connections and come home and read the book. Those 'somewheres' aren't all great houses or North London bus routes; there are gardens, monuments, museums, churches and a surprising quantity of stained glass. There are walks both urban and rural, where you can explore real landscapes or imaginary haberdasher's shops. There's the club where Buck's Fizz was invented and a pub where you can eat Sherlock's Steak & Ale Pie. There's a railway station where you can stroke the muzzle of one of the world's most famous and endearing bears.

You can start in Cornwall and work your way up to the Scottish Highlands, taking detours to Northern Ireland in the west and Norfolk in the east. Or you can simply amble over to the place nearest to you. Wherever you are in the United Kingdom, you're never far from something associated with a good book.

A NOTE ON VISITING ARRANGEMENTS

Among the many things that have changed as a result of the Covid-19 pandemic are the opening hours of public places. It's also much more likely than it used to be that you'll have to book in advance rather than just turning up. Please check with the site before attempting to visit anywhere mentioned in this book.

1

———

CHAPTER ONE

LONDON

Poets' Corner, Westminster Abbey

GEOFFREY CHAUCER, EDMUND SPENSER AND OTHERS

www.westminster-abbey.org

What better place to start a voyage of literary discovery? A visit to Westminster Abbey is high on any list of heritage destinations in London: don't miss the comparatively new Queen's Diamond Jubilee Galleries, where many of the abbey's treasures are displayed in the thirteenth-century triforium (an arcade above the arches of the main body of the church) and where the views alone are worth the entrance fee. There's also a clue in the name of Poets' Corner: a visit here will yield great dividends in terms of luminaries to whom you can pay your respects.

From the galleries, come back to earth and make your way to the South Transept, where many of Britain's most illustrious writers are celebrated. The tradition of burying poets here began with Geoffrey Chaucer (c. 1340–1400), author of *The Canterbury Tales* (see page 109), although he earned the honour not through his verse but because he was Clerk of the King's Works, responsible for repairs at the abbey. He didn't get the current monument until 1556, by which time his poetry and his influence on the English language were highly regarded; another poet, Nicholas Brigham, had Chaucer's bones moved to their current location and erected a marble tomb for them. Brigham also wrote the Latin inscription, which begins:

> *Of old the bard who struck the noblest strains*
> *Great Geoffrey Chaucer, now this tomb retains.*

Some forty years later, another poet, Edmund Spenser (c. 1553–1599), whose epic *The Faerie Queene* had been written in celebration of Elizabeth I, asked to be buried nearby; it may be that linking himself with his illustrious predecessor was an attempt to ensure that posterity continued to admire him. Certainly the inscription on Spenser's memorial, despite its erratic spelling, is not exactly modest: it describes him as: 'The prince of poets in his tyme whose divine spirit needs noe other witnesse then the works which he left behinde him'.

Spenser's choice of burial site set a precedent – two great poets side by side began to constitute a 'corner' and in the ensuing centuries they were joined by the Jacobean dramatist Francis Beaumont (1584–1616), the lexicographer Samuel Johnson (see page 39), the playwright and politician Richard Brinsley Sheridan (1751–1816), Charles Dickens (see pages 33, 35 and 111), the ashes of Rudyard Kipling (see page 104) and many, many more. Other literary giants who aren't buried here have memorials in the form of inscribed busts, statues, hanging tablets or stones in the floor: these include Shakespeare, Jane Austen, William Blake, the Brontë sisters, Alfred, Lord Tennyson, and, in the twentieth century, T. S. Eliot, P. G. Wodehouse, Philip Larkin and Ted Hughes, all of whom have mentions elsewhere in this book. It's a veritable roll call of British men – and to a lesser extent women – of letters. Space being now at a premium, there is also a stained-glass memorial window which glows, when the light is right, with that vivid electric blue you get only in stained glass. Installed in 1994 with room for twenty names, it currently has only seven incumbents: an eclectic mix of writers that includes

ohn. del.   J.Bluck Aquat

ENTRANCE into POETS CORNER
Westminster Abbey.

| ohn Dryden. | 83. Martha Birch. | 84. A. Cowley. | 85. I. Roberts. | 86. G. Chaucer. | 87. I. Phillips. | 88. B. Booth |
| 4. Drayton. | 90. Ben. Johnson. | 91. S. Butler. | 92. E. Spencer. | 93. I. Milton. | 94. Gray. | 95. C. Anstey |

Publish'd Nov.r 1811, for R.Ackermann's Westm.r Abbey, at 101 Strand, London.

A Part of Prior's Monument.

Shakespeare's contemporary Christopher Marlowe (see page 109), Elizabeth Gaskell (page 156) and Oscar Wilde (page 24).

Memorials in Poets' Corner vary from the grandiose to the surprisingly modest. Charles Dickens's grave is covered by a small stone bearing only his name and the dates of his birth and death; he specified in his will 'that my name be inscribed in plain English letters on my tomb ... I rest my claims to the remembrance of my country upon my published works'.

It's perhaps appropriate that one of the grandest and most eloquent monuments should be Shakespeare's. He is commemorated by a life-sized statue in white marble, with the heads of Elizabeth I, Henry V and Richard III carved into the pedestal on which he leans. In his hand he carries a scroll bearing part of a speech by Prospero in *The Tempest*:

> *The Cloud capt Tow'rs,*
> *The Gorgeous Palaces,*
> *The Solemn Temples,*
> *The Great Globe itself,*
> *Yea all which it Inherit,*
> *Shall Dissolve;*
> *And like the baseless Fabrick of a Vision*
> *Leave not a wreck behind.*

As in Southwark Cathedral (see page 46), you can rely on Shakespeare – and on Prospero in particular – to remind you that life is short. Yet Poets' Corner also brings to mind the rest of that classical aphorism: life may be short, but art endures. Perhaps Spenser was right – what matters are the works you leave behind you.

Theatreland
IVOR NOVELLO, NOËL COWARD
AND HAROLD PINTER

www.delfontmackintosh.co.uk/theatres/
novello-theatre
www.delfontmackintosh.co.uk/theatres/
noel-coward-theatre
www.haroldpintertheatre.co.uk

The first decade or so of this century saw a wave of theatres being renamed: three in the space of six years abandoned their old names and took on the mantle of great twentieth-century playwrights. In 2005 the Strand (on the Aldwych) became the Novello; the following year the Albery (in St Martin's Lane) became the Noël Coward; and in 2011 the Comedy (just off Leicester Square) was renamed in honour of Harold Pinter, who had died three years earlier. A leisurely half-hour stroll will take in all three.

The Novello dates from 1905 and was built as a 'reverse pair' to the Aldwych Theatre, which stands just along the road from it, on the other side of the Waldorf Hotel. A

Grade II listed building, its English Heritage listing describes it endearingly as 'Lively Free Classicism of vaguely Beaux Arts derivation'. A plaque outside tells you that 'Ivor Novello, 1893–1951, Composer and Actor Manager, lived and died in a flat on the top floor of this building'. He'd been there since 1913, and from 1935 onwards it was rare for a Novello musical not to be playing in the West End. Writing both words and music, often directing and starring as well, he gave the British public exactly what they wanted during some very dark years: romantic melodramas, such as *Glamorous Night* (1935) and *Careless Rapture* (1936), with faintly absurd plots and great tunes. The plaque that adorns his birthplace in Cardiff is rather more evocative than the London one: 'This boy became a Ruritanian King who gave his people dreams and songs

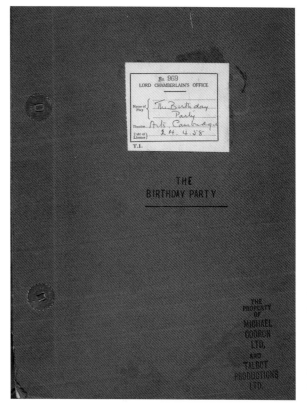

to sing.' His shows are rarely revived, but the songs can still bring a tear to the eye and the Ivors – the songwriters' equivalent of the Oscars – are named after him.

The architect of the Novello – W. G. R. Sprague, who was responsible for several London theatres – had designed the Noël Coward two years earlier; 'Free Classical eclecticism' is English Heritage's somewhat disparaging description, though the interior is more approvingly described as being 'in restrained French neo-classical taste'. The connection with Coward (1899–1973) is that in 1920 he appeared there in his own light comedy *I'll Leave It To You*: it was the first time one of his plays had been performed in the West End. It provoked the *Observer*'s critic to opine that if its author could 'overcome a tendency to smartness', he would 'probably produce a good play one of these days'. The critic wasn't wrong: Coward went on, of course, to write *Private Lives* (1930), *Present Laughter* (1939), *Blithe Spirit* (1941) and others that are frequently revived, though not necessarily at 'his' theatre.

From the Noël Coward, you can walk behind the National Portrait Gallery, past the statue of the great Victorian actor Henry Irving, and on to a rather soulless side street off Leicester Square to find the Harold Pinter. It's older than the other two – first opened in 1881 – and less imaginative in appearance, being a classical design with painted stucco. A number of works by Pinter (1930–2008) had been performed here in the last years of his life and the change of name was a tribute to the man regarded as one of the great and most influential British playwrights of his age. His first play, *The Room*, premiered in

1957; his second, *The Birthday Party* (now regarded as a classic), in 1958. So original was Pinter's approach – a threatening tone interspersed with apparent trivialities, non sequiturs and the famous long pauses – that as early as 1960 the *Times* critic could describe another writer's work as having 'Pinteresque overtones' and assume that readers would know what was meant.

So whether your taste is for Novello's lavishly staged Ruritania, Coward's timeless wit or Pinter's veiled menace, there should be something here, in this compact area of the West End, to please you. And that, as a sinister character in *The Birthday Party* says, is more than true. It's a fact.

The Sherlock Holmes

ARTHUR CONAN DOYLE

www.greeneking-pubs.co.uk/pubs/greater-london/sherlock-holmes

The 1951 Festival of Britain, celebrating the centenary of Prince Albert's Great Exhibition in Hyde Park in London, was designed to be a 'tonic for the nation' – not an international exposition as its predecessor had been, but a nationwide cultural event to raise the spirits of a country still in the grip of post-war austerity. One of its many exhibitions was to be found at Abbey House, 215–229 Baker Street, an art deco building erected in the 1930s as the headquarters of the Abbey National Building Society, at an address that encompassed Sherlock Holmes's fictional 221B.

That exhibition included a painstaking reconstruction of Holmes and Watson's sitting room, with a rack of bottles containing the detective's chemicals on one wall, his violin tucked away in a corner, a pipe on the crowded mantelpiece and just below this a Persian slipper holding tobacco, one of the many features of Holmes's untidiness that enabled Watson to give himself 'virtuous airs' by comparison. There was even a waxwork bust of the great detective himself, shown rather alarmingly with a bullet hole through his forehead. This is a reference to the story 'The Adventure of the Empty House', the one in which Holmes returns after being believed dead for three years; he sets a model of himself in the window at Baker Street to entrap the friends of the late Professor Moriarty when they attempt to murder him. The ruse succeeds, the waxwork is duly shot and the evil Colonel Sebastian Moran arrested.

The Festival of Britain's exhibit also contained a great deal of Holmes memorabilia, including a 1914 poster advertising a performance of 'The Speckled Band' at the Grand Theatre, Southampton, and a copy of Holmes's monograph on the distinction between the ashes of various tobaccos ('with 140 illustrations in colour').

After the festival closed, the exhibition went on a world tour, and on its return in 1957 was purchased by the Northumberland Arms pub just off Trafalgar Square. This may be the expensive hotel mentioned in 'The Adventure of the Noble Bachelor', where a bed for the night costs eight shillings and a glass of sherry eightpence; it's certainly adjacent to the Turkish baths where Holmes and Watson relax at the beginning of 'The Adventure of the Illustrious Client'. If you take a few steps along the lane by the side of the pub and look up and to your right, you can still see one of the entrances to the baths:

the mosaics and decorative rounded arches have a vaguely Turkish appearance and give a tiny suggestion of the luxury that once awaited anyone who ventured inside to sweat away the cares of the day.

Anyway, to get back to 1957, the Northumberland Arms changed its name to the Sherlock Holmes and the exhibition it had bought can be seen on its upper floor to this day.

If the name isn't enough to lure you in, a friendly sign outside the pub welcomes hounds, 'Baskerville or otherwise', and the windows are etched with images of Holmes, Watson and their creator Sir Arthur Conan Doyle (1859–1930), not to mention the trademark violin, magnifying glass, pipe and deerstalker. The pub offers a Holmes ale and a Watson porter and, if you're lucky, a gin of the week called Watson at the Sherlock. There's not much in the stories to indicate that Holmes cared a great deal about food (at the end of 'The Adventure of the Dying Detective' he suggests to Watson that 'something nutritious at Simpson's would not be out of place', but this is after he has been fasting for three days to convince people that he is indeed dying, and he's already admitted that giving up tobacco was the really irksome thing). Still, it would be churlish to quibble at the 'Sherlock Classics' on a menu that includes Sherlock's Steak & Ale Pie, Watson's British Chicken & Woodland Mushroom Pie and Lestrade's Sausage & Mash. You have to admire the cheerful way in which the pub enters into the spirit of its theme.

But wait a minute. Did Moriarty, who famously perished at the Reichenbach Falls in 1893, really – as the menu suggests – eat scampi, a term first recorded in the *Oxford English Dictionary* in 1928? Hmm.

Collier's

Household Number for November

Sherlock Holmes

In this Number Solves
The Mystery of

The
Norwood Builder

Another Tribute to Sherlock Holmes

www.sherlock-holmes.co.uk

Holmes and Watson's faithful housekeeper, Mrs Hudson, wouldn't have approved of people shooting waxworks on her property. For something that comes closer to her standards of domesticity, head back to Baker Street and the Sherlock Holmes Museum at what is now designated Number 221B. There you can see the study, the various bedrooms and an array of wax models portraying scenes from the stories; you can also read extracts from Dr Watson's diaries. For purists there's a particularly nice touch. In 'A Scandal in Bohemia', Holmes explains to Watson the difference between 'seeing' and 'observing'. Watson admits, when asked, that he has seen the steps which lead up from the hall to the study, perhaps hundreds of times:

'Then how many are there?'
'How many? I don't know.'
'Quite so! You have not observed. And yet you have seen. That is just my point. Now, I know that there are seventeen steps, because I have both seen and observed.'

At the museum, the first-floor study is reached by a staircase of precisely seventeen steps.

Jeeves and Wooster's Mayfair

P. G. WODEHOUSE

Pelham Grenville Wodehouse (1881–1975) didn't spend much of his life in London, though a blue plaque in Dunraven Street, Mayfair, marks his one-time residence. A lot of his fiction is set nearby, and you can do an enjoyable, if entirely imaginary, Jeeves and Wooster walk around the area. Start in Berkeley Square, where Bertie Wooster lives when he isn't in the middle of imbroglios in a succession of country houses. Jeeves's club, the Junior Ganymede, is in nearby Curzon Street, and Bertie's Drones is in Dover Street – though Wodehouse is said to have modelled the Drones on Buck's Club in Clifford Street, where the Buck's Fizz was invented. Buck's was founded just after the First World War by a Captain Buckmaster, who wanted something less stuffy than the well-established clubs in St James's (such as, perhaps, the Athenaeum, the inspiration for Wodehouse's Demosthenes Club, to which the formidable 'nerve specialist' Sir Roderick Glossop belongs). Whether Captain Buckmaster specifically wanted his members to organise a Fat Uncles' Sweepstake or to play practical jokes on each other so that one of them fell into the club swimming pool in full evening dress, as members of the Drones do, is not recorded. Buck's Club is housed in an elegant Georgian red-brick building with a handsome nineteenth-century lamp-holder over the doorway, but sadly (as far as the passer-by in search of a 'tissue-restorer' is concerned) it is open only to members.

There used to be a genuine Drones Club in St George Street, a few minutes' walk from the fictional one; there was also for a long time a Drones restaurant in Pont Street, Belgravia. Again, sadly, these are no longer with us. If you want to follow in the footsteps of Catsmeat Potter-Pirbright, Oofy Prosser and their ilk, enlivening your dining experience by throwing bread rolls around, the choice of restaurant is nowadays up to you. But you'd probably be wise to avoid Barribault's. This upper-crust establishment appears in a number of stories (and Wodehouse gives it several different locations), but wherever it is situated it remains intimidating:

> *It can make the wrong sort of client feel more like a piece of cheese – and a cheap yellow piece of cheese at that – than any other similar establishment in the world. The personnel of its staff are selected primarily for their ability to curl the upper lip and raise the eyebrows just that extra quarter of an inch which makes all the difference.*

Decidedly not a place for being boisterous with the bread rolls.

Bertie's Aunt Dahlia's town house is conveniently just round the corner from him, at 47 Charles Street; it's been converted into offices now, but the immaculate sheen on the brass doorknocker suggests there may still be a zealous housemaid in residence. Dahlia, you will remember, is Bertie's 'good and deserving aunt', not to be confused with Aunt Agatha, 'who eats broken bottles and wears barbed wire next to the skin' (and who mercifully resides a safe distance away in Hampshire).

Finally, it is worth toddling along Bond Street in search of Eulalie Soeurs, the ladies' lingerie emporium that was the guilty secret of Bertie's arch-nemesis, the would-be fascist dictator Roderick Spode. Dread of exposure puts an end to Spode's ability to bully, for, as Bertie rightly puts it:

You can't be a successful Dictator and design women's underclothing … One or the other. Not both.

Mimicking Jeeves's response to this observation, you may like to murmur to yourself, 'Precisely, sir.'

The Café Royal
OSCAR WILDE
www.hotelcaferoyal.com

Dropping into the Café Royal, a stone's throw from Piccadilly Circus, you could easily imagine yourself back in 1894, on the fateful day when the Marquess of Queensberry saw his son, Lord Alfred Douglas, having lunch with the notorious Oscar Wilde
(1854–1900). The playwright – whom Queensberry later accused, in a bizarre misspell-
ing, of 'posing as a Sondomite' – had already scandalised society with his only novel, *The
Picture of Dorian Gray* (1891) and its alleged promotion of homosexuality. In the opening
chapter the artist, Basil Hallward, shows the portrait to his friend Lord Henry Wotton
and extols its subject's beauty. It's only after this that we meet Dorian for ourselves:

> *Lord Henry looked at him. Yes, he was certainly wonderfully handsome, with
> his finely-curved scarlet lips, his frank blue eyes, his crisp gold hair. There was
> something in his face that made one trust him at once. All the candour of youth was
> there, as well as all youth's passionate purity. One felt that he had kept himself
> unspotted from the world. No wonder Basil Hallward worshipped him.*

Few people would bat an eyelid nowadays, but Victorian London – and especially the
Marquess of Queensberry – was disgusted. So for Wilde to be having lunch *in a public
restaurant* with the Marquess's son was the last straw, and set in train the series of lit-
igations that eventually sentenced Wilde to hard labour in Reading Gaol, destroyed
his health as well as his reputation and led him to die, aged only forty-six, in exile and
squalor in Paris.

The Café Royal days, though, saw Wilde at the height of his fame, at the centre of
London's literary elite. In the place where artists, writers and musicians flocked to see and
be seen, and which also boasted perhaps the best wine cellar in the world, he would lunch
with George Bernard Shaw (see page 130), the influential American editor Frank Harris
and the artist James McNeill Whistler. Others who might be passing through included the
brilliant young artist Aubrey Beardsley – no stranger to scandal himself, having produced
some decidedly erotic illustrations for the 1894 edition of Wilde's play *Salomé*.

Extensively and expensively restored between 2008 and 2012, the Café Royal retains
much of the gilded glory of Wilde's heyday. For the best of sheer belle époque glamour,
make for the former Grill Room, now known as the Oscar Wilde Lounge, where you can
have afternoon tea. Be sure to splash out on a glass of champagne. He would have done.

If this sounds as if it's beyond your budget, head to Charing Cross, where in a pedes-
trianised area between the station and Trafalgar Square you'll find Maggi Hambling's
1998 sculpture *A Conversation with Oscar Wilde*. Part memorial, part green granite sarcophagus masquerading as a chaise longue, it's adorned with a bust of the writer, smiling
and holding a cigarette. 'Sit down,' he seems to be saying. 'Make yourself comfortable.
Tell me the gossip. Gossip (to quote a character in *Lady Windermere's Fan*) is charming!'
In real life, it's unlikely that many people got a word in when Oscar was in full flow, so
take the opportunity while you can.

Albany

**LORD BYRON, ERNEST WORTHING
AND OTHERS**

The name of this apartment complex on Piccadilly has been much argued about over the years: should it have a definite article or not? Not is generally the preferred answer, on the basis that The Albany sounds like the name of a pub. Before it was (the) Albany, it was Melbourne House, childhood home of Sir William Lamb (later the Prime Minister Lord Melbourne). So its earliest literary connection may be said to be with Sir William's wife Lady Caroline (1785–1828), the one who had a highly publicised affair with Lord Byron (1788–1824) and described him as 'mad, bad and dangerous to know'. Rejected by her lover, Lady Caroline took her revenge in a way that was as public as the affair had been: she published their story in a Gothic novel called *Glenarvon*, which depicted not only Byron and William Lamb, but also other members of the family and of Georgian society in easily recognisable guise. It led to Lady Caroline's social ruin and didn't do Byron's reputation much good either.

By the time this was going on, the Lambs had moved out of Melbourne House and in 1802, after a decade as the residence of Frederick, Duke of York and Albany (hence the modern name), the mansion was converted into sixty-nine apartments (or 'sets') that were let to unmarried gentlemen. From the first it attracted members of the literary world, both in fact and in fiction. Oddly enough, one of the earliest writers to take up residence there was Lord Byron, and Lady Caroline, never one to let an opportunity for outrageousness pass her by, caused one of its earliest scandals: after Byron had ended their affair and at a time when no decent woman would be seen within Albany's portals, she entered his set disguised as a boy. Finding him absent, she left him a note saying, 'Remember me, Byron', which provoked the unloving response:

Remember thee! Aye, doubt it not.
Thy husband too shall think of thee.
By neither shalt thou be forgot,
Thou false to him, thou fiend to me!

Today, you don't have to be a man or disguised as a man to visit Albany, although you can't get beyond the courtyard without an invitation. That courtyard is worth a stroll, though, because it is a step back in time, a dignified haven only a few steps from bustling Piccadilly. The house is three storeys high, a picture of Georgian elegance, and flanks three sides of the yard; if you are of an architectural bent you can admire the pulvinated friezes. Alternatively, savour the list of famous literary residents: Arnold Bennett, Bruce Chatwin, Graham Greene, Aldous Huxley, J. B. Priestley, Terence Rattigan and, in a rare departure from the 'no women, no pets, no musical instruments' rule, the romantic novelist Georgette Heyer and the novelist and journalist Sybille Bedford, who for a while slept on Huxley's sofa ('not quite long enough').

There's an array of fictional residents, too, notably Jack Worthing, posing as his non-existent but reprehensible brother Ernest in Oscar Wilde's *The Importance of Being Earnest*. There's also a minor character in Wilde's *The Picture of Dorian Gray* (Lord Fermor, 'a genial if somewhat rough-mannered old bachelor, whom the outside world called selfish because it derived no particular benefit from him') and, going down the social scale somewhat, the moneylender 'Fascination' Fledgeby in Dickens's *Our Mutual Friend*, who is miserly even about breakfast:

> *Present on the table, one scanty pot of tea, one scanty loaf, two scanty pats of butter, two scanty rashers of bacon, two pitiful eggs, and an abundance of handsome china bought a secondhand bargain.*

But the best description perhaps comes in the novels by E. W. Hornung (1866–1921) about the gentleman thief Raffles, who also plays cricket for England (as an amateur or 'gentleman', of course):

> *The room was the good-sized, square one, with the folding doors, the marble mantel-piece, and the gloomy, old-fashioned distinction peculiar to the Albany. It was charmingly furnished and arranged, with the right amount of negligence and the right amount of taste.*

So stand in that courtyard and imagine Lady Caroline Lamb's hysteria, Oscar Wilde's cucumber sandwiches or Raffles's whisky and soda – all human life has passed here.

A Piccadilly footnote: you might expect Dorothy L. Sayers's aristocratic detective Lord Peter Wimsey – a bachelor until he is well into his forties – to be an Albany resident, but no. He has rooms at 110A Piccadilly, a fictional address further down the street, opposite Green Park.

'The African's' Tomb, Tottenham Court Road
OLAUDAH EQUIANO
amchurch.co.uk

On the fringes of Fitzrovia, on the side of a nondescript building belonging to University College London, is a plaque with an unusual dedication: to Olaudah Equiano (1745–1797), 'the African'. On this site, we are told, he lived and published in

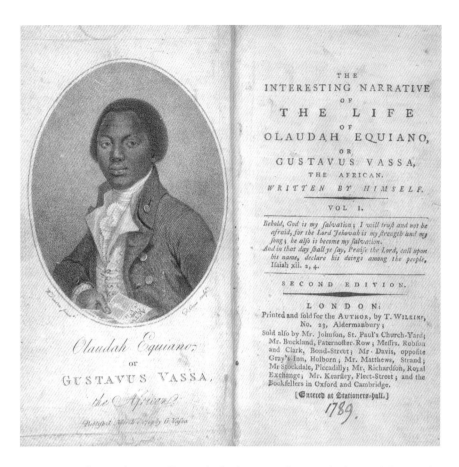

THE

INTERESTING NARRATIVE

OF

THE LIFE

OF

OLAUDAH EQUIANO,

OR

GUSTAVUS VASSA,

THE AFRICAN.

WRITTEN BY HIMSELF.

VOL I.

*Behold, God is my falvation; I will truft and not be
afraid, for the Lord Jehovah is my ftrength and my
fong; he alfo is become my falvation.
And in that day fhall ye fay, Praife the Lord, call upon
his name, declare his doings among the people.*
Ifaiah xii. 2, 4.

SECOND EDITION.

LONDON:
Printed and fold for the AUTHOR, by T. WILKINS,
No. 23, Aldermanbury;
Sold alfo by Mr. Johnfon, St. Paul's Church-Yard;
Mr. Buckland, Paternofter-Row; Meffrs. Robfon
and Clark, Bond-Street; Mr. Davis, oppofite
Gray's-Inn, Holborn; Mr. Matthews, Strand;
Mr Stockdale, Piccadilly; Mr. Richardfon, Royal
Exchange; Mr. Kearfley, Fleet-Street; and the
Bookfellers in Oxford and Cambridge.

[Entered at Stationers-hall.]

1789.

Olaudah Equiano,

or

GUSTAVUS VASSA,

the African.

1789 'his autobiography on suffering the barbarity of slavery, which paved the way for its abolition'. The book was entitled *The Interesting Narrative of the Life of Olaudah Equiano, or Gustavus Vassa, the African,* so before you've even opened it you have an indication of the indignities – and, of course, much worse – that slaves suffered: Equiano was more than once given a new name at the whim of a new master.

Equiano had been born free in what is now Nigeria, where his father was wealthy enough to own slaves himself, but he was kidnapped as a child and taken as a slave to the Caribbean. His account of his experiences on the journey is chillingly matter-of-fact:

I became so sick and low that I was not able to eat, nor had I the least desire to taste any thing. I now wished for the last friend, death, to relieve me; but soon, to my grief, two of the white men offered me eatables; and, on my refusing to eat, one of them held me fast by the hands, and laid me across I think the windlass, and tied my feet, while the other flogged me severely ... the crew used to watch us very closely who were not chained down to the decks, lest we should leap into the water: and I have seen some of these poor African prisoners most severely cut for attempting to do so, and hourly whipped for not eating.

Having survived these horrors, Equiano lived an extraordinary life. Accompanying his master to sea during the Seven Years War (1756–63), he served both as a valet and as a ship's hand while barely into his teens. Unusually for a slave he was taught to read and write, and became a valuable agent in his master's trading enterprises, travelling as far afield as the Arctic, Madeira and Philadelphia, where he was impressed by the preaching of the English evangelist George Whitefield. At the age of not much more than twenty he was able to buy his freedom (for about £5,500 in today's terms) and set up in business on his own. From then on he was based in London, where he became involved in the emerging campaign to abolish the slave trade, travelling the country to lecture on the subject. By the time he came to publish his memoir, he was sufficiently well connected for his subscribers to include His Royal Highness the Prince of Wales and His Royal Highness the Duke of York (the future King George IV and his brother), as well as numerous members of the peerage, the aristocracy and the church. In a dedication to 'the Lords Spiritual and Temporal, and the Commons of the Parliament of Great Britain', Equiano wrote that the chief design of 'the following genuine Narrative' was:

> *to excite in your august assemblies a sense of compassion for the miseries which the Slave-Trade has entailed on my unfortunate countrymen. … May the God of heaven inspire your hearts with peculiar benevolence on that important day when the question of Abolition is to be discussed, when thousands, in consequence of your Determination, are to look for Happiness or Misery!*

It was nearly twenty years before the Slave Trade Act made the trade illegal throughout the British Empire, and a further twenty-five before slavery itself was banned, but there's no doubt that the *Interesting Narrative*, which was hugely successful and reprinted eight times in the few years that remained of the author's life, was a major factor in changing public opinion.

Equiano was buried in the small churchyard adjoining the Whitefield Tabernacle (one of several founded by followers of the evangelist mentioned a moment ago) in Tottenham Court Road, where he is assumed to have worshipped. The tabernacle was destroyed during the Second World War and replaced by a building now occupied by the American International Church. The graveyard, too, has disappeared; it lies beneath a children's playground and a small public park, meaning that there is somewhere pleasant for you to sit and ponder this remarkable man.

A near contemporary of Equiano, Ottobah Cugoano was born in present-day Ghana around 1757 and, like Equiano, was kidnapped into slavery as a boy. He too endured the horrors of captivity in the Caribbean and eventually gained his freedom in London, where he became a servant to the artists Richard and Maria Cosway. A plaque on the wall of their former home at 80–82 Pall Mall commemorates him as an 'author and anti-slavery campaigner'. His book of *Thoughts and Sentiments on the Evil and Wicked Traffic of the Slavery and Commerce of the Human Species*, in the collection of the British Library, is as chilling as Equiano's and if anything even more impassioned: Africans, he wrote,

> *are born as free, and are brought up with as great a predilection for their own country, freedom and liberty, as the sons and daughters of fair Britain.*

The 'Ministry of Truth', Malet Street

GEORGE ORWELL

www.senatehouseevents.co.uk

Winston kept his back turned to the telescreen. It was safer, though, as he well knew, even a back can be revealing. A kilometre away the Ministry of Truth, his place of work, towered vast and white above the grimy landscape. ... The Ministry of Truth – Minitrue, in Newspeak – was startlingly different from any other object in sight. It was an enormous pyramidal structure of glittering white concrete, soaring up, terrace after terrace, 300 metres into the air. From where Winston stood it was just possible to read, picked out on its white face in elegant lettering, the three slogans of the Party:

WAR IS PEACE
FREEDOM IS SLAVERY
IGNORANCE IS STRENGTH

The Ministry of Truth contained, it was said, three thousand rooms above ground level, and corresponding ramifications below.

This passage is taken from George Orwell's *Nineteen Eighty-Four* (1949), but in real life it's a description of Senate House in Malet Street, the imposing art deco administrative centre of the University of London. During the Second World War it was co-opted as the headquarters of the Ministry of Information, a government department which existed only during the two world wars and was in charge of propaganda: a suitably Orwellian concept. The building is accessible only to those visiting the library or attending events but, if you can get in, the galleried foyer, the main staircase and some of the halls that are available for hire are frankly glorious; from the outside you can see why the building has been described as Stalinist and why Winston Smith looked at it with such dread.

Best known now for his novels, George Orwell (1903–1950) was one of the finest journalists of his day and was described (by *Newsweek* magazine in 1969) as 'the foremost architect of the English essay since Hazlitt, perhaps since Dr Johnson'. As Hazlitt had died in 1830 and Johnson in 1784, this was a formidable compliment. If you want to celebrate Orwell's journalistic style in the capital, your best bet is the 1933 memoir *Down and Out in Paris and London*, in which he details the time he spent in the company of tramps, learning to live – 'food, bed, tobacco, and all' – at the rate of half a crown (12½p) a day. He covered a lot of ground during this time, but perhaps the benches along the Embankment, where people sleep rough to this day, are as evocative as any landmark. Here Orwell recorded the reflections of his friend Bozo:

Sometimes, he said, when sleeping on the Embankment, it had consoled him to look up at Mars or Jupiter and think that there were probably Embankment sleepers there. He had a curious theory about this. Life on earth, he said, is harsh because the planet is poor in the necessities of existence. Mars, with its cold climate and scanty water, must be far poorer, and life correspondingly harsher. Whereas on earth you are merely imprisoned for stealing sixpence, on Mars you are probably boiled alive. This thought cheered Bozo, I do not know why. He was a very exceptional man.

An Abolitionist's Plaque

MARY PRINCE

On the wall of Senate House, Malet Street – on which Orwell based his Ministry of Truth, effectively a monument to slavery (see page 30) – is an unobtrusive plaque that you could easily walk past without noticing. It tells you simply that 'Mary Prince, abolitionist and author, lived in a house near this site 1829'.

Mary Prince (c. 1788–after 1833) may not be a household name, but as the first woman to publish a memoir about slavery (and possibly the first black woman to publish any memoir in Britain), she surely deserves to be. Born in Bermuda, the daughter of slaves, she was herself first sold into slavery at the age of ten. Her account of the brutality of her life is unsparing:

When we were ill, let our complaint be what it might, the only medicine given to us was a great bowl of hot salt water, with salt mixed with it, which made us very sick. If we could not keep up with the rest of the gang of slaves, we were put in the stocks, and severely flogged the next morning.

In 1828 Mary was brought to London, where trading in slaves had been abolished, but owning them was still legal. She was in poor health and unable to work hard enough to satisfy her master and mistress:

When the great washing came round, which was every two months, my mistress got together again a great many heavy things, such as bed-ticks, bed-coverlets, &c. for me to wash. I told her I was too ill to wash such heavy things that day. She said, she supposed I thought myself a free woman, but I was not; and if I did not do it directly I should be instantly turned out of doors.

In due course she was indeed turned out of the house and eventually found work with the Scottish abolitionist Thomas Pringle. He gave her the opportunity to write and to publish her life story, *The History of Mary Prince*, in 1831. The book caused outrage among opponents of the anti-slavery movement and provoked two libel cases, at both of which Mary testified. At the same time, its emphasis on personal details and the day-to-day sufferings of a slave introduced a new aspect to the abolitionist debate and made a not insignificant contribution to the passing of the Slavery Abolition Act in 1833. After that, we don't know what happened to her. Did she gain her freedom? Did she return to Antigua and the husband from whom she had been forcibly separated years earlier? Did she succumb to the ill health that had dogged her for much of her life? No one is sure. An exhibition about slavery at the Museum of London Docklands acknowledges Mary Prince's 'crucial role in the abolition campaign', but the woman herself seems to have vanished from the records. Yet thanks to that brief period in the limelight, she made a lasting change.

The Dickens Museum
CHARLES DICKENS

dickensmuseum.com

Charles Dickens (1812–1870) had various addresses in London over the years, but 48 Doughty Street, Bloomsbury – now the Dickens Museum – is the only one you can visit. He moved there with his wife Kate and infant son, also Charles, in 1837 and lived there less than three years, but that period marked the beginning of his break-through from jobbing journalist and sketch writer to hugely successful novelist. To visit the museum is to get an impression of just how manically productive he was – you can see the study in which he sat conscientiously every morning, writing solidly for four hours and producing in remarkably short time *Nicholas Nickleby*, *Oliver Twist* and the later instalments of *The Pickwick Papers*.

You also gain an insight into his private life. Two more children were born here and Kate's seventeen-year-old sister Mary, who lived with them, died. Dickens was so grief-stricken that he missed that month's deadlines for the next instalments of his books – unheard of for someone with his journalistic background. He later used Mary as a model for many of the improbably pure and innocent female characters

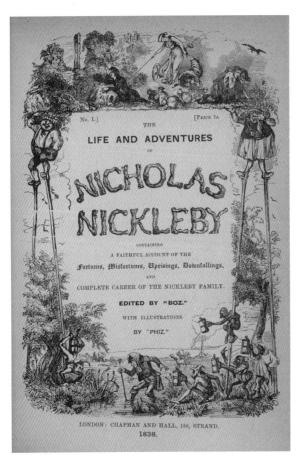

who people his novels: Rose Maylie in *Oliver Twist*, Little Nell in *The Old Curiosity Shop* and Florence Dombey in *Dombey and Son*.

As you progress through the house you can see that he was becoming prosperous: there's a pump in the kitchen, meaning that water was effectively 'on tap' and no one had to go out into the street with a bucket to collect it. The cosy nursery provides a stark contrast to Dickens's own street-roaming childhood when his father was imprisoned for debt and, as he himself said, he could easily have turned into the sort of 'little criminal' he immortalised in *Oliver Twist*. But, lest we forget those dismal years, there's also an iron grille from the Marshalsea Prison, through which the elder Dickens would have gazed out onto the outside world.

In the dining room you're back to prosperity: the table is set for a lavish dinner, while in a corner cabinet nestles a set of silver ladles used for serving punch. They're decorated with images of characters from *The Pickwick Papers* and were presented to Dickens by his publishers to celebrate his finishing the book.

During his Doughty Street years he was also an increasingly important member of London literary circles: friends came round in the evening, not only for dinner and conversation, but also to listen to Dickens reading extracts from his latest writings. In later life he became renowned for his public readings – a first for an established author, and eventually an even greater money-spinner than the books themselves. They were more like theatrical one-man shows than simple readings, and in the museum you can see the copies that he used as scripts, with significant passages underlined, serious social commentary (which he considered inappropriate for an evening of light entertainment) crossed out and handwritten 'stage directions' to himself in the margin. There's also the reading desk which he dismantled and took with him when he did his reading tours of the United States.

There's always something unusual going on in Doughty Street, too: special exhibitions in recent years have included 'Dickens and the Business of Christmas', acknowledging the extraordinary influence that *A Christmas Carol* has had on the way we celebrate, and 'Dickens the Campaigner', emphasising the concern for social justice that underpins much of his work.

In contrast to all this energy, the museum's café, in the peaceful courtyard at the back of the house, is one of the most delightful in London. It's a pleasure to sit there and relax while contemplating Dickens's remarkable work ethic. Be careful which seat you choose, though, for as he himself wrote (in *Martin Chuzzlewit*) 'the privileges of the side-table' include 'the small prerogatives of sitting next the toast, and taking two cups of tea to other people's one'.

Dickens's London
CHARLES DICKENS

www.viaducttavern.co.uk

the-old-curiosity-shop.com

Quite a few of Dickens's heroes start life outside London and come to the metropolis to seek their fortune. Because they come from different parts of the country and arrive in different parts of town, we get various first impressions, but dirt and confusion seem to loom large. In *Oliver Twist*, Fagin's den is in Saffron Hill, the dirtiest and most wretched place that Oliver has ever seen:

> *Covered ways and yards, which here and there diverged from the main street, disclosed little knots of houses, where drunken men and women were positively wallowing in the filth; and from several of the door-ways, great ill-looking fellows were cautiously emerging, bound, to all appearance, on no very well-disposed or harmless errands.*

In *Great Expectations*, Pip, also newly arrived, finds himself in Smithfield:

> *the shameful place, being all asmear with filth and fat and blood and foam, seemed to stick to me. So, I rubbed it off with all possible speed by turning into a street where I saw the great black dome of Saint Paul's bulging at me from behind a grim stone building which a bystander said was Newgate Prison. Following the wall of the jail, I found the roadway covered with straw to deaden the noise of passing vehicles; and from this, and from the quantity of people standing about, smelling strongly of spirits and beer, I inferred that the trials were on.*

And *Bleak House* famously begins with a description of 'implacable November weather':

> *As much mud in the streets, as if the waters had but newly retired from the face of the earth, and it would not be wonderful to meet a Megalosaurus, forty feet long or so, waddling like an elephantine lizard up Holborn-hill. Smoke lowering down from chimney-pots, making a soft black drizzle, with flakes of soot in it as big as full-grown snowflakes – gone into mourning, one might imagine, for the death of the sun.*

Things have changed quite a bit since Dickens's time, obviously. Even in November,

F.P.Millhorpe

"Has it long gone the half-hour?"

Holborn is less muddy than it used to be, and Saffron Hill is disappointingly salubrious. The meat market in Smithfield is still there, but today's hygiene standards have put paid to the worst of the filth, fat, blood and foam; the area abounds with smart restaurants and coffee shops. You can still get a bit of ghoulish pleasure by venturing round the corner, as Pip did. Newgate Prison is long gone: the Central Criminal Court or Old Bailey, which for centuries stood alongside the prison, now occupies part of its site. Some of the prison cells, however, can still be seen (by prior arrangement) under the Viaduct Tavern in Newgate Street – a resplendent Victorian gin palace from whose windows you can see the site where public hangings took place until 1868.

Less ghoulishly, you can visit the Old Curiosity Shop in Portsmouth Street (close to Lincoln's Inn, which features prominently in *Bleak House*). Sitting rather incongruously among the recently refurbished buildings of the London School of Economics, it's a quaint, crooked sixteenth-century structure that ranks as one of the city's oldest shops, among the few to survive the Great Fire of 1666. In the course of its history it has been both a dairy and a bookstore, as well as an antiques shop; now it specialises in upmarket shoes, including a style called Quilp, after the villain of *The Old Curiosity Shop*. The shop wasn't given its current name until after Dickens's novel was published, but may well have been his inspiration: he was living just round the corner and is known to have visited it. He describes Little Nell's home as:

> *one of those receptacles for old and curious things which seem to crouch in odd corners of this town and to hide their musty treasures from the public eye in jealousy and distrust. There were suits of mail standing like ghosts in armour here and there, fantastic carvings brought from monkish cloisters, rusty weapons of various kinds, distorted figures in china and wood and iron and ivory: tapestry and strange furniture that might have been designed in dreams.*

It's hard to believe that he didn't have his own local curiosity shop in mind.

Bunhill Fields

WILLIAM BLAKE

www.cityoflondon.gov.uk/things-to-do/city-gardens/find-a-garden/bunhill-fields-burial-ground

www.sjp.org.uk

Surviving today as a 4-acre site just outside the City of London, Bunhill Fields became a formal burial ground at the time of the Great Plague in 1665. I say 'formal' because its name derives from 'Bone Hill' and it may have been used as a cemetery as far back as Saxon times; it's certainly on record that a thousand cartloads of human bones were brought here when St Paul's charnel house (a vault where human remains were stored) was demolished in 1549. Its significance from the seventeenth century until 1854, when it was deemed to be full and closed for further burials, was that it was not consecrated ground attached to an Anglican church. This made it particularly popular with Non-conformists (Protestant Christians who were not members of the Church of England). Such people were often also known as Dissenters, and a number of the writers who were eventually laid to rest in Bunhill Fields seem to have made a point of voicing their dissent. John Bunyan (see page 128) is one example; Daniel Defoe (1660–1731), author of *Robinson Crusoe* and of various political and religious pamphlets that were always getting him into trouble, is another. A third, who is buried close to them, is the writer, artist, engraver and mystic William Blake (1757–1827).

Unlike his cemetery companions, Blake never actually served a prison term, though he was at one point charged with assaulting a soldier who had trespassed in his garden and with uttering seditious expressions against the king. Best remembered now as the author of the decidedly unseditious 'Jerusalem', he took a fair few risks with his anti-clerical writings and his publications included such controversial titles as *There Is No Natural Religion* and *All Religions Are One,* while his *The Marriage of Heaven and Hell* includes a section in which he sides with the character of Satan in Milton's *Paradise Lost.*

For a while Blake had a wealthy patron in the poet William Hayley (1745–1820), hugely popular in his day but derided by Byron and regarded by Southey as good in 'everything except his poetry'. For three years, from 1800 to 1803, Blake lived near Hayley in the Sussex village of Felpham and worked with him. You can walk past his cottage in the aptly named Blakes Road and a stained-glass window installed as recently as 2011 in the church of St Mary's commemorates his work. In it, two angels stand in adjacent panels, each carrying a sphere adorned with imagery from Blake's writings and art: Adam and Eve after the Fall, a serpent, a tiger (or Tyger) and other birds and beasts. Below them, panels depicting images from nature are framed by lines from 'Auguries of Innocence':

To see a World in a Grain of Sand
And a Heaven in a Wild Flower
Hold Infinity in the palm of your hand
And Eternity in an hour

It's part of the appeal of this modern window, designed by stained-glass artist Meg Lawrence, that it feels entirely in keeping with the tone of this twelfth-century church. It's as beautiful and as full of complicated messages as Blake could have wished.

Blake returned to the capital in 1804 and, despite his energy, his versatility and his undoubted if unconventional brilliance, he never made much money. When he died, he was buried in an unmarked spot in Bunhill Fields; the headstone indicating that he and his wife Catherine lay 'near by' wasn't erected until 1927, the hundredth anniversary of his death. Then in 2018, after years of detective work on the part of two enthusiasts, the site was pinpointed more accurately and a new stone commissioned: it describes Blake as 'Poet, Artist, Prophet'.

In 2011 Bunhill Fields was declared a Grade I park, indicating that the site is of 'exceptional interest'. At the time, the English Heritage historian who advised the government on granting this status remarked:

Paradoxically, the fact that many of those buried here would cheerfully have damned one another to hell on some minute point of theological dispute has brought them all together in this peaceful place ... Many of these people suffered a lifetime's persecution for their beliefs before coming to rest here.

There's another tribute to Blake to be found nearer the centre of London. Although his father was a Dissenter, the baby William was baptised into the Church of England, in the spectacular Grinling Gibbons font in St James's, Piccadilly. The Blake Society, whose mission is to 'continue the work that Blake began: exploring new modes of expression, and awakening the artist and prophet in each individual', is based at the church and holds regular meetings there. And if you're feeling energetic there's always the Autumn Equinox procession on Primrose Hill (see page 57).

Dr Johnson's House
SAMUEL JOHNSON
www.drjohnsonshouse.org *Closed on Sundays and Bank Holidays.*

You always get the impression that Samuel Johnson (1709–1784) was something of a smart alec, fond of the sound of his own voice. Certainly his oft-quoted maxims suggest that he was good at coining phrases that would find their way down to posterity: his famous definition of oats as 'a grain, which in England is generally given to horses, but in Scotland supports the people' and his view that a woman preaching was 'like a dog's walking on his hind legs. It is not done well; but you are surprised to find it done at all' surely can't have come off the top of his head. So you may well visit his house in Gough Square, a peaceful spot just off Fleet Street, with a certain amount of trepidation: you feel you ought to go, but you're not really expecting to like it.

If that is the case, you're in for a pleasant surprise. Johnson came from an unpretentious background in Lichfield and never really hit the big time financially. He won a place at Oxford but left after little more than a year because he couldn't afford the fees. When, in 1746, he was commissioned by a consortium of booksellers-cum-publishers to write what turned out to be his great *Dictionary of the English Language,* he was a struggling hack. After it was published in 1755, he was acclaimed for his scholarship; seven years later, he was awarded an annual pension of £300 by the king, but that made him comfortable rather than rich. The house in Gough Square, in which he lived from 1748 to 1759, is modest, unassuming and welcoming.

It's a four-storey town house, and the only one of a late seventeenth-century development to survive. After Johnson's time it was used as a hotel, a print shop and a storehouse and was 'forlorn and dilapidated' when newspaper magnate Cecil Harmsworth bought it in 1911. His intention was always to open it to the public as 'Dr Johnson's House' and he restored many of the original features, including formidable fireplaces, a pine staircase that extends up to all four storeys (and provides a downward view to be avoided by the faint-hearted), and such quirky security devices as a heavy chain with a corkscrew latch and a spiked iron bar over the fanlight in the front door. On the first floor can be seen hinged panels that close to divide one large room into two smaller ones with a landing between; on the ground floor there is a powder closet in which Johnson would have stored his wigs.

Very little of the furniture and décor is Johnson's own, however. There's no pretence that the house is 'as he would have left it', though you can see his walking stick and a letter case that belonged to him. It is predominantly a museum dedicated to his life and work. But Harmsworth was adamant that everything in it should be *appropriate* to Johnson – he apparently turned down an offer of Chippendale furniture which, although of the right period, would have been beyond Johnson's means. He also refused to exhibit Johnson's death mask – 'too gloomy' – though, according to the custom of the time, the artist Joshua Reynolds had ordered one to be made and multiple copies seem to have been handed out to the deceased's friends. The Department of Anatomy at Edinburgh University owns a cast, and a bust based on it is in the collection of the National Portrait Gallery in London, should you be interested.

The dictionary was a labour of considerable love. Failing to enlist the support of a wealthy patron that might have underwritten such an undertaking, Johnson set to work more or less on his own. According to *The Making of Johnson's Dictionary* by Swiss academic Allen Reddick:

> *At large tables in a garret in Gough Square, Johnson gathered thousands of quotations from past English writers, with his only assistance provided by a rag-tag group of predominantly Scottish ne'er-do-wells.*

The garret is the high point (in more ways than one) of the house in Gough Square. Here you can leaf through a copy of the dictionary and marvel at its extraordinary range and depth. Dip in anywhere and you find gems:

> *Orniscopist: one who examines the flight of birds in order to foretell futurity.*

Or this splendid alternative to what we now call a wishbone:

> *Merrythought: a forked bone on the body of fowls; so called because boys and girls pull in play at the two sides, the longest part broken off betokening priority of marriage.*

The dictionary is not perfect – Noah Webster (1758–1843), the first great American lexicographer, complained that not a single page was correct. Even if that remark can be dismissed as sour grapes or professional jealousy, it's hard to deny that defining 'network' as 'any thing reticulated or decussated, at equal distances, with interstices between the intersections' is perhaps a bit obscure. In the end there is something endearing about the man, not known for his modesty, who could say of his own work that:

> *Dictionaries are like watches, the worst is better than none, and the best cannot be expected to go quite true.*

The GREAT FIRE of LONDON in the Year 1666.

Pepys's London
SAMUEL PEPYS

www.ahbtt.org.uk

saintolave.com

Many London tour groups offer a 'Pepys walk', a guide to Pepys's London, but there's no reason why you shouldn't organise one for yourself, reliving the horrors of the Great Fire of 1666, which Samuel Pepys (1633–1703) experienced at first hand and which he described in probably the greatest diary ever published.

At the time of the fire, Pepys was living in Seething Lane, a few minutes' walk from the Tower of London. This was official accommodation, next to the Navy Office where he worked, and the existing Seething Lane Gardens must be very close to where he recorded that he had buried his wine and expensive Parmesan cheeses to protect them from the fire.

Just moments away, in the direction of the river, is the church of All Hallows by the Tower, from which he watched the fire spread across the City:

*I up to the top of Barking steeple, and there saw the saddest sight of desolation that I
ever saw; every where great fires, oyle-cellars, and brimstone, and other things burning.
I became afeard to stay there long, and therefore down again as fast as I could, the fire
being spread as far as I could see it.*

Having survived the fire, All Hallows was badly damaged in the Blitz and rebuilt in the
1950s, but the seventeenth-century brick tower – the one that Pepys climbed via what is
now called the Pepys door – is still intact.

Pepys's parish church wasn't All Hallows, though. It was St Olave, described by John
Betjeman (see page 60) as 'a country church in the world of Seething Lane' and by
its own website as having 'the timeless atmosphere of a modest ancient parish church
in the heart of the modern City'. The flames of the Great Fire are said to have come
within 90 metres or so of the building, which was saved only because the wind changed
direction and carried the conflagration away. Another victim of Second World War
bombing, it too retains its seventeenth-century tower; the rest was rebuilt in its original
(fifteenth-century) style. Pepys referred to it affectionately as 'our own church', though
he more than once complained of hearing a dull sermon here. When his wife Elizabeth
died in 1669, at the age of only twenty-nine, she was buried in St Olave and Pepys had
a monument erected in her memory – a bust that leans out from the wall, as if keeping
an eye on the place where her husband used to sit, in the gallery opposite, which has
long since been dismantled. Pepys himself lived for another thirty-four years and died
in Clapham, but his body was carried back to St Olave and buried close to Elizabeth's;
his memorial now stares back at hers across the nave.

To return to the days of the Great Fire, Pepys got as far west as St Paul's and watched
it being destroyed:

*saw all the towne burned, and a miserable sight of Paul's Church; with all the roofs
fallen, and the body of the quire [choir] fallen into St. Fayth's.*

He also collected and kept by him:

*a piece of glass of Mercers' Chappel in the street, where much more was, so melted and
buckled with the heat of the fire, like parchment.*

If you continue to walk west, you'll come to a plaque commemorating Pepys's birth,
in Salisbury Court, just off Fleet Street; it's in the shadow of St Bride's Church, where
he was christened. Further west again, close to Charing Cross Station, is Buckingham
Street, where he lived in post-diary days (1679–88) before retiring from public life after
the enforced abdication of James II: another plaque marks the spot, at Number 12.

Although Pepys spent much of his working life at court at Whitehall and his leisure
time in the taverns of Southwark, he'll be forever associated with the City and those terrifying days and nights in early September 1666, when 'all over the Thames, with one's
face in the wind, you were almost burned with a shower of firedrops'. Wander along
Seething Lane and the streets around it with Pepys's words ringing in your ears and you
can imagine that you can still smell the smoke.

CHAPTER ONE: LONDON

Hawksmoor's Churches

PETER ACKROYD

www.stgeorgesbloomsbury.org.uk

www.ccspits.org

stanneslimehouse.org

www.st-alfege.org.uk

www.stgeorgeintheeast.org

stml.org.uk

I f you have a day to spare, you can do a walking tour of Nicholas Hawksmoor's six London churches; if not, skip the one in Bloomsbury and the one in Greenwich and you'll find four reasonably close together. Hawksmoor (c. 1661–1736) may be less famous than his mentor Christopher Wren, but he was a genius in his own right. He contributed to Castle Howard (see page 126) and Blenheim Palace and was one of several architects commissioned in 1711 to build fifty new churches to support London's burgeoning population.

The six wholly designed by Hawksmoor are St George's Bloomsbury; Christ Church Spitalfields; St Anne's Limehouse; St Alfege Greenwich; St George in the East; and St Mary Woolnoth. They're all fine examples of English baroque, with all the fancy adornment that that term implies. In his *England's Thousand Best Churches,* Simon Jenkins remarks that Hawksmoor is 'never retiring' and his churches are 'in a class of their own, powerful and eccentric'. Jenkins speaks of the 'barley-sugar columns and cherubs galore' in St Mary Woolnoth and describes the west front of Christ Church Spitalfields as 'a soaring compilation of architectural shapes, apparently intended purely as theatre'. The distinctive 'pepper pot' towers of St George in the East survived the Second World War bombing that destroyed the original interior; the architectural historian Ian Nairn, writing about the 1960s restoration, said, 'This is a stage somewhere beyond fantasy ... it is the more-than-real world of the drug addict's dream.'

In short, there is much to admire and to gasp at, before you delve into anything more sinister.

Among the forms that Hawksmoor garnered 'from an entire thesaurus of styles and motifs' (according to architecture journalist Gillian Darley), there are undeniable pagan and pre-Christian influences. The steeple of St George's Bloomsbury, resembling a stepped pyramid and inspired by the Mausoleum at Halicarnassus, one of the Seven Wonders of the Ancient World, is perhaps the most famous. It may be these touches that gave rise to the theory – which apparently has little other foundation – that Hawksmoor was some sort of Satanist. It has further been suggested that he arranged his buildings to cast a spell over the City: you can (at a pinch) plot them on a map to produce the Egyptian symbol of the Eye of Horus. You may think this is a touch fanciful; it's nevertheless the idea that Peter Ackroyd (born 1949) uses as a backdrop to his 1985 novel *Hawksmoor.*

This is an elaborate postmodern detective story whose narrative flits between the eighteenth century and the present day. The historical part concerns an architect – Ackroyd calls him Nicholas Dyer, but he's clearly based on Hawksmoor – whose interest in the dark arts lures him to introduce blasphemous elements, not to mention corpses, into the churches he builds. In the modern section, Hawksmoor is the name Ackroyd gives to the detective tracking down a serial killer whose murders all take place in or around – you've guessed it – a Hawksmoor church.

Occult psychogeography – the study of the influence of the environment on the mind and behaviour – may or may not be your thing, but it's a great excuse to visit and marvel at some of the most individualistic churches in London. Though you might prefer not to do it after dark.

Brick Lane
MONICA ALI

www.visitlondon.com/things-to-do/place/279336-brick-lane-market *The market is open on Sundays only, but there's plenty to see on other days.*

*B*rick Lane, the debut novel by Monica Ali (born 1967), was published in 2003 and anyone walking down Brick Lane then would have seen what her protagonist Nazneen saw. Nazneen is a young woman fresh from 'the village' back in Bangladesh and she's come to London as the result of an arranged marriage. She speaks little English and rarely goes out. So when one evening she does venture out on a bus, the neighbourhood is a revelation to her:

The shops were lit up still. Leather shops, dress shops, sari shops, shops that sold fish and chips and samosas and pizzas and a little bit of everything from around the world. Newsagents, hardware shops, grocers, shops that sold alcohol, shops whose windows were stacked with stools and slippers and cassette tapes and seemed to sell nothing but were always full of men in Panjabi-pyjamas, smoking and stroking their beards. Between the lights were black patches where the windows were boarded or the For Sale signs were hung.

Later in the book, she's walking a step behind her husband down Brick Lane itself:

In the restaurant windows were clippings from newspapers and magazines with the name of the restaurant highlighted in yellow or pink. There were smart places with starched white tablecloths and multitudes of shining silver cutlery. In these places the newspaper clippings were framed. The tables were far apart and there was an absence of decoration that Nazneen knew to be a style.

Walk up Brick Lane from Whitechapel Road today and your first impression is that nothing much has changed. There are still shops selling roll upon roll of fabric, Bangla restaurants, Indian restaurants, shops selling brightly coloured sweets, mini-supermarkets selling a little bit of everything. Even an area where skateboarders practise sounds familiar:

The graffiti on the shed walls had kaleidoscoped to a dense pattern of silver and green and peacock blue, wounded here and there with vermilion, the colour of mehindi on a bride's feet.

Nazneen's world is not destined to remain so hemmed in. Inspired partly by her relationship with a young Muslim radical, partly by (of all people) the ice-skaters Torvill and Dean, she learns to take control of her life. As she blossoms in the book, so does Brick Lane as you walk along it today. Go on a Sunday, head a block or two further north and you'll find yourself in the middle of a bustling market offering antiques, bric-a-brac, jewellery and vintage clothing – much of it in the shadow of the Old Truman Brewery, now a gallery and arts centre. The street may be best known for its curry houses, but there's a surprising number of pizzerias and some famous bagel bakeries. There's a vegan Italian and Korean fusion restaurant. There's even a display of street art based round multi-coloured images of broccoli. And why not? As Nazneen's friend Razia says in the last line of the book, 'This is England. You can do whatever you like.'

Razia is talking about going ice-skating in a sari; I'm talking about quirky fusion restaurants and DayGlo-coloured broccoli. The bagel shops, of course, reflect a period of Jewish immigration, while in nearby Hanbury Street a plaque on the wall of Hanbury Hall refers to an earlier time when the recent arrivals were French Huguenots. These Protestants escaping Catholic persecution in their homeland built themselves a chapel at Number 59 Brick Lane. That was in 1743; for part of the nineteenth and twentieth centuries it was a synagogue, and since 1976 it's been a mosque. As Razia (firmly) and Nazneen (more diffidently) would testify, in Brick Lane there's room for it all.

Southwark Cathedral
CHAUCER, SHAKESPEARE AND OTHERS
cathedral.southwark.anglican.org

Tucked away in the shadow of the Shard and behind the foodie bustle of Borough Market, Southwark Cathedral is a bit of an undiscovered gem. Catch it on the right day and its tawny stonework positively glows in the sun. Inside you can tick a good few literary figures off your list. The stained-glass windows above the north aisle (on the left as you go in) include memorials to Oliver Goldsmith (1730?–1774), Samuel Johnson (see page 39), John Bunyan (page 128) and Geoffrey Chaucer (page 109), all of whom lived in the vicinity at some point. Goldsmith's makes reference to his poem 'The Deserted Village' and 'other works in prose and poetry'; Johnson's to his great dictionary; and Bunyan's to his *Pilgrim's Progress*, an allegorical and highly moral tale not much read nowadays but whose characters Giant Despair and Mr Worldly Wiseman and locations such as Vanity Fair and the Slough of Despond were once guaranteed to keep children awake at nights.

Chaucer's memorial, as you might expect, depicts *The Canterbury Tales*, with a parade of pilgrims setting off from the nearby Tabard Inn. Geoffrey himself appears in a roundel at the top of the window, flaunting a strikingly scarlet turban-like headdress; below him is no mere inn sign, but a full-scale herald's tabard, with the tower of Southwark Cathedral behind; and below that the pilgrims themselves, headed by the monk and two more prosperous-looking gentlemen – the merchant and the squire, perhaps. They've hardly started on their journey but they look a bit bored already; the stories they are

about to tell each other will be a welcome relief from the tedium of covering the 55-mile pilgrimage at a sedate walking pace.

The climax of the piece (at the bottom, and therefore easiest to see) is St Thomas Becket, the murdered Archbishop of Canterbury, whose shrine in the cathedral there is the reason for all this palaver. He's richly dressed, as befits his station; he carries a staff in the form of a cross in his left hand and has his right hand raised, as if to bless the pilgrims as they set off on their journey. The whole thing is the work of Victorian glass manufacturer Charles Kempe (1837–1907), who was responsible for an enormous amount of stained glass all over the country, from Liverpool's Anglican Cathedral to the memorial to Jane Austen (see page 96) in Winchester Cathedral. It was installed in 1900 to mark the 500th anniversary of Chaucer's death.

Across the way, in the south aisle and within spitting distance of Shakespeare's Globe Theatre (see page 48) is the memorial to our greatest playwright. His window, by stained-glass designer Christopher Webb (1886–1966), replaced one destroyed during the Second World War and depicts various characters from Shakespeare's plays. Prospero, the magician from *The Tempest*, is centre stage, with the sprite Ariel flying above him and the monster Caliban grovelling at his feet; the scene is headlined by the speech in which Prospero speaks of the transience of life ('We are such stuff / As dreams are made on, and our little life / Is rounded with a sleep').

Webb was obviously in a reflective mood when he produced this work, as along the bottom we see the Seven Ages of Man from *As You Like It*, ending with decrepitude: 'second childishness and mere oblivion / Sans teeth, sans eyes, sans taste, sans everything'. Webb can't be held entirely responsible for this pessimism, however, because the window stands above – and looks as if it is growing from – a statue of Shakespeare himself (Henry McCarthy, 1911). In this, the Bard is depicted reclining in a Bankside meadow with, on the day I visited, his hand holding a sprig of fresh rosemary ('for remembrance', as Ophelia tells us). His head rests on his other hand and he stares rather blankly into the middle distance: judging by his expression he could easily be wondering whether to be or not to be.

Shakespeare's Globe
WILLIAM SHAKESPEARE
www.shakespearesglobe.com

Can this cock-pit hold
The vasty fields of France? Or may we cram
Within this wooden O, the very casques
That did affright the air at Agincourt?

That's part of the prologue to Shakespeare's *Henry V*, in which the Chorus asks the audience to use their imagination, to accept that the battle scenes with their huge armies are actually taking place within 'this wooden O' – the circular Globe Theatre. Tradition has it that *Henry V* was the first play staged at the original Globe, in 1599. If that is so, this was the first speech ever uttered there, so the Chorus is not only asking the audience to suspend disbelief about spectacular crowd scenes and the fact that the action flits back and forth between England and France, but it's also introducing them to a new venue.

That Globe burned down in 1613, apparently because sparks from an onstage cannon set the thatched roof alight during a performance of Shakespeare's *Henry VIII*. The theatre was rebuilt in 1614, then closed by order of Parliament in 1642 and pulled down two years later. It might have remained a forgotten piece of history, of interest only to Shakespeare scholars, had it not been for the energy and determination of the American actor and director Sam Wanamaker (1919–1993). The fulfilment of his long-term dream created a loving replica, reproducing as accurately as possible the dimensions and look of the original. The timbers are held together using wooden pegs, as they would have been in Shakespeare's (1564–1616) day; the ornate pillars that support the roof over the stage are made of green oak, the same wood the original builders would have used, and carved using the same techniques. One noticeable difference, though, is the location: the Thames is narrower now than it was in the sixteenth century, with the result that the original site is some 180 metres inland from the current one. It's also partly covered by listed buildings that Wanamaker's project wasn't allowed to disturb. Today's theatre, mimicking the riverside position of its predecessor, is built on land that wasn't there 400 years ago.

The modern Shakespeare's Globe, as it is always called, opened in 1997, with, appropriately enough, a production of *Henry V*. Ever since, an annual 'season' has run from mid-April to mid-October and most but not all of the repertoire is by the Bard. Some of the audience sits on benches that are sheltered from the elements, but there's also an open-air yard where you stand (and, if you're at the front, lean on the stage) as the 'groundlings' did in Shakespeare's day. True to their period, productions often end with dances and feature ancient instruments; the comedies tend to be boisterous and bawdy; and if anything requires blood, you can expect no shortage, from *Measure for Measure* (a severed head in a bag) to *Titus Andronicus* (gore *everywhere*). It seems likely that the man who wasn't above having a character's eyes gouged out on stage (*King Lear*) or a murdered corpse uncovered to cries of 'O piteous spectacle! ... O most bloody sight!' (*Julius Caesar*) would have approved.

S. PAULES CHURCH

Three Cranes

The Stilliarde

The Gally fuste

ᴁESIS

The Globe

Angela Carter's South London
ANGELA CARTER
brixtonmarket.net

The novels and short stories of Angela Carter (1940–1992, whose archive is held by the British Library) are renowned for their vivid, unfettered originality. To do a tour of her part of South London, you need to take a bit of her imagination with you. 'Welcome to the wrong side of the tracks!' says the narrator, Dora Chance, in the opening lines of *Wise Children*. 'Me and Nora, that's my sister, we've always lived on the left-hand side, the side the tourist rarely sees, the *bastard* side of Old Father Thames ...' The river, she later explains, 'lies between Brixton and glamour like a sword'.

Carter's last novel before her untimely death, *Wise Children* is a celebration of many things: of theatre and dancing and singing, of duality (almost everyone in the novel is a twin), of intellectual pursuits and earthy fun. In among all this is a celebration of that wrong side of the tracks, where Carter lived for the last sixteen years of her life and wrote many of her best-known works.

The Chances – generations of them, as the novel floats back and forth through time – live in Bard Road in Brixton: it doesn't exist, but with Shakespeare being such a dominant feature of the book, you can't blame the author for pretending that it did. It's possible to locate it fairly accurately: we know that from the attic you can see all the way to Westminster and St Paul's, and it isn't far from Electric Avenue, home of Brixton Market, with its lights 'glowing like bad fish through a good old London fog'. The market is a good place to start a Carter fantasy tour. In real life it describes its stalls as 'eclectic'; depending on the day of the week you can find anything from exotic cuisine to hand-knitted tea cosies or vintage shoes and gloves. Or, as Dora puts it:

> *You can buy anything you want in Brixton market. We got stockings with little silver stars all over, 'more stars than there are in Heaven', recollected Nora.*

After the tangible colours and flavours of Brixton Market, your imagination has to kick in. The Kennington Theatre, where the Chance twins appeared in panto ('Would you believe a live theatre in Kennington, once upon a time?'), is no more: once described as one of the most sumptuous in Europe, it was badly damaged by Second World War bombs and replaced by a nondescript block of flats. Clapham High Street is still there, but it's unlikely that you'll find the haberdasher's shop above which:

> *once upon a time, there was an old woman in splitting black satin pounding away at an upright piano ... and her daughter in a pink tutu and wrinkled tights slapped at your ankles with a cane if you didn't pick up your feet high enough.*

Once you've indulged these flights of fancy, however, a short walk away, at 107 The Chase, you *will* find the house where Carter spent those last, productive years, the house where she tutored Kazuo Ishiguro and entertained other younger writers, such as Salman Rushdie and Ian McEwan, who went on to great things. Her study, according to her friend, the journalist Susannah Clapp, was 'unadorned', but other parts of the house

had a carnival atmosphere more in keeping with the mind that produced *Wise Children* and *Nights at the Circus*:

> *violet and marigold walls, and scarlet paintwork. A kite hung from the ceiling of the sitting room, the shelves supported menageries of wooden animals, books were piled on chairs. Birds ... were released from their cages to whirl through the air.*

A blue plaque on the wall outside tells us merely that Angela Carter lived here from 1976. Again, you should give your imagination free rein. Clearly what she did was more exciting than that bald statement makes it sound.

A Different View of Brixton

C. L. R. JAMES AND BERNARDINE EVARISTO

If Angela Carter's whimsy isn't to your taste, you can skip the whole 'Clapham High Street and pink tutu' diversion (see page 50) and focus on some more down-to-earth aspects of Brixton. Just round the corner from Electric Avenue and the market is Railton Road, much in the news during the 1981 riots but today an unremarkable residential street. It was once the home of a group of radical Caribbean-born intellectuals, notably the Trinidadian Cyril Lionel Robert James (1901–1989): a plaque on the wall of Number 167 identifies the house where he lived and died. This house was also for almost twenty years in the 1970s and 1980s the headquarters of the political magazine *Race Today*, edited by James's nephew and protégé, the broadcaster and campaigner Darcus Howe (1943–2017). It's now the headquarters of the Brixton Advice Centre and its windows are adorned with what it describes as a 'dynamic visual arts installation' celebrating the building's cultural heritage. This depicts James, Howe and other 'local heroes' including dub poet Linton Kwesi Johnson (born 1952, pictured opposite) and – surprisingly to those who aren't well up on the history of Railton Road – the popular Trinidadian pianist Winifred Atwell (c. 1910–1983), the first black person to have a number one hit in the UK singles chart. She's here because she also ran a hairdressing salon just up the road.

To revert to C. L. R. James: in addition to his political writing, much of which concerned the struggles of working people and campaigned for Caribbean independence, he was the cricket correspondent of what was then the *Manchester Guardian*. With *Beyond a Boundary*, which he described as 'neither cricket reminiscences nor autobiography', he produced what is widely regarded as the best book ever about cricket, or perhaps any sport. An unexpected item on the CV of a man who met Trotsky.

Brixton has undergone its share of transformations over the years. In *Girl, Woman, Other* by Bernardine Evaristo (born 1959), radical feminist playwright Amma buys a property here in the 1990s, having lived in squats or slept on other people's sofas for years. At that time, it's 'crime-addled but affordable', populated by 'alternatives' like her. Twenty years on, she and a friend look disapprovingly around the bar of the Ritzy cinema, hating:

> *the interlopers who were colonizing the neighbourhood, who patronized the chi-chi eateries and bars that now replaced a stretch of the indoor market previously known for stalls selling parrot fish, yam, ackee, Scotch bonnet peppers, African materials, weaves, Dutch pots, giant Nigerian land snails and pickled green eggs from China.*

These interlopers are people who 'loved slumming it in SW2 or SW9' but 'couldn't hide the fact that SW1 or SW3 were in their DNA'. At the same time, Amma's teenage daughter Yazz dismisses what she calls her mother's whinges:

> *as if she herself wasn't part of the gentrification of Brixton years ago*
> *as if she herself isn't a frequenter of the artsy hotspots like the Ritzy*
> *as if she herself didn't take Yazz to one of the very champagne bars she supposedly scorns to celebrate passing her 'A' levels a year early.*

Evaristo doesn't pass judgement on these views. In her world, as in Brixton's, there's room for both champagne and Scotch bonnet peppers. And probably for boogie-woogie pianists who run hairdressing salons, too.

Post-*Windrush* West London
ANDREA LEVY AND SAM SELVON

Earl's Court and Notting Hill must have been baffling to the Caribbean immigrants of the 1940s and 1950s: cold, grey and full of people who didn't want you to be there. For an eye-opening journey back to this place and time, try taking Andrea Levy (1956–2019) and Sam Selvon (1923–1994) with you.

In Levy's *Small Island*, Hortense, newly arrived from Jamaica in 1948, is pleasantly surprised by the place she is going to live:

> *The house, I could see, was shabby. Mark you, shabby in a grand sort of a way. I was sure this house could once have been home to a doctor or a lawyer or perhaps a friend of a friend of the King. Only the house of someone high-class would have pillars at the doorway. Ornate pillars that twisted with elaborate design. The glass stained with coloured pictures as a church would have. It was true that some were missing, replaced by cardboard and strips of white tape. But who knows what devilish deeds Mr Hitler's bombs had carried out during the war?*

That's before she discovers that she, a qualified teacher, and her husband Gilbert, who served in the Royal Air Force on behalf of what he thinks of as the Mother Country, are occupying just one room of this shabby-grand house and are expected to step into the gutter to allow a white person to pass them in the street.

Hortense and Gilbert's room is in Nevern Street, Earl's Court – it doesn't exist, but Nevern Square, Nevern Place and Nevern Road do, and those grand houses with the fancy pillars are still there. Most of them have been smartened up a bit since Mr Hitler's bombs, some of them turned into hotels, some of them looking as if they could do with smartening up again. To a Londoner, this is just London, but to anyone who wasn't used to a big city built mostly in brick, it would have been impressive.

From Nevern Square, a walk through the expensive real estate between Kensington Gardens and Holland Park will take you to Notting Hill, the scene of Selvon's *The Lonely Londoners,* written and set a few years after the events of *Small Island*. Moses, a Trinidadian like his creator, has been living there for some time and has become an unwilling mentor to naïve new arrivals. World-weary and homesick, he tries to explain London to them:

> *It divide up in little worlds, and you stay in the world you belong to and you don't know anything about what happening in the other ones except what you read in the papers. Them rich people who does live in Belgravia and Knightsbridge and up in Hampstead and them other plush places, they would never believe what it like in*

*a grim place like Harrow Road or Notting Hill ... they don't know nothing about
hustling two pound of brussel sprout and half-pound potato, or queuing up for fish and
chips in the smog.*

Not only that, but wherever Moses's protégés go they will be given the worst jobs, paid
less than their white counterparts or told there are no vacancies. And everyone will
assume they are Jamaican. Daunted when he discovers how right Moses is, newcomer
Galahad looks at his own hand and wonders, 'Why the hell you can't be blue, or red or
green, if you can't be white?'

London is also filthy. Selvon was writing before the introduction of the 1956 Clean
Air Act; when Moses blows his nose on a foggy night, his white handkerchief turns
black. It's all a long way from that fanciful place where Hugh Grant fell in love with
Julia Roberts.

While you're in the area, if you're a fan of Martin Amis (born 1949) you may be disappointed to know that the pub in Portobello Road on which the disreputable Black
Cross in *London Fields* is said to be based closed some years ago; the building now houses
an upscale Japanese restaurant. An example of life imitating Hugh Grant rather than
Moses and Galahad.

THE
LONELY
LONDONERS

Samuel
Selvon

Robin Adler

THE AUTHOR

SAMUEL SELVON was born in Trinidad of Indian parents. He
went to school and college on the Island, and during the war
served for five years as a telegraphist in a mine-sweeper.
After the war, he worked on *The Trinidad Guardian*, and
began to write short stories in his spare time, several of which
were accepted by the B.B.C. Encouraged by this success, he
came to England, bringing with him the manuscript of a
novel called A BRIGHTER SUN, which was published by
Wingates in 1952 and by Viking in the United States. He
was awarded a Guggenheim Fellowship for his second novel,
AN ISLAND IS A WORLD. THE LONELY LONDONERS is his third
novel and the second to be published in America.

ST MARTIN'S PRESS

103 Park Avenue, New York

ST
MARTIN'S
PRESS

Paddington Station
MICHAEL BOND
www.thisispaddington.com

London has no shortage of statues of the literary great and good, but there can't be many cuter than the one at Paddington Station of everyone's favourite marmalade-eating bear. (With no disrespect intended to everyone's favourite honey-eating bear, see pages 57 and 103.) A bronze by Marcus Cornish (born 1964) sits by Platform 1, near where Paddington first met the Brown family, and shows him perched on the suitcase that had been 'wanted on voyage', looking round rather wistfully for someone who might take him home.

Venture into the enclosed Lawn area of the station, where the shops and cafes are, and in the Paddington Shop you'll be greeted by another statue of our hero, in colour this time, raising his red hat and looking altogether more cheerful. You'll also find, alongside an astonishing range of merchandise – do we really need Paddington skittles or a Paddington music box? – a biographical sketch of his adventures so far. A useful reminder, for those who discovered him via the 2014 film, that *A Bear Called Paddington* first appeared in book form in 1958 and that it and the many sequels by Michael Bond (1926–2017) have been translated into forty languages, including Latin.

Paddington's adventures were by no means confined to the station that gave him his name. So his shop will also supply you (free of charge) with a leaflet detailing the Pawprint Trails that families can explore in the area. Some of the connections to Paddington Bear are on the tenuous side, but it's an incentive to meander through the newly revamped Paddington Basin of the Grand Union Canal. Here, the highlight for children has to be the Water Maze (Merchant Square), described in the leaflet as 'an interactive water sculpture ... a set of water jets arranged in three concentric circles which rise and fall in turn, creating random openings in each circle'. It's a genuine maze, in the sense that there's a centre to be reached, and Paddington would have been good at it, because, as he once explained to Mr Gruber, 'You have to be good at mazes if you are brought up in Darkest Peru. Some of the forests there are very thick.' Basically it's an excuse for kids to run around and get wet; and of course it wouldn't have been there when Paddington was living in the area, but these are mere quibbles. It's an excellent place to sit and eat your marmalade sandwiches.

On the other side of the Westway, a little searching brings to light another recent addition to the area: a trio of steel sculptures commemorating famous local residents. Michael Bond, cradling Paddington in his arms, stands alongside computing genius Alan Turing and pioneering nurse Mary Seacole: surely one of the strangest juxtapositions ever thought of, in a tiny park beside the church of St Mary's on Paddington Green.

Delightful though the Pawprint Trail is, however, it's the bronze statue in the station that brings Paddington (Bear, not Station) to life. It's all you can do not to pat that outstretched muzzle and assure the recently arrived stowaway that everything will be all right.

In fact, if you look a little closer, you'll see that Paddington's muzzle is a good bit shinier than the rest of him. *Lots* of passers-by have succumbed to the urge to stroke it.

Primrose Hill/Regent's Park
DODIE SMITH AND A. A. MILNE

www.zsl.org

Imagine that, Heaven forbid, your children had been kidnapped and, in the days before social media, you wanted to raise the alarm with as many connections as possible. Where would you go?

To the place where you got the best phone signal, obviously.

That's effectively what Pongo and Missis did in Dodie Smith's *The Hundred and One Dalmatians:* they went to Primrose Hill to join what Smith (1896–1990) called the Twilight Barking, because reception was bad in their part of Regent's Park. The Twilight Barking was a system known to all dogs, a way of 'keeping in touch with distant friends, passing on important news, enjoying a good gossip'. It was this system that set a country-wide network of dogs searching for the stolen puppies and enabled the parents to rescue not only their own offspring, but also eighty-two others from the wicked hands of Cruella de Vil.

There isn't a Dalmatian monument on Primrose Hill, but the hill is noticeable enough to help you understand why barking carried a long way. There isn't a monument as such at all; instead there is an edging in York stone, with an inscription from William Blake (see page 37):

I have conversed with the spiritual sun. I saw him on Primrose Hill.

There are Druidic connections with Primrose Hill dating back to Blake's time (and still an annual procession at the time of the Autumn Equinox); it's also one of only six protected viewpoints in London, with the height of the trees controlled so as not to restrict the view, so who knows what (or whom) Blake might have seen here?

Coming back to earth for a moment, Primrose Hill is an extension of Regent's Park, separated from it by the Regent's Canal and within easy earshot of London Zoo, where you can rub shoulders, as it were, with another childhood favourite. For this is where the young Christopher Robin Milne first met an American black bear called Winnipeg

(or Winnie) that had been given to the zoo in 1914 by a Canadian soldier. In the introduction to *Winnie-the-Pooh*, A. A. Milne (1882–1956) explains that his son once had a favourite swan that he called Pooh:

> *and when we said good-bye, we took the name with us, as we didn't think the swan would want it any more.*

As Christopher Robin was devoted to the zoo's bear, his own teddy somehow became Winnie-the-Pooh.

Sadly, in Regent's Park you can no longer whisper something to the third keeper from the left and be let into the bear enclosure, as Christopher Robin was – they're less relaxed about such things nowadays, and anyway the bears have moved out to the Zoological Society of London's other zoo, at Whipsnade in Bedfordshire. But you can still see the statue of the original Winnie and her Canadian benefactor, near the war memorial and Butterfly Paradise, and another of her on her own, near the Mappin Terraces. If you're dedicated enough you may still earn A. A. Milne's approval:

There are some people who begin the Zoo at the beginning, called WAYIN, and walk as quickly as they can past every cage until they get to the one called WAYOUT, but the nicest people go straight to the animal they love the most, and stay there.

Or you can cross back over the road, head up Primrose Hill again and, as the sun goes down, listen to the dogs barking, social networking in a uniquely canine way.

Another Zoo Connection

www.zsl.org

Here's a strange claim to fame. Christina Rossetti (1830–1894) is almost certainly the only Victorian poet to include a wombat in her verses. She lived most of her adult life within easy reach of Regent's Park, worshipping at Christ Church, Albany Street (now St George's Cathedral) and ending her days in Torrington Square, Bloomsbury, where she is commemorated by a stone plaque on the wall of Number 30. Her brother, the Pre-Raphaelite artist Dante Gabriel Rossetti (1828–1882), was passionate about wombats, kept two as pets, produced several drawings of them and – many years before Christopher Robin Milne visited his beloved bear (see page 57) – spent hours at the Wombats' Lair in the zoo. It's very tempting indeed to believe that Christina went with him. One of her best-known poems, 'Goblin Market', contains these lines, describing the various goblin merchants that the heroines encounter:

One had a cat's face,
One whisk'd a tail,
One tramp'd at a rat's pace,
One crawl'd like a snail,
One like a wombat prowl'd obtuse and furry,
One like a ratel tumbled hurry skurry.

Nobody who hadn't seen a wombat in the flesh could have written that description.

St Pancras Station
JOHN BETJEMAN

Poet Laureate from 1972 until his death, John Betjeman (1906–1984) was also the most popular poet of his generation, famous for his easy, approachable verse about the subaltern's yearning for Miss Joan Hunter Dunn and friendly bombs falling on Slough. An affable personality with a pleasant round face and slightly dishevelled appearance, he further endeared himself to the public when, in 1973, he made a nostalgic documentary for the BBC entitled *Metro-Land*; Clive James, then television critic for the *Observer* newspaper, dubbed it an 'instant classic'. Metro-Land was the name given by the Metropolitan Railway to the area northwest of London that its trains served; it was a marketing gimmick from the early years of the twentieth century when, according to Betjeman, Wembley was 'an unimportant hamlet, where for years the Metropolitan didn't bother to stop'. The idea was that City clerks would be seduced by names like Harrow Garden Village into buying dream homes in these semi-rural developments and travelling to work by train. The documentary was a paean to Englishness and English suburban life, and Betjeman's commentary, partly in verse, was a perfect accompaniment to the joys of Neasden, Pinner and St John's Wood.

Betjeman was also a passionate advocate of great architecture in general and Victorian architecture in particular, at a time when the latter was deeply unfashionable and derided by many experts. He was one of a number of prominent people who protested unavailingly against the demolition of the distinctive Doric arch at Euston Station (the main entrance to the original station, which had opened in 1837) when the terminus was rebuilt in the 1960s. He was more successful when, a few years later, British Rail proposed to demolish St Pancras Station and the adjoining Midland Grand Hotel – both classic examples of Victorian Gothic. The support of the respected architectural historian Sir John Summerson, enlisted by Betjeman, was crucial in saving both buildings and in gaining them the Grade I listed status they enjoy today.

So, when St Pancras was redeveloped in 2007 to accommodate the Eurostar trains, Betjeman was an obvious subject for a statue on the concourse. Sculpted in bronze by Martin Jennings (born 1957), who was also responsible for the statue of Philip Larkin in Hull (see page 165), the poet clutches his trademark trilby hat to his head as he gazes upwards at the famous iron and glass roof. Jennings's work was praised for capturing Betjeman's characteristic scruffiness – his unbuttoned raincoat apparently blows in the wind, his tie is fastened askew and he carries, of all unassuming things, a shopping bag. The siting of the statue is significant, too: in a quiet tribute to the poet's quintessential Englishness, it is nowhere near the bustling international area, with its trains for Lille, Paris and Brussels. If you encounter John Betjeman, you are more likely to be heading for Luton or Nottingham or Sheffield, though you'll end up zooming past Metro-Land rather more quickly than he did half a century ago.

NW
ZADIE SMITH

If John Betjeman (see page 60) is too old-fashioned for you, get off the metaphorical Metro-Land train at Willesden Green and discover the northwest London of Zadie Smith (born 1975): the 'Willesden kaleidoscope', from which the 52 bus will take you west towards Knightsbridge and you can watch 'the many colours shade off into the bright white lights of town', or east towards Harlesden where 'white fades to yellow fades to brown, and then Harlesden Clock comes into view, standing like Queen Victoria's statue in Kingston – a tall stone surrounded by black'. If you don't want to bother with the bus, a short walk will take you up to Cricklewood Broadway, which suicidal Archie realises is a strange choice of place to do away with himself and where halal butcher Mo fights a daily battle against pigeons and their mess.

This is all from Smith's first novel, *White Teeth*, published in 2000; since then, and particularly since the publication of *NW* in 2012, she's come to be regarded as one of the finest chroniclers of modern London. Though perhaps not so much a chronicler as a painter; even more than Monica Ali in *Brick Lane* (see page 45), she is creating a collage, a collection of odds and ends pasted together apparently at random to make a whole. Or, as she says about Willesden, a kaleidoscope, a complex pattern of changing shapes and colours.

The city of *NW* is diverse, lively, humorous, but often fraught with tension. It's a place that even the Tube map can't quite comprehend:

It did not express his reality. The centre was not 'Oxford Circus' but the bright lights of
Kilburn High Road. 'Wimbledon' was the countryside, 'Pimlico' pure science fiction.
... Who lived there? Who even passed through it?

Walk through the streets of NW and you'll see the same buildings Smith sees: the Hindu
temple on Willesden Lane that 'has the colours of a block of Neapolitan ice cream and
is essentially the same shape. A block of Neapolitan ice cream with two upturned cones
at either end.' The ancient but unnamed church that Natalie plans to attend so that her
children can get into a 'good' school is clearly St Mary's in Neasden Lane, bizarrely
situated in a patch of green just off the North Circular: it's been there (in the book as in
real life) since AD 938 – 'out of time, out of place. A force field of serenity surrounds it.'
To Irish Pauline, that's its attraction: 'I wouldn't be liking the newer churches, no ... You
can be surer of the older ones, so you can.'

As you walk, you'll see the people Smith sees, too. Outside the temple, elderly
Hindus 'wear their saris and jumpers and cardigans and thick woolly socks. They look
like they have walked to Willesden from Delhi, adding layers of knitwear as they progress northwards.' On the estate of 'five blocks connected by walkways and bridges and
staircases, and lifts that were to be avoided almost as soon as they were built', bored
children 'kicked a dented can over and over' or 'had a long branch he held loosely in his
hand, letting it collide with whatever got in its way'.

Away from the estate, though, look at the houses and, like Smith, you'll be reminded
of John Betjeman: the whole area created back in the 1880s, 'an optimistic vision of
Metroland ... Well-appointed country living for those tired of the city. Fast-forward.
Disappointed city living for those tired of their countries.'

That's a pessimistic view of NW. In Smith's world, the diverse elements of that kaleidoscope constantly jostle for position. They're by no means all bright and cheerful: they
can be drug-fixated, crime-ridden or miserably trapped in a life that may be rich or poor
but isn't what they would have chosen for themselves. But some of them cling on to their
potential. As they jostle, they do what a kaleidoscope is meant to do: produce an endless
variety of intriguing shapes.

Keats House, Hampstead

JOHN KEATS

www.cityoflondon.gov.uk/things-to-do/attractions-museums-entertainment/keats-house
Normally open Wednesday–Sunday only.

If you've ever thought that the lines:

> *My heart aches, and a drowsy numbness pains*
> *My sense, as though of hemlock I had drunk*

were a gloomy way to start a poem about a nightingale, wend your way to John Keats's
house in Hampstead, take in the sorrowful details of his brief life (1795–1821) and you'll

A View on Hampstead Heath looking towards London

be a bit more sympathetic. Losing his father when he was eight, his mother when he was fourteen, a younger brother before that brother was out of his teens, and himself succumbing to the family curse of tuberculosis when he was twenty-five, he didn't have much to be cheerful about.

His house in Hampstead, however, is for the most part charming (we'll come back to the bit that isn't in a moment), with lines from his poetry adorning the walls: my favourite was 'The great beauty of Poetry is, that it makes every thing every place interesting'. Your first impression is that for a failed medical student/as yet unrecognised poet, young John was doing pretty well for himself, living here. That's before you realise that he was sharing the house with its owner, his friend Charles Brown, and that in their day it was divided in two and they occupied only half of it. They each had a study on the ground floor and a bedroom above, but the spacious and elegant sitting room at the end of the corridor wasn't built until some twenty years after Keats moved on.

Nonetheless it was during his time here that he enjoyed what is often called his *annus mirabilis* – the 'marvellous year', spanning late 1818 and early 1819, when he wrote not only 'Ode to a Nightingale' (composed, according to Brown, under the plum tree in the garden), but also his odes to Psyche, on a Grecian Urn and on Melancholy, among others.

It was shortly after this that Fanny Brawne and her mother moved into the other half of the house. Fanny and Keats met constantly in the garden they shared, and fell famously and passionately in love. When Keats's tuberculosis confined him to bed, as it soon did, he lay in Brown's study, which overlooked the garden, so that he could watch

Fanny as she walked there. Today, one of the rooms at her end of the house is furnished as if it were her sitting room, with a pretty little writing desk and a mannequin displaying the style of dress she would have worn on those walks. The lovers now communicated by letter; hers have not survived, but his are regarded as some of the most ardent ever written: 'I have been astonished that Men could die Martyrs for religion,' he told her. 'I have shudder'd at it – I shudder no more. I could be martyr'd for my Religion – Love is my religion – I could die for that – I could die for you.' And much more in the same vein.

Keats moved to Rome for the sake of his health in September 1820 and died there less than six months later; you have to go to Italy for the end of his story. But what you read in this cosy house in Hampstead, about this immensely talented and achingly youthful man facing his own end – about him beginning to cough up blood and recognising it as his 'death-warrant' – is deeply moving.

Oh, and the bit that isn't charming? A cabinet upstairs contains Keats's death mask – a cast of his face taken shortly after death. This wasn't unusual in his day; a death mask was often taken as a memento, or as the basis for a portrait (compare the story of Dr Johnson, page 39). What is more unusual is that there is also a life mask, placed alongside the death version. The label tells us that Keats had to lie very still and breathe through straws while his friend, the painter Benjamin Haydon, cast his face in plaster – he wanted to use Keats's likeness as one of the crowd in his great work *Christ's Entry into Jerusalem*, which also features the faces of Voltaire and Wordsworth (the finished painting is in the collection of Mount St Mary's Seminary in Cincinnati, Ohio, should you be passing). The label in Keats House continues, 'Can you tell which mask is which?' I couldn't, and nowhere in the house could I find the answer. Fascinating, just a touch disturbing, but not inappropriate for a life that was so overshadowed by death.

London's Victorian Cemeteries
RADCLYFFE HALL, GEORGE ELIOT AND OTHERS
www.kensalgreencemetery.com

highgatecemetery.org

By the 1820s the churchyards that had traditionally accommodated most of London's dead were, frankly, full to overflowing. Various Acts of Parliament in the 1830s sought to remedy this by creating cemetery companies, whose purpose was to establish burial grounds away from the heavily populated inner city, and by 1841 what became known as the 'Magnificent Seven' were, as it were, open for business. They were Kensal Green, West Norwood, Highgate, Abney Park, Brompton, Nunhead and Tower Hamlets; not all of them are worth including on a literary cemetery-crawl, but visits to Kensal Green and Highgate will pay dividends.

Cremation wasn't legalised in Britain until 1885, so these cemeteries were well used and well known. G. K. Chesterton's poem 'The Rolling English Road' (in which 'the rolling English drunkard' recalls, among other inebriated evenings, 'the night we went to Birmingham by way of Beachy Head') ends with the cheering words:

For there is good news yet to hear and fine things to be seen,
Before we go to Paradise by way of Kensal Green.

Writing these lines in 1914, Chesterton (1874–1936) could safely assume that his public would know what he meant. He himself didn't end up in Kensal Green (he's in the Roman Catholic cemetery in Beaconsfield). Its most famous literary occupants are the great Victorian novelists William Makepeace Thackeray (1811–1863) and Anthony Trollope (1815–1882); George Grossmith (1847–1912), co-author of the comic masterpiece *Diary of a Nobody*; the poet Thomas Hood (1799–1845), a local boy perhaps best known for 'I remember, I remember/The house where I was born'; and, more recently, the playwright Harold Pinter (see page 16).

If you have a liking for cemeteries, Kensal Green is a pleasant place to wander and has some spectacular Victorian mausoleums, but for real atmosphere you need to go to the West Cemetery at Highgate (previous page), which can be visited only on a guided tour. Overgrown and rambling, this is a haunting place – almost literally, as in the 1960s it featured in many a Hammer Horror film. Its literary highlight can be found in the Circle of Lebanon, so named because of the ancient cedar tree which was its focal point until disease felled it in 2019. Here you can pay homage to the doyenne of lesbian literature, Radclyffe Hall (1880–1943), whose partly autobiographical novel *The Well of Loneliness* (1928) was banned for its positive depiction of same-sex relationships between women. Hall's vault is inscribed with lines chosen by the author's lover Una, Lady Troubridge and taken from Elizabeth Barrett Browning's 'Sonnets from the Portuguese, 43':

And, if God choose,
I shall but love thee better after Death.

As Hall shares her tomb with an earlier lover, Mabel Batten, these words may well be a deliberate defiance of the social conventions that all three women challenged during their lives.

The Rossettis are in the West Cemetery, too – not only Christina (see page 59), but also her parents, her brother Dante Gabriel and his wife and muse Lizzie Siddall.

Across the road in the East Cemetery, which you can wander into at will, you'll find the grave of another unconventional novelist, George Eliot (real name Mary Ann Evans, 1819–1880). The author of *Middlemarch*, considered by many to be the greatest English novel of the nineteenth century (see page 147), scandalised society by openly living with a married man at a time when adulterous affairs were condoned only if they were conducted with discretion; and after his death marrying a man twenty years Eliot's junior. Both of these men, George Lewes and John Cross, are buried near to the author's tombstone. There's nothing defiant about the inscription, though; it's taken from one of Eliot's own poems:

O May I join the choir invisible
Of those immortal dead who live again
In minds made better by their presence.

If that rather Victorian sentiment isn't to your taste, you may prefer to contemplate the most famous monument of all, that of Karl Marx (1818–1883), with its large bronze head sitting atop a marble pedestal. The pedestal is inscribed with quotations from *The Communist Manifesto*, most conspicuously its closing words, 'Workers of All Lands Unite'. It dates only from the 1950s, when it was funded by the Communist Party of Great Britain, and is a Grade I listed structure – the highest accolade it can get. It doesn't inspire universal approval, however: it's not only been vandalised, but has also twice been the subject of bomb attacks.

Marx's collaborator Friedrich Engels (1820–1895) lived in Regent's Park Road,

Primrose Hill, for twenty-four years and has a plaque at Number 122; at his request he was cremated and his ashes scattered off Beachy Head, near Eastbourne.

Still a bit heavy? Then go and look for Douglas Adams (1952–2001): the headstone is simple enough, but admirers leave a colourful array of pens and pencils in a flowerpot in front of it, and a marker bearing the number '42' is stuck in the earth nearby. Fans of Adams's *Hitchhiker's Guide to the Galaxy* series will, of course, be aware that forty-two turns out to be the answer to the Ultimate Question of Life, the Universe, and Everything. Perhaps, somewhere beyond the grave, Adams has come up with a better question than 'What do you get when you multiply six by nine?'

Strawberry Hill House, Twickenham
HORACE WALPOLE

www.strawberryhillhouse.org.uk

Horace Walpole (1717–1797) isn't much read nowadays, but his hugely successful *The Castle of Otranto* once sent shivers running down the spine of the English reading public. It was this and other far-fetched Gothic tales that inspired Jane Austen's *Northanger Abbey* and set its heroine Catherine Morland imagining all sorts of horrid goings-on in the abbey of the title.

SOUTH FRONT of STRAWBERRY HILL, the Seat of the HON. H. WALPOLE.

Word lovers may know Walpole because it was he who coined the glorious word *serendipity*, claiming to have read a Persian fairy tale called *The Three Princes of Serendip* in which the princes possessed the gift of accidentally making pleasant discoveries.

Walpole was also, like most literate people of his era, an inveterate letter-writer, and in his case a particularly gossipy one: if you want the dirt on anyone in Regency society, his correspondence is a good place to start. Here's a snippet, chosen at random from many possibilities; it's a reminiscence of the courts of the first two King Georges, which – as the son of Britain's first Prime Minister, Sir Robert Walpole – Horace had visited frequently as a child:

George II., no more addicted than his father to too much religious credulity, had yet implicit faith in the German notion of vampires, and has more than once been angry with my father for speaking irreverently of those imaginary bloodsuckers.

You can see that the man had an eye for foibles.

Even before *Otranto* became a bestseller, Walpole was wealthy enough to build himself a residence at Strawberry Hill, in the fashionable Thames-side location of Twickenham (in those days far enough from town for a home there to count as a 'country retreat'). Instead of a tasteful villa, he went for a Gothic castle, festooned with pinnacles and battlements, inspired by the architecture he had seen while making the Grand Tour across Europe as a young man. Not one for hiding his light under a bushel, he graciously permitted visitors – no more than four a day, and no children – to take guided tours under the aegis of his housekeeper. He entertained royalty, the aristocracy and foreign diplomats and, when he was inspired by a nightmare to write *Otranto*, he had it printed on the private printing press he set up in his grounds.

He also amassed a vast art collection and published an inventory of it, remarking that 'In truth my collection was too great already to be lodged humbly'. Sadly it was dispersed after his death, although much of it was later re-collected by an American enthusiast and can be seen in the Lewis Walpole Library at Yale. In its heyday it must have been quite a sight: the list of contents of Walpole's China Room covers twelve pages; he owned a collection of miniatures which he described as 'the largest and finest in any country'; and he indulged a taste for such oddities as the spurs William III wore at the Battle of the Boyne and a lock of Edward IV's hair 'cut from his corpse at St George's Chapel at Windsor'. He also possessed an enormous number of portraits of himself, including at least twenty-six by the German-born society painter John Giles Eccardt, produced in the space of a mere nine years. Today you can still admire (you'd surely be expected to) one of these in the Blue Bedchamber. It shows Walpole in his late thirties, clearly prosperous and gazing out at the viewer with a shrewd look and the tiniest glimmer of a smile. Perhaps he was aware of his own foibles, too: perhaps, when he said, with a typical lack of restraint, that his country home was 'a very proper habitation for the author of *The Castle of Otranto*', his tongue was ever so slightly in his cheek.

2

CHAPTER TWO

SOUTHWESTERN ENGLAND

A Tour of Cornwall

DAPHNE DU MAURIER AND WINSTON GRAHAM

www.nationaltrust.org.uk/trails/frenchmans-creek-circular-walk

www.poldarkmine.org.uk *The mine is generally open from April to October, closed on Sundays, Mondays and some Bank Holidays. This information is subject to change: be sure to check in advance.*

The disappointment of a literary tour of Cornwall is that you can't visit Manderley, the great house haunted with memories that is at the heart of Daphne du Maurier's *Rebecca*.

Well, obviously you can't, because – spoiler alert – it burns down at the end of the book. More tangibly, Menabilly, du Maurier's Cornish home near Fowey, is in private hands and (like Manderley) can't be seen from the road. Du Maurier (1907–1989) lived there from 1943 to 1969; at the time she was writing *Rebecca* (published in 1938) she was based on the other side of the Fowey River. She could certainly have been inspired by the mystery surrounding Menabilly, which was largely neglected by its owners and falling into ruins. For the interior of Manderley she is said to have drawn on Milton Hall near Peterborough, which she had visited as a child and which had impressed her with its 'big house feel'. Its elegant Palladian exterior would have been no use to her, though: it could surely not frighten anyone the way Manderley frightened the second Mrs de Winter.

Another disappointment to du Maurier fans, though in a different way, is Jamaica Inn. Haunt of smugglers in the novel of the same name, it now offers a Museum of

Smuggling alongside the pub. You can't fault the location – high up on Bodmin Moor, miles from anywhere and, on the right day, as bleak a spot as you'll find this side of Wuthering Heights (see page 166). There's a bit of a theme-park feel to it, though ...

Frenchman's Creek, now, that's another matter. It's part of the Helford River, much deeper into Cornwall, beyond Falmouth, and there's a beautiful circular walk to be done along it, taking in the idyllic Helford village and the local woods. Go in springtime and any disappointment you feel at not meeting French pirates will be more than made up for by the glories of the daffodils and wild garlic.

Thanks to the recent television series, though, *Poldark* rather than du Maurier is what most people have on their mind when they go to Cornwall. Winston Graham (1908–2003) set his 'novels of Cornwall' in the coastal and mining area centred on Truro: at the beginning of the fourth of them, *Warleggan,* he refers to 'that coastal triangle lying between Truro, St Ann's and St Michael' and mentions six houses 'inhabited by gentlefolk' of which Ross and Demelza's Nampara, to the east of the fictional St Ann's, is the smallest. In the 1970s television series the coast further south and west, near the real-life St Just, was used for Nampara Cove; more recently parts of the filming were done on the north coast, at Porthcothan, and others down beyond Penzance, at Porthcurno.

The less glamorous side of Poldark life can be explored at the Poldark Tin Mine at Helston. It's perfectly safe, as all the literature and the staff will be quick to tell you, but clambering through its low, damp tunnels with water rushing around you, you have no difficulty in imagining how poor Francis Poldark came to drown in a place like this. Lots of people will think this is great fun; anyone of a nervous or claustrophobic disposition may prefer just to stand on almost any part of this glorious coastline and imagine little smuggling boats landing on moonless nights, with Ross Poldark, almost certainly shirt-less, helping to unload their cargo.

Literary Stained Glass

www.kingarthursgreathalls.co.uk

It's difficult to pick a favourite when you're offered Thomas the Tank Engine (see page 171), Alice in Wonderland (page 182), Narnia (page 124) and William Blake (page 38). For truly overwhelming wow factor, it's worth heading to Cornwall, to the comparatively modern (1930s) King Arthur's Great Halls in Tintagel, to marvel at the seventy-two (count them – seventy-two) panels designed by Arts and Crafts artist Veronica Whall (1887–1967) and depicting the legends and the coats of arms of the Arthurian knights.

Arthurian romance, particularly *Le Morte d'Arthur* by Thomas Malory (c. 1415–1471) was immensely popular in Victorian times (think of Tennyson's 'The Lady of Shalott' and John Waterhouse's Pre-Raphaelite painting of the same subject). It was also a huge inspiration for William Morris (1834–1896) and other leading lights of the Arts and Crafts movement. One of these was Veronica Whall's father, Christopher Whall (1849–1924), the pioneering stained-glass artist who was his daughter's principal teacher and mentor. He must have been a good one: at the age of thirteen she was adept enough to contribute a panel to the work he was producing for Gloucester Cathedral, regarded as his masterpiece.

Veronica's panels in Tintagel cover an extraordinary spectrum of colours, from blood red to deepest indigo, and convey piety, passion, anxiety and adventure. Her subjects include the young Arthur drawing his sword out of a stone; the older king knighting one of his entourage; and various heraldic devices accompanied by quotations drawn from the Bible, Shakespeare and other poets. The round table in the Great Hall is helpfully engraved with place settings: 'Here ought to sit King Arthur', 'Here ought to sit Sir Galahad' and so on. If you want to absorb the gist of the Arthurian legend without having to plough through a lengthy fifteenth-century text, this is without a doubt the place to come.

While you're here, of course, you should take the short stroll down to the sea and marvel at what remains of Tintagel Castle. The ruins add enormous drama to what is traditionally said to be Arthur's birthplace. Apart from the legend having inspired Richard, Earl of Cornwall, to build the castle, though, it is nothing to do with King Arthur; it dates only from the thirteenth century, some seven hundred years after he is supposed to have lived. If the tides are kind, you can walk along the beach to Merlin's cave, where Arthur's father is said to have given his baby son into the care of the great wizard. Whether or not you believe in the legends surrounding Arthur and his knights, there are few places more magical in all of Britain.

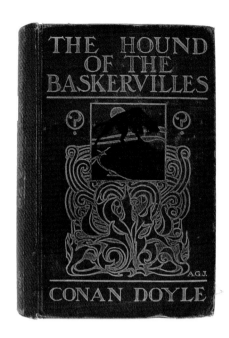

Unless they take the view that there is no such thing as bad publicity, the people in charge of tourism on Dartmoor don't have much cause to be grateful to Arthur Conan Doyle (1859–1930). Not only does he endow the moor with a huge and ferocious hound, but he also gives it a feature called Grimpen Mire whose remorseless quicksand sucks ponies and humans to their death. He doesn't make the weather conditions sound very inviting either:

Every minute that white woolly plain which covered one half of the moor was drifting closer and closer to the house. Already the first thin wisps of it were curling across the golden square of the lighted window ... As we watched it the fog-wreaths came crawling round both corners of the house and rolled slowly into one dense bank, on which the upper floor and the roof floated like a strange ship upon a shadowy sea.

All this, of course, is from the Sherlock Holmes novel *The Hound of the Baskervilles*, in which Holmes and Watson are invited to Devon by Sir Henry, who is threatened with the same mysterious and possibly supernatural fate as some of his ancestors at Baskerville Hall.

The story was partly inspired by an existing Dartmoor legend about a local squire called Richard Cabell, who lived at Brook Hall, near Buckfastleigh. Cabell died in 1677 and was believed to have sold his soul to the Devil. A 1907 guide to Devonshire tells us that he had:

such an evil reputation that he was placed under a heavy stone, and a sort of penthouse was built over that with iron gratings to it to prevent his coming up and haunting the neighbourhood. When he died the story goes that fiends and black dogs breathing fire raced over Dartmoor and surrounded Brooke, howling.

You can see the Cabell family mausoleum in the churchyard of the Holy Trinity Church, Buckfastleigh, on the edge of Dartmoor National Park, although Richard's name doesn't feature on the tomb's inscription. Perhaps he has wandered off on the Devil's business.

Conan Doyle wasn't entirely maligning the geography of Dartmoor, either. There *are* areas of treacherous peat bog, and it can be pretty bleak and breezy on a bad day. The Visit Dartmoor website also has a cheery list of mysterious happenings, bottomless lakes

and people being hounded to their deaths off a granite outcrop called the Dewerstone, so one more haunting tale isn't likely to bother them. Pick a good day, though, and the views are magnificent, the bird life extraordinary and the villages as pretty as any in England. In daylight, any substantial quadruped you come across is more likely to be a Dartmoor pony than a gigantic hound. By night, though, you might want to be just a little bit cautious ...

Agatha Christie's Devon

AGATHA CHRISTIE

www.burghisland.com

www.torquaymuseum.org *Closed on Sundays.*

www.nationaltrust.org.uk/greenway *Open April till October only.*

Isolation is a feature of many a traditional murder mystery. The secluded country house, the snowed-in pub, the village where any stranger sticks out like a sore thumb are all very convenient for the novelist wanting to limit the number of suspects. What better location, then, than an island that is accessible only by a causeway and is completely cut off at high tide? Such a place is Burgh Island in Devon, where Agatha Christie (1890–1976)

wrote and set two of her novels, *And Then There Were None* (published in 1939 under a now taboo title) and *Evil Under the Sun* (1941). In the former, eight guests are mysteriously invited to visit the island, where they and the two servants are all accused (by means of a gramophone recording) of murder. They are themselves then murdered one by one, following the pattern of the nursery rhyme which ends with the book's title:

> *Ten little Soldier Boys went out to dine;*
> *One choked his little self and then there were nine.*
>
> *Nine little Soldier Boys stayed up very late;*
> *One overslept himself and then there were eight*

... and so on.

The tension, which increases as fewer and fewer of the group are left alive, and the odds against which of them is the killer shorten, ranks this as one of Christie's scariest works (eat your heart out, *Mousetrap*). It's also the bestselling crime novel of all time.

And Then There Were None has been filmed many times, but never actually at Burgh Island. The 2001 version of *Evil Under the Sun*, starring David Suchet, however, used the hotel and its beaches to full advantage. In this novel, an actress who seems to be having an affair with another guest is murdered in a lonely cove, which can be reached only by boat or by climbing down a long ladder from the clifftop. Here, the mystery is all about timing: how could it have been done, when absolutely everybody's movements are accounted for? And who was heard running a bath at the odd hour of just before lunch?

To this day, the Burgh Island Hotel rejoices in the art deco style of the 1920s, when it was built and became immensely popular. The decorative highlight is the domed ceiling of the Palm Court Lounge, which the website describes as 'a mesmerising kaleidoscope of blues, greens and turquoise'. Lucky guests can stay in the Beach House, built specifically as a retreat for Dame Agatha. Others may revel in rooms and suites named after previous visitors (both real and fictional), including Noël Coward, the aviator Amy Johnson and, inevitably, Hercule Poirot. Highlight of any visit is the black-tie dinner in the Grand Ballroom, which offers an outside dance floor under the stars. Everything about Burgh Island enters into the spirit of the Jazz Age and the 'bright young things' of Agatha Christie's youth: it has been said of the Grand Ballroom dinners that it is impossible to be overdressed.

The less extravagant may choose to do their sleuthing in another part of Devon, the Agatha Christie Gallery in Torquay Museum. Here, enthusiasts can find furniture, props and costumes from the *Poirot* and *Miss Marple* television series, as well as information about the writer's life, copies of first editions, photographs and other memorabilia. It's more conventional than a glamorous evening on Burgh Island, but it's fun (you can even do an Agatha Christie quiz as you go round), and you don't have to worry about anyone slipping cyanide into your cocktail.

For a more outdoor setting, head to Greenway, Dame Agatha's holiday home from the 1930s until her death. As with Dickens and Gad's Hill Place (see page 113), it was somewhere she had known from childhood and had always thought was the most beautiful of the many properties on the River Dart. When it came on the market, she couldn't resist snapping it up (for £6,000). She described it in her autobiography as:

> *a white Georgian house of about 1780 or '90, with woods sweeping down to the Dart below, and a lot of fine shrubs and trees – the ideal house, a dream house.*

Not only that, but the gardens are full of woodland walks and boast a two-storey boathouse with a balcony, the setting for the murder in *Dead Man's Folly*. You can't go anywhere in Agatha Christie's footsteps without experiencing a certain frisson.

'Doone Valley', Exmoor
R. D. BLACKMORE

www.visit-exmoor.co.uk

www.visit-exmoor.co.uk/coleridge-way/point-of-interest/oare-church

Richard Doddridge Blackmore (1825–1900) was one of the most successful novelists of his time, but *Lorna Doone* is the only one of his works that is remembered today. Whether you've read it or not, if you've ever been anywhere near Exmoor, you'll have come across the name.

The fictitious Doones are a clan of outlaws, based on similar historical clans that existed in the area in the seventeenth century. The beautiful Lorna is betrothed, against her will, to her wicked cousin Carver Doone. She falls in love with a local farmer, John Ridd, and they plan to marry, but Carver bursts in during the ceremony and shoots her. It's a lot more complicated than that and, spoiler alert, everything turns out all right in the end (except for Carver Doone, obviously, who gets his deserts), but that brief summary is enough to enable you to appreciate what you see in Doone Valley.

Starting in the hamlet of Malmsmead, not far from Lynton, you can do a delightful circular walk. The stream known as Bagworthy Water flows through Malmsmead and is crossed by a seventeenth-century stone bridge and an older ford. The walk takes you along the stream, past the R. D. Blackmore memorial stone, through woods and valleys and across moorland – it is stunningly beautiful, though bleak and best avoided in bad weather, and perhaps at its loveliest in daffodil time.

The literary highlight of the walk is the tiny church of St Mary, Oare, where Blackmore's grandfather was rector from 1809 to 1842. You wouldn't think there would be much of a congregation out here: even local boy John Ridd, narrating the novel, describes 'the sloping little churchyard of Oare' as:

> *as meek a place as need be, with the Lynn brook down below it. There is not much of company there for anybody's tombstone, because the parish spreads so far in woods, and moors, without dwelling-house.*

Something keeps it going: there's been a church on the site for 800 years and the nave and inner chancel of the present one date back to the fifteenth century. It has eighteenth-century box pews and pulpit, a fifteenth-century piscina, a Norman font and a plaque commemorating Blackmore: it makes him look like a particularly benevolent and bewhiskered character from Dickens and describes him, in an epitaph we could all aspire to, as having had 'a certain grand and glorious gift of radiating humanity'.

St Mary's real importance for our purposes is that it is where Carver Doone so rudely interrupted John and Lorna's wedding. You'll look in vain for bloodstains on the altar, but the church's austere beauty, its views and its loving tribute to its most famous son more than make up for that. Wear sturdy walking boots to get there, though.

Westward Ho!
CHARLES KINGSLEY
www.visitdevon.co.uk/northdevon/explore/
villages-and-towns/westward-ho

Charles Kingsley's *Westward Ho!* (1855) is another hugely successful Victorian novel that may not have an enormous twenty-first-century fan base (see 'Doone Valley', page 76). In fact, in Evelyn Waugh's *The Ordeal of Gilbert Pinfold* (1957), the paranoid Gilbert, imagining he is being persecuted by strange voices in the course of a sea voyage, chooses the most boring book he can find in the ship's library and reads it aloud to them until they beg him to stop: that book is *Westward Ho!*

Nonetheless *Westward Ho!* has the rare distinction for a novel of having given its title both to a hotel and to the town that grew up around it; there was even a short-lived railway link that would never have been needed if Kingsley's novel had not been such a success. It is a historical adventure set against the background of Sir Francis Drake's naval battles with the Spaniards, but the hero is a Devon lad, and much of the story takes place near his home town of Bideford. Kingsley (1819–1875) had intended his title to mean something along the lines of 'Go west, young man', but when the popularity of the novel attracted people to holiday in North Devon the name was annexed by entrepreneurs building a hotel to cash in on the new demand; Westward Ho! soon came to refer to the surrounding area as well.

Today, Westward Ho! is a seaside resort in the North Devon Area of Outstanding Natural Beauty, a great place for surfing and other water sports, as well as a starting point for stunning walks along the cliffs. The original Westward Ho! Hotel isn't there any more, but there are plenty of alternatives. A drive to Bideford itself, 3 miles inland, takes you along Kingsley Road to a rather grand white marble statue of the author in Victoria Park, overlooking the Torridge River. It shows him in an academic gown, a quill pen in his right hand and two books in his left, reminding us that he wasn't merely a popular novelist: he was also a university professor, a social reformer, a rector in the Church of England, a chaplain to Queen Victoria and the purveyor of some unattractive views on the Irish, Jews, Catholics and Americans. He's best remembered, however, for his jingoistic historical novels and moral tales for children, such as *The Water-Babies*. Also for inadvertently creating the only place name in Britain that includes an exclamation mark.

Back in Westward Ho! itself, you can see a memorial to another, better-remembered author. Rudyard Kipling (see page 104) spent part of his childhood here and the first stanza of his poem 'If—' (once voted the nation's favourite) is set in granite along the promenade. Perhaps, if Kingsley had been writing half a century later, there might have been a seaside resort in Devon called You'll Be a Man, My Son! – with, of course, an exclamation mark.

Coleridge Cottage, Nether Stowey

SAMUEL TAYLOR COLERIDGE

www.nationaltrust.org.uk/coleridge-cottage

www.visit-exmoor.co.uk/coleridge-way/
coleridge-way-home-page

www.groupaccommodation.com/properties/
greta-hall-keswick-cumbria-lake-district

Most of us think of Samuel Taylor Coleridge (1772–1834) as one of the 'Lake Poets', but he famously failed to finish his poem 'Kubla Khan' because he was interrupted by 'a person from Porlock' while he was living in Somerset. This was in 1797 and he was staying, for the sake of his health, at an isolated farmhouse not far from Porlock itself. But for most of the three years he was in the West Country he lived in a house you can visit, now known as Coleridge Cottage, in Nether Stowey. Not only 'Kubla Khan', but also 'The Rime of the Ancient Mariner' (said to have been inspired by nearby Watchet Harbour) and the lyrical 'Frost at Midnight' were written in these years; in fact, 'Frost at Midnight' describes the poet sitting by this very fireside after the rest of the household has gone to bed:

save that at my side
My cradled infant slumbers peacefully.

Coleridge was only in his mid-twenties at this time, but he was already notorious as a radical, a supporter of the democratic ideals behind the French Revolution and an opponent of the slave trade; he was unhappily married and subject to both depression and physical ailments which were treated with laudanum and led to his becoming dependent on opium. You can find out all about this rather glum life in the cottage, which – having spent much of the nineteenth century as an inn before being 'saved for the nation' in 1893 – has been restored to something that Coleridge would have recognised. Trinkets ranging from his inkwell to locks of his hair are on display, and you can listen to extracts from his poetry as you wander through the garden.

Coleridge was an indefatigable walker, one of the first Englishmen to indulge in hill-walking for pleasure, at a time when walking was generally regarded as a means of getting from A to B for those who couldn't afford carriages or horses. His neighbours in Somerset regarded this as decidedly eccentric, but the twenty-first century takes a more tolerant view and has established a waymarked Coleridge Way, starting (or finishing) at the cottage in Nether Stowey and covering 51 miles through glorious Exmoor countryside to Porlock and Lynmouth on the North Devon coast. One of the macabre highlights of the route is Felons Oak, on the edge of Langridge Wood. It's the site of an ancient tree from which convicted felons were hanged, their bodies left to decompose as a grim deterrent to other potential malefactors. Local legend has it that, after the three-hundred-year-old tree was felled, you could hear the rattle of chains if you put your ear to the stump, but in Coleridge's day there might easily have been a rotting corpse to speed the energetic hiker on his way.

It was after this period that Coleridge moved to the Lakes, and you can follow in his footsteps here, too. Greta Hall in Keswick is better known as the home of another Lake Poet, Robert Southey (1774–1843), who lived there from 1804 until his death, but Coleridge and his family had been there for three years before that. Coleridge had moved to Cumberland (as it was then called) in order to be near his friends the Wordsworths, and from Keswick he frequently walked to Grasmere to visit them, a distance of some 13 miles. As he had in Somerset, he tramped endlessly over the district's many hills and it's said that on his way to Grasmere he was once side-tracked into climbing Helvellyn and arrived at his destination well after dark.

Coleridge was passionate about the Lake District; in his narrative ballad *Christabel* there are references to Bratha Head, Windermere and other features of the local scenery; and, with one of the most forced rhymes ever contrived, he even worked Helvellyn into a short poem called 'The Knight's Tomb':

Where is the grave of Sir Arthur O'Kellyn?
Where may the grave of that good man be?
By the side of a spring, on the breast of Helvellyn,
Under the twigs of a young birch tree!

You can stay at Greta Hall: it's now a rather luxurious self-catering holiday rental, with a Southey Wing and a Coleridge Wing, the original slate flag floor, 3 acres of garden, fishing rights on the Greta River and the possibility of wild swimming in nearby Derwentwater. All very lovely, but the real tribute to Coleridge would be to put your boots on, get out on the fells and absolutely not worry about being home in time for tea.

Jane Austen's Bath

JANE AUSTEN

janeausten.co.uk/blogs/arts-and-entertainments/the-upper-rooms

thepumproombath.co.uk

Jane Austen gives us two conflicting views of Bath: that of the young, impressionable Catherine Morland in *Northanger Abbey*:

> *I shall never be in want of something to talk of again to Mrs. Allen, or anybody else. I really believe I shall always be talking of Bath, when I am at home again - I do like it so very much. ... Oh! Who can ever be tired of Bath?*

and that of the more mature, more melancholy Anne Elliot in *Persuasion*:

> *She persisted in a very determined, though very silent disinclination for Bath; caught the first dim view of the extensive buildings, smoking in rain, without any wish of seeing them better; felt their progress through the streets to be, however disagreeable, yet too rapid.*

Catherine has never been away from home before and sees everything through fresh, excited eyes; Anne has been to Bath more than once and been unhappy there. Also, she is arriving in January, so is perhaps seeing the city at its more joyless – though to be fair it does rain a *lot* in Bath: its annual rainfall is an astonishing 30 per cent higher than London's.

Climate apart, if you're an Austen fan, you're more likely to side with Catherine than with Anne. One of the joys of Bath is how Jane Austen-like parts of it still are: you can go shopping in Milsom Street, where Admiral Croft in *Persuasion* scoffed at a painting of a ship in a printshop window ('What queer fellows your fine painters must be, to think that anybody would venture their lives in such a shapeless old cockleshell as that'); and you can visit the Upper Rooms, the eighteenth-century assembly rooms in Bennett Street, described on their completion as 'the most noble and elegant of any in the kingdom'. It was here that Catherine Morland first attended a ball, though she had no acquaintance and no one to dance with. The four rooms are still much as they used to be, with a Ball Room, Card Room and Tea Room all leading off the Great Octagon, and imposing enough that you can imagine a thousand people crammed in there at a time, exchanging gossip and commenting on each other's taste in dress. The Upper Rooms were so called to distinguish them from the older 'Lower Rooms' (where Catherine first met Henry Tilney, shortly after the disappointing debut just mentioned), but the latter were destroyed by fire in 1820.

The other fashionable occupation in Jane Austen's time (she lived from 1775 to 1817) was to 'take the waters' in the Pump Room, or at least to promenade there in the early part of the day. The supposedly health-giving waters come from the natural springs that encouraged the Romans to settle in the area 2,000 years ago and that gave Bath its name. Located above the Roman Baths, the Pump Room today is an elegant restaurant that retains many of the original Georgian features, including a marble vase from which the spa water still pours. You can drink it if you choose, though people are rather more sceptical nowadays about its ability to cure gout or any of the other disorders from which members of eighteenth-century society suffered.

As long as you have an umbrella, Bath is a delight at any time of year, but dedicated Janeites will want to go in September, for the annual ten-day Jane Austen Festival. Here you can attend talks on her works or, if you prefer, dress up in Regency costume to take part in a parade and various balls in the Assembly Rooms and Pump Room. Practise your curtsey and dig out the lovely sprigged muslin dress that's been hanging at the back of your wardrobe for too long.

WEST FRONT of the ABBEY CHURCH at BATH.

Another View of Bath

MARY SHELLEY

http://posp.co.uk/st-pancras-old-church

The story of Mary Shelley, née Godwin (1797–1851), writing *Frankenstein* during a wet summer holiday in Switzerland with her married lover and future husband, Percy Bysshe Shelley, and Lord Byron (see page 142), has been told and retold. Less well known, perhaps, is that, on her return to England, she, Shelley and her stepsister, who was pregnant by Byron, lived for a while in that most respectable of resorts, Bath. It was here that Mary expanded what had originally been a short story and turned it into the novel that is widely regarded as the world's first work of science fiction. At the time of writing, there are plans to open a Frankenstein museum, celebrating this immensely influential work and covering Mary's 'tragic personal life, literary career and the novel's continuing relevance today in regards to popular culture, politics, and science'.

The museum will be situated in a Georgian terrace just three doors along from the Jane Austen Centre. That's in Gay Street, though Mary lived – appropriately enough, given the eerie nature of her tale – in Abbey Churchyard. By the time she moved to Bath, Austen had long since decamped to Chawton (see page 94), so we'll never know what these chalk-and-cheese novelists would have made of each other as neighbours.

Mary's parents were the philosophers William Godwin (1756–1836) and Mary Wollstonecraft (1759–1797), who is regarded as one of the earliest feminists. The older Mary's best-known work, *A Vindication of the Rights of Woman*, put forward radical views on the education of women, deploring the fact that men had been more anxious to make women into 'alluring mistresses than affectionate wives and rational mothers' and that:

the civilised women of this present century, with a few exceptions, are only anxious to inspire love, when they ought to cherish a nobler ambition, and by their abilities and virtues exact respect.

Powerful stuff in the 1790s.

Wollstonecraft died of septicaemia a few days after her daughter was born, so something else we will never know is what she would have thought of the younger Mary's unconventional lifestyle. She was buried in the churchyard of St Pancras Old Church in London, where her daughter had frequent assignations with Shelley at the start of their relationship and where in 1814 they declared (and, according to legend, consummated) their mutual passion and made plans for their elopement to France.

There's still a memorial to Wollstonecraft and Godwin at St Pancras, but in 1851 their remains were taken to Bournemouth and buried there in the churchyard of St Peter's; when Mary Shelley died two years later, she was interred alongside them. A lock of both Mary and Percy Bysshe Shelley's hair, along with an alleged fragment of the latter's ashes, are among the more unusual finds in the collections of the British Library.

Burying the family in Bournemouth was probably a good decision. Only a few years after this, Charles Dickens (see pages 33, 35 and 111) published *A Tale of Two Cities* (admittedly set during the French Revolution some decades earlier) and mentions the old church of St Pancras as a place where Jerry Cruncher, describing himself as an 'honest tradesman', practises his profession. As that profession is grave-robbing, anyone who had had their mortal remains moved to Bournemouth must have been breathing a (posthumous) sigh of relief. Today, the substantial green space of Old St Pancras churchyard is a peaceful spot where you can also find an ancient ash tree. It's known as the Hardy Tree because it was growing here in the 1860s when a young Thomas Hardy (see page 89) was supervising the excavation of part of the graveyard to make way for the building of St Pancras Station. There is also a substantial Victorian Gothic memorial known as the Burdett-Coutts Memorial Sundial, after the wealthy nineteenth-century philanthropist Angela Burdett-Coutts, who had it erected to commemorate the many people whose graves had been disturbed in the course of the churchyard's long history.

So, while there is no lingering sign of Frankenstein, perhaps the memory of Jerry Cruncher lives on.

Burnt Norton to East Coker

T. S. ELIOT

www.nationaltrail.co.uk/en_GB/attraction/cotswold-way-marker-stone-chipping-campden

www.eastcoker.com/tseliot.html

A tour of the sites of Thomas Stearns Eliot's *Four Quartets* will take you across a substantial chunk of southern England, from Gloucestershire ('Burnt Norton') and Somerset ('East Coker'), then back in time to the London of the Blitz ('The Dry Salvages') and on to Huntingdonshire ('Little Gidding').

Burnt Norton is a seventeenth-century manor house situated in the grounds of Hidcote Manor, near Chipping Campden. It's in private ownership, so you have to be content to stare and ponder its strange history. Originally known as Norton House, it was owned in the eighteenth century by a slightly deranged baronet who built an extravagant new mansion next door to it for his mistress. After she left him, he burned the new house down one night in a drunken fit, losing his own life and damaging the original manor into the bargain. When it was refurbished it was given its current name as a result.

When Eliot (1888–1965) happened upon it in 1934, it was deserted and neglected – inspiration enough for a poem that begins with its narrator recalling a moment in a garden and leads into a meditation on the nature of time and the importance of grasping the moment. Eliot was clearly in melancholic mood: most people find Chipping Campden attractive but he, not renowned for looking on the bright side, described it as having an 'olde worlde atmosphere stinking of death'. Even he couldn't find fault with the view from the hills around the town, though. On a clear day it is breathtaking, extending to the Brecon Beacons to the west and the Shropshire Hills to the north – perhaps 50 miles as the crow flies.

Chipping Campden also marks the northern end of the Cotswold Way, a National Trail, courtesy of which the energetic can walk the 102 miles to Bath. The marker stone near the Market Hall contains a quotation not from 'Burnt Norton' but from 'East Coker': 'Now the light falls across the open field, leaving the deep lane shuttered with branches, dark in the afternoon' – an odd choice, you might think, because most people setting off for an eleven-day walk would start rather earlier in the day.

No matter.

For 'The Dry Salvages' (named after a rock formation off the coast of Massachusetts, where he had spent time as a child) and 'Little Gidding', Eliot drew on his own experience of the Blitz, recounting an imagined encounter with Dante during an air raid and using the theme of fire to reflect on destruction, purification and renewal. Little Gidding itself is a village between Huntingdon and Peterborough, which in the seventeenth century was home to a strict High Anglican religious community. This was reviled for being 'popish' by the Puritans of the 1630s and 1640s, and so there is little for the visitor to see except the church of St John, restored in the eighteenth century but with the font and lectern dating from its earlier incarnation. Eliot is thought to have visited only once, but his importance to the village lives on in an annual festival in July.

'East Coker' may be the second of the *Quartets* but the village in Somerset after which it is named is worth visiting last because it is where Eliot's ashes are buried. East Coker was the home of his ancestors: a Sir Thomas Elyot lived here in the sixteenth century and it's from here that the family emigrated to the recently established colony of New England. Although the poem, like the other *Quartets,* is meditative, dealing with issues of life, death and spirituality, it is full of rural references – a 'deep lane' that 'insists on the direction into the village' or 'snowdrops writhing under feet / And hollyhocks that aim too high'. Even today there's a remarkable tranquillity about the village, the lanes that approach it being particularly narrow, the thatch and the amber-tinted stone feeling as if they have been there since time immemorial. Eliot's memorial plaque in the church of St Michael and All Angels fittingly features the first and last lines of 'East Coker': 'In my beginning is my end' and 'In my end is my beginning'.

In between these inspirational visits to the countryside, Eliot lived most of his adult life in London and you can track down at least three plaques: on the former offices of the publisher Faber & Faber in Thornhaugh Street, Bloomsbury, where he worked as an editor for many years; on one home in Crawford Street, Marylebone; and on his final address, in Kensington Court Place, where he moved in 1957. A year before he died, he was visited there by, of all people, the comedian Groucho Marx. Groucho, having done his homework in order to impress the Nobel laureate with his knowledge of his works, found that Eliot was much more interested in discussing Marx Brothers films. Perhaps he wasn't so relentlessly melancholic after all.

Lyme Regis
JANE AUSTEN AND JOHN FOWLES

http://www.lymeregis.org
www.landmarktrust.org.uk/news-and-events/visiting-landmarks/visiting-belmont
www.southwestcoastpath.org.uk

If you went to the cinema in the 1980s, you probably have firmly fixed in your memory the iconic image of the French lieutenant's woman, played by Meryl Streep, huddled in a black cloak on the wind- and wave-swept Cobb at Lyme Regis, in the film version of John Fowles's 1969 novel. You may even remember the novel's alluring opening line:

'An easterly is the most disagreeable wind in Lyme Bay', which encourages 'a person of curiosity', watching a couple walking down the quay when the wind is blowing, to draw certain conclusions about the nature of their relationship.

Alternatively, you may remember the Cobb as the place, in *Persuasion* by Jane Austen (1775–1817), where Louisa Musgrove insisted on jumping down the steps over and over again, inevitably falling and cracking her head and making Captain Wentworth realise that Anne Elliot's persuadability – as opposed to Louisa's headstrongness – isn't such a bad thing after all.

Jane Austen's characters, visiting out of season, headed straight for the sea. 'There is nothing to admire in the buildings themselves,' Austen observes, so:

> *the remarkable situation of the town, the principal street almost hurrying into the water, the walk to the Cobb, skirting round the pleasant little bay, which, in the season, is animated with bathing machines and company; the Cobb itself, its old wonders and new improvements, with the very beautiful line of cliffs stretching out to the east of the town, are what the stranger's eye will seek.*

John Fowles (1926–2005) wrote *The French Lieutenant's Woman* while living in a remote farmhouse on the fringes of Lyme. After three years he moved closer to the centre of town, to Belmont, one of the many elegant villas that sprang up in coastal places in the eighteenth century, when the idea that sea bathing and sea air were good for you took off and seaside holidays became popular. Belmont is now owned by the Landmark Trust, which means you can stay in it, and from Fowles's first-floor writing room you can gaze out over the Cobb, as he did. It isn't generally open to the public, though there are several open days each year.

Despite Jane Austen's disparaging remarks about the buildings, there's great pleasure to be gained from walking through the medieval and Georgian parts of Lyme. But the real joy for committed walkers is the Undercliff, an extraordinary tumbled stretch of coastline created through a series of landslides and now part of the South West Coast Path: it's been described (in an episode of the BBC's *Coast and Country Auctions*) as the closest thing to subtropical jungle that we have in the United Kingdom. It's in this magical place that, in *The French Lieutenant's Woman*, Charles encounters Sarah sleeping in a sun trap on a grassy slope. In an erotically charged scene (this is the 1860s, remember, and she is generally considered to be a 'fallen' woman), he observes her lying with 'her right arm thrown back, in a childlike way. A scattered handful of anemones lay on the grass around it' and he becomes convinced of her innocence, 'of her being unfairly outcast'.

This sort of encounter may not happen to you, but the scenery, the birds and the wild flowers – Charles notices eyebright, birdsfoot and vivid green clumps of marjoram – make the effort worthwhile. And you should make a point of looking back towards the Cobb and admiring what Fowles described as 'quite simply the most beautiful sea rampart on the south coast of England'.

The horror of that moment
to all who stood around!

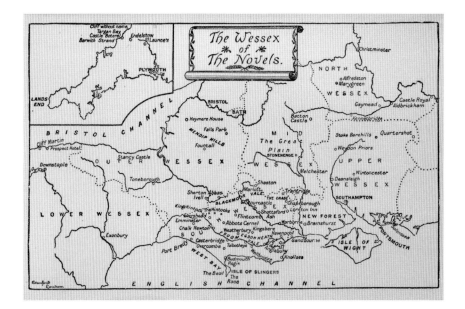

Dorchester

THOMAS HARDY

www.nationaltrust.org.uk/hardys-cottage

www.nationaltrust.org.uk/max-gate

'What an old-fashioned place it seems to be!' said Elizabeth-Jane, while her silent mother mused on other things than topography. 'It is huddled all together; and it is shut in by a square wall of trees, like a plot of garden ground by a box-edging.'...

To birds of the more soaring kind Casterbridge must have appeared on this fine evening as a mosaic-work of subdued reds, browns, greys, and crystals, held together by a rectangular frame of deep green. To the level eye of humanity it stood as an indistinct mass behind a dense stockade of limes and chestnuts, set in the midst of miles of rotund down and concave field.

Casterbridge (in Thomas Hardy's 1886 novel *The Mayor of Casterbridge*) is Dorchester; a rather romanticised Dorchester, as Hardy (1840–1928) remembered it from childhood, although he lived there most of his life. There can be few authors so closely identified with an area and a landscape. 'Hardy's Wessex' was the author's invention: by his own admission he 'disinterred' the name from the pages of English history because the novels he intended to write 'seemed to require a territorial definition of some sort to lend unity to their scene' and 'the area of a single county did not afford a canvas large enough for this purpose'. The area is not very clearly defined – it extends in some books as far west as Devon and in others as far north and east as Oxford. In any case, it is centred on his home town and is the setting for all his major novels.

Hardy's Cottage, that romantic combination of thatch and cob that is everyone's idea of a country cottage, is in the village of Higher Bockhampton, about 3 miles from Dorchester itself. It's not only the author's birthplace, but also the place where he wrote the early novels *Under the Greenwood Tree* (1872) and *Far from the Madding Crowd* (1874). The setting is idyllic – roses round the doorway, ancient woodland all around – but the rooms are spartan, reflecting the way the young Hardy would have lived. By the time he was forty-five, however, he was successful enough to move into something larger and more luxurious and, having trained as an architect, was able to design it himself. This was Max Gate, a Queen Anne-style, red-brick status symbol, showing that the humbly born author was moving up in the world. It's only 3 miles from the cottage, but a world apart in other ways. Here he wrote *Tess of the d'Urbervilles* (1891) and *Jude the Obscure* (1895), both of which scandalised his Victorian public so much that he gave up writing novels and devoted himself to poetry. He lived at Max Gate for the rest of his life and, although most of his ashes are interred at Poets' Corner in Westminster Abbey (see page 14), his heart is buried under a modest monument in the local Dorset churchyard, St Michael's of Stinsford. In a touching posthumous tribute, a later Poet Laureate, Cecil Day-Lewis (1904–1972), who had no connection with Dorset but was a great admirer of Hardy, was, at his own request, buried there too.

Two hours' brisk walk from Max Gate is the Hardy monument, towering above Black Down hill. This is a memorial to the other Dorset Thomas Hardy – the naval one, of Battle of Trafalgar/'Kiss me, Hardy' fame. No relation, no literary connections, but the site of the monument provides a great view over the landscape that was the other Thomas Hardy's lifeblood and inspiration.

3

CHAPTER THREE

SOUTHERN ENGLAND

Farringford House, Isle of Wight

ALFRED, LORD TENNYSON

farringford.co.uk

www.visitisleofwight.co.uk

Following the death of Wordsworth in 1850, Alfred Tennyson (later Lord Tennyson, 1809–1892) became Poet Laureate and, as was the norm in those days, remained in that post for the rest of his long life. Looking for a country retreat, in 1853 he moved, with his wife Emily, to the Isle of Wight and settled at Farringford House, a mansion on the western tip of the island, beyond Freshwater Bay. Emily had fallen in love with the view; Alfred, inviting a friend to visit, described it as the place:

> *Where, far from noise and smoke of town,*
> *I watch the twilight falling brown*
> *All round a careless order'd garden,*
> *Close to the ridge of a noble down.*

Another visitor, the novelist Anne, Lady Ritchie, noted:

> *The house at Farringford seemed like a charmed palace, with green walls without, and speaking walls within. There hung Dante with his solemn nose and wreath; Italy gleamed over the doorways; friends' faces lined the passages, books filled the shelves, and a glow of crimson was everywhere; the oriel drawing-room window was full of green and golden leaves, of the sound of birds and of the distant sea.*

CHAPTER THREE: SOUTHERN ENGLAND

When the Tennysons first came to Farringford it was a fairly standard Georgian villa enlivened by bits of Gothic ornamentation such as arched, rather cathedral-like windows and castellated parapets. Alfred and Emily were responsible for many additions and improvements, often supervised by Emily while her husband was travelling. As well as a sizeable extension, providing a large room for parties on the ground floor with a library above, she put in bay windows to make the attic rooms light and airy; installed a grand arch in the hall; and inserted the dormer window in Tennyson's attic study: it still provides a glorious westward view across the Downs to the Needles.

Tennyson thought that the Isle of Wight would be a quiet haven away from the bustle of London. He'd failed to take into account just how much of an attraction he was: his visitors included the Italian nationalist Giuseppe Garibaldi and Queen Victoria's consort Prince Albert, whose summer residence, Osborne House, was only a short drive away. So many friends and random celebrity seekers flocked to see him that he eventually bought Aldworth House, situated in what is today called Tennyson's Lane, near Haslemere in Surrey, and retreated there for the summer months. He continued to spend the quieter winters at Farringford, appreciating the beauty that was such an inspiration to him.

Today, the gardens are as much an attraction as the house – both Tennysons were keen gardeners and the planting in the walled kitchen garden, one of their favourite spots, has been recreated following descriptions in Emily's journal and paintings by their artist friend Helen Allingham.

You can also follow in Alfred's footsteps by walking on what are now called the Tennyson Downs, as he did every day, remarking that the air was worth 'sixpence a pint' (a decent sum, making it more expensive than gin) and revelling in the dramatic views. A stiffish climb across springy grass takes you to the Tennyson Monument, a towering Celtic cross on the highest point of the Downs, on the site of a beacon that once warned of any threatened invasion. You can also visit the local church, All Saints' in Freshwater, where Emily and the couple's eldest son are buried and where the inscription accompanying a marble bust of the poet tells us that his happiest days were passed at Farringford. Tennyson himself, as befits the longest-serving Poet Laureate ever, can be found in Poets' Corner, Westminster Abbey (see page 14).

Emsworth Museum
P. G. WODEHOUSE

emsworthmuseum.org.uk *Open weekends and Bank Holidays, Easter till end October only.*

Before he became a writer, Pelham Grenville Wodehouse (1881–1975) had worked in banking with spectacular lack of success, resigning just before he would have been sacked on the grounds of innumeracy and the unacceptable habit of writing ideas for plots on pages he subsequently tore from the bank's ledgers. Free to embark on a writing career, he went to visit a friend who was teaching in a small school in Hampshire, fell in love with the town and lived there for the next ten years.

The town was called Emsworth, the school was Emsworth House and its headmaster a man named Deverall Hall. Wodehouse never taught there, but he lived next door and helped the boys with amateur dramatics and cricket. The house he lived in was called Threepwood.

Fans of his work will have noticed some familiar names in that last paragraph. They were the inspiration for the pig-loving Earl of Emsworth in the Blandings Castle series, his roguish brother Galahad ('Gally') Threepwood and, with a slight adjustment to spelling, Deverill Hall in King's Deverill, one of the many places where (in this case in the 1949 novel *The Mating Season*) Bertie Wooster came dangerously close to having to marry the dreadful Madeline Basset. Only a couple of miles to the west of Emsworth is Warblington, which became the surname of one of Lord Emsworth's married sisters, and almost as close if you head east is Bosham, the courtesy title given to his lordship's son George. Chichester Clam, Boko Fittleworth and Roberta Wickham are only three more in a long list of characters whose names were inspired by local places. Wodehouse drew on his surroundings for settings, too: Emsworth House School, thinly disguised as Sanstead, is the setting for *The Little Nugget* (1913) and the fictional town of Belpher, which features in *A Damsel in Distress* (1919), is undoubtedly Emsworth.

Sadly Emsworth House School no longer exists, but Threepwood does. There is a P. G. Wodehouse gallery in the local museum, dedicated to his life and work, and the Emsworth Maritime and Historical Trust organises Wodehouse Walks round the town.

Jane Austen's House, Chawton
JANE AUSTEN
janeaustens.house *Open Thursday to Sunday only.*
www.winchester-cathedral.org.uk

In 1809, shortly after moving to the house where she would live for most of the rest of her life, Jane Austen (1775–1817) penned a mock-Byronic piece of doggerel about it:

> *Our Chawton home – how much we find*
> *Already in it, to our mind.*
> *And how convinced that when complete,*
> *It will all other Houses beat*
> *That ever have been made or mended,*
> *With rooms concise, or rooms distended.*

She seems to have been right: it's a house in which she was content. After an unsettled decade that had involved several changes of home, the death of her father and associated financial difficulties, Jane – along with her mother, sister and a woman friend – was back to within 20 miles of where she was born, in a cottage on the substantial estate her brother had inherited. Two hundred years after her death, there's still a gentleness

about it that reflects the quiet, domestic life she lived here. Her letters are full of gossip, interest in the wellbeing of friends and family, the beauty of the garden and the possibility of 'a great crop of Orleans plums, but not many greengages' – the normal day-to-day concerns of any early nineteenth-century woman in comfortable but not wealthy circumstances.

Yet it was in this tranquil place and time that she revised earlier drafts of *Sense and Sensibility*, *Pride and Prejudice* and *Northanger Abbey*, became a published – and critically acclaimed – author and subsequently wrote *Mansfield Park*, *Emma* and *Persuasion*. It's a prodigious output over a mere eight years, the latter part of which was troubled by ill health.

The house is a substantial, seventeenth-century red-brick affair – rather bigger than what we would call a cottage today – but the memory you are most likely to take away with you is one of smallness. The walnut table at which Jane wrote is *extraordinarily* small. The explanation (taken from her nephew's memoir of her) was that she didn't want anyone beyond the immediate family circle to know about her writing, and always 'wrote upon small sheets of paper which could easily be put away, or covered with a piece of blotting paper'. If you pay a visit to the British Library in London, you can see her

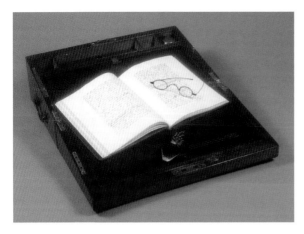

portable 'writing-box' and spectacles on display in the Treasures Gallery. Yet despite this apparent modesty, there is no doubt that, when success came, she enjoyed it: 'Make everybody at Hendon admire "Mansfield Park",' she wrote to a niece who was visiting friends shortly after that novel was published.

You'll also notice how small Jane herself was: both her bed and a robe of hers that is on display might be more suited to today's average twelve-year-old.

As for the garden, the cottage-garden flowers, the herbs, both medicinal and culinary, the climbers and the old roses would all have been familiar to Jane and there's an old oak tree believed to be descended from one she planted herself. There are also two particularly beautiful curved seats, engraved with words she wrote to the Prince Regent's personal librarian in a letter dated 1 April 1816. She was declining his invitation to write something less provincial, more aristocratic, which might earn her the prince's sponsorship:

> *I could not sit seriously down to write a serious Romance under any other motive than to save my Life, & if it were indispensable for me to keep it up & never relax into laughing at myself or other people, I am sure I should be hung before I had finished the first Chapter.*

A refusal to compromise your principles for monetary gain can rarely have been so charmingly or so modestly written.

The Austens worshipped at the local church, St Nicholas, and Jane's mother and sister, both named Cassandra Austen, are buried there. Jane herself lies, as befits a Hampshire author of such renown, in Winchester Cathedral. In fact, she is there for the simple reason that she died in Winchester, 16 miles from Chawton, where she had gone to be close to a doctor during her last illness. She much admired the cathedral and a friend seems to have pulled strings to get permission for her to be buried there. Jane's funeral and original gravestone were modest, the latter referring to her as the daughter of a deceased local minister rather than as a novelist. That inscription is still there, but over the years following her death her fame increased and her memorials in the cathedral expanded accordingly: there are now also a brass plaque beginning with the words 'Jane Austen, known to many by her writings ...', a memorial window and a statue of her sitting, quill pen in hand, head bent in concentration, at a replica of that tiny table in the cottage at Chawton.

Brighton
GRAHAM GREENE
www.brightonpier.co.uk

AN ENTERTAINMENT BY GRAHAM GREENE

The holiday crowd ... came in by train from
Victoria every five minutes, rocked down
Queen's Road standing on the tops of the
little local trams, stepped off in bewildered
multitudes into fresh and glittering air:
the new silver paint sparkled on the piers,
the cream houses ran away into the west
like a pale Victorian water-colour; a race
in miniature motors, a band playing,
flower gardens in bloom below the front,
an aeroplane advertising something for the
health in pale vanishing clouds across the sky.

Sounds nice, doesn't it? It's the opening of Graham Greene's 1938 novel *Brighton Rock*. A typical jolly Bank Holiday at the seaside. Except that, at the beginning of the paragraph, we've read, in the book's very first line:

Hale knew, before he had been in Brighton
three hours, that they meant to murder him.

From that moment on, everything about Greene's Brighton is threatening. You can be slashed with a razor blade at the races or pushed to your death down the stairs of a shabby boarding house; even a drive out into the country, towards the comfortable villas of Rottingdean and Peacehaven, carries the terrifying knowledge that Pinkie, the teenage gangster haunted by dreams of hell and damnation, has a bottle of vitriol in his pocket and is ready to throw it at you.

There are lots more cheerful things to do in Brighton than follow in Pinkie's ill-fated footsteps, but the book is full of real locations, painstakingly described, that you can seek out if you wish. The Palace Pier is now a Grade II listed building and still offers the traditional fairground attractions that Pinkie would have seen when he paid his threepence and went through the turnstile:

past the peepshows, the slot-machines and the quoits to a shooting-booth. The shelves of
dolls stared down with glassy innocence, like Virgins in a church repository.

Some of it is a bit more high-tech nowadays and it may cost you more than threepence. There's rather less Catholic angst, though, and there are still dodgems and a ghost train and side shows where you can win a rubber duck.

If you head west along the seafront you'll pass the Royal Albion, the Old Ship, the Grand and the Metropole (now part of the Hilton chain) – all hotels that get passing mentions in *Brighton Rock*. You won't see the Cosmopolitan, though. Greene (1904–1991) is believed to have based this on the Bedford, which was destroyed by fire in 1964 and rebuilt as a Holiday Inn. Today you can revel in the fact that Charles Dickens wrote *Dombey and Son* while staying in the original Bedford in the 1840s. Sadly, however, you are unlikely to see the mobster Colleoni walking across 'an acre of deep carpet from the Louis Seize writing room', nor to spot 'a woman in mauve with an untimely tiara … writing a letter in a jumble of chinoiserie'.

You can still buy traditional Brighton rock, with the resort's name all the way through it, or a personalised version to use as wedding favours or even to celebrate your favourite football team. You can visit the local distillery and buy Brighton Gin Rock to use in mint-flavoured cocktails. But it's hard to avoid another memory of Pinkie's short and ill-fated career. As his nemesis, Ida, says in the novel, people don't change:

It's like those sticks of rock: bite it all the way down, you'll still read Brighton.

In Graham Greene's Brighton, even the confectionery has a hint of menace.

Monk's House, Rodmell
LEONARD AND VIRGINIA WOOLF
www.nationaltrust.org.uk/monks-house

Leonard (1880–1969) and Virginia Woolf (1882–1941) discovered Monk's House in Rodmell in 1919 when they were looking for a country retreat; they owned it and loved it for the rest of their lives and it became their permanent home after they were bombed out of London in 1940. Although it had 'no buses, no water, no gas or electricity', Virginia wrote that it had 'great charms' – and it certainly gave them peace and quiet in which to write. Virginia's sister Vanessa Bell and a fellow member of the Bloomsbury set, Duncan Grant (see page 100), contributed to the décor; their artworks adorn the walls, and a set of table and chairs which they painted, with Virginia's initials worked into the design, can still be seen in the sitting room.

On the windowsill in the same room is a bust of Virginia by the sculptor Stephen Tomlin (1901–1937). Tomlin took seven years to persuade Virginia to sit for him and the moment she agreed she regretted it. She hated, as her nephew and biographer Quentin Bell put it, to be 'peered at'; she refused to endure more than six sittings, meaning that the sculpture was left unfinished, the eyes blank, and showing, as Leonard wrote, 'a shadow of her misery … frozen into the clay of the portrait'. Unfinished or not, as a study of anguish, it is compelling.

Virginia famously decreed that a woman must have 'money and a room of her own if she is to write fiction'. At Monk's House she had more than a room – she had a shed known as the 'writing lodge' in the orchard, an even more tranquil spot than the house

itself. She headed down here to work 'with the regularity of a stockbroker' and produced many of her most famous books here, surrounded by cigarette ends, scraps of paper and discarded pen nibs.

To the Woolfs, 'the shape and fertility and wildness of the garden' had been one of the great attractions of Monk's House. Over the years Leonard created a beautiful English country garden, with amazing views over the Downs at any time of year but perhaps at their most beautiful in the spring when the orchard is in blossom. Virginia drew great inspiration from both garden and views, not least in her short story 'In the Orchard':

> There were twenty-four apple-trees in the orchard, some slanting slightly, others growing straight with a rush up the trunk which spread wide into branches and formed into round red or yellow drops. Each apple-tree had sufficient space. The sky exactly fitted the leaves. When the breeze blew, the line of the boughs against the wall slanted slightly and then returned.

It's good to know that this unhappy woman had somewhere that, in the periods of respite between her bouts of depression, brought her joy. She drowned herself in the nearby River Ouse and her ashes are buried in the garden at Monk's House, under a lead cast of the bust that caused so much heart-searching.

Leonard Woolf survived his wife by twenty-eight years and died at Monk's House. His ashes lie alongside Virginia's, the site also marked by a bronze bust.

But if you're thinking, 'Hold on, these are the Bloomsburys. Shouldn't we take a look at Bloomsbury?', the most rewarding place to visit is Tavistock Square Gardens. Leonard and Virginia lived in this London square at no. 52 from 1924 to 1939, running the Hogarth Press and publishing the likes of T. S. Eliot (see page 84), E. M. Forster and Katherine Mansfield. The gardens are dominated by a statue of Gandhi in the centre and a conscientious objectors' memorial stone at one end, but another cast of that same bust of Virginia is tucked away in one corner and a helpful information board points you in the direction of a ginkgo biloba tree dedicated to Leonard. Slap bang in the middle of London, it's a tranquil place in which to reflect on the lives of two writers who loved tranquillity.

Charleston, West Firle
THE BLOOMSBURYS
www.charleston.org.uk *Entry to the house is by guided tour only: you're advised to book in advance.*

If you've ever thought that the Bloomsbury set were a bit of an arty-farty self-indulgent lot, a visit to their home at Charleston will put you right. Duncan Grant (1885–1978), a conscientious objector during the First World War, was obliged to do 'work of national importance' as an alternative to military service, and for much of the war he did just that on a local farm twelve hours a day, six days a week, acquiring such calluses on his hands that he couldn't paint. Conscientious indeed.

A group of the Bloomsburys – Duncan Grant, his lover David Garnett (another conscientious objector), Vanessa Bell and her two young sons – moved to this sixteenth-century farmhouse in 1916. It was at the recommendation of Vanessa's sister, Virginia Woolf, who, with her husband Leonard, had a country home nearby, and knew that the men would be able to find work in the area. From then on and for more than sixty years, Charleston became a focus of Bloomsbury intellectual and artistic endeavour, not to mention Bohemian living. The economist John Maynard Keynes spent extended periods here and, when he married in 1925, leased a farm only a few hundred metres away. Vanessa's husband, the art critic Clive Bell (with whom she remained friendly until her death in 1961, although theirs was a marriage in name only from about 1916 onwards), was another frequent visitor, sometimes with a mistress in tow. Others who formed part of the circle included the Woolfs, the novelist E. M. Forster and Grant's cousin, the biographer Lytton Strachey. Angelica, the daughter of Vanessa Bell and Duncan Grant, was born at Charleston on Christmas Day 1918; she subsequently married David Garnett and became the artist known as Angelica Garnett. With all the comings and goings, the *ménages à trois* and the changing of partners that went on, living at Charleston must have been stimulating but unsettling. Angelica later described her childhood there as 'a precarious paradise'.

Charleston was an unremarkable farmhouse when the first Bloomsburys moved in, but they set about making it uniquely their own. As Vanessa's son Quentin Bell put it: 'Restoration or conservation seemed too dull a solution; it was much more fun to invent something new and change the entire aspect of a room.' The living room/schoolroom that became Clive Bell's study when he moved into the house in 1939 is dominated by a glorious marquetry table that had been a wedding present to him and Vanessa, but that

is about the only substantial piece of furniture in the house that has no Bloomsbury mark on it. The critic and artist Roger Fry (another of Vanessa's lovers) designed the unusual fireplace so that it juts out into the room in an effort to provide more heat in a cold house; Vanessa decorated both this and the window embrasures, while Duncan Grant painted the door panel. The same 'go on, you have a go' attitude can be seen throughout the house: Grant's bedroom features paintings by Vanessa, but he himself designed the carpet and the stool cover. The guest bedroom frequently occupied by Maynard Keynes contains a door panel in stained glass created by Quentin Bell.

And so it goes on. In fact, Keynes's bedroom is the least 'arty' room in the house, and perhaps the one with the strongest literary connections: it was here that he wrote the work that made him famous, *The Economic Consequences of the Peace*, a denunciation of the Treaty of Versailles signed after the end of the First World War. Some fifteen years later, Clive Bell composed his memoir *Old Friends* in the study, and Vanessa in particular was a voluminous letter-writer – some three thousand of her letters survive and give a remarkable, not to say bawdy, insight into the unconventional lives everyone led at Charleston.

The house is breathtaking – possibly even exhausting, given the hugely eclectic range of art that penetrates almost every nook and cranny. The true joy of Charleston, though, is its walled garden, another creation of Bell and Grant, following designs by Fry. It has a pond lined with tiles placed so that their reflection can be seen in the water; an abundance of sculpture, much of it by Quentin Bell; and lush cottage-garden planting, with rampant hollyhocks in the summer and plenty of fruit trees. If you go in the spring, when the tulips and blossom are at their best, you'll come away with a memory that won't fade in a hurry.

To round off the visit, if you're grave-hunting you don't have far to go: St Peter's Church, Firle, is only a couple of miles away. Duncan and Vanessa lie side by side in the churchyard, with Angelica appropriately at their feet and Quentin a short distance away.

Literary Gardening

www.nationaltrust.org.uk/sissinghurst-castle-garden
www.nationaltrust.org.uk/knole

Opening times of gardens and buildings vary throughout the year at both properties.

Throughout this book you'll find reference to authors who loved and were inspired by their gardens, from Henry James in Rye (see page 106) to Beatrix Potter in the Lake District (page 174). Perhaps the author most closely associated with her garden is Vita Sackville-West (1892–1962), and the association came about through an accident of chromosomes. It would never have happened if she had been born a boy.

Vita and her husband, the politician and writer Harold Nicolson (1886–1968), bought Sissinghurst Castle in Kent as a ruin in 1930 and created, in no particular order: a rose garden; a white garden designed in the hope that 'the great ghostly barn owl will sweep silently across a pale garden, next summer, in the twilight'; a cottage garden; a lime walk; an orchard; a nuttery full of Kentish cobnuts ... Sissinghurst has become one of the most visited gardens in Britain, and rightly so. You can also climb the tower in which Vita did her writing and enjoy spectacular panoramic views.

Vita's most successful novel, however, was written before she ever set eyes on Sissinghurst. She was born, her parents' only child, about 20 miles away, at Knole, a beautiful and vast fifteenth-century house set in 1,000 acres of parkland. She loved the place passionately but, owing to what she described as 'a technical fault' (being female), she was unable to inherit it and, after her father's death in 1928, she had to see it pass into the hands of a cousin. *The Edwardians*, written shortly afterwards, has been described as a love letter to Knole. In its opening chapter, nineteen-year-old Sebastian has climbed onto the roof and looks down over an estate that closely resembles Vita's childhood home:

Acres of red-brown roof surrounded him, heraldic beasts carved in stone sitting at each corner of the gables. Across the great courtyard the flag floated red and blue and languid from a tower. Down in the garden, on a lawn of brilliant green, he could see the sprinkled figures of his mother's guests, some sitting under the trees, some strolling about; he could hear their laughter and the tap of the croquet mallets. Round the garden spread the park; a herd of deer stood flicking with their short tails in the shade of the beeches.

If you visit Knole today you probably won't be allowed to climb on to the roof, but you should still recognise a lot of the details of Vita's description. And if you visit Sissinghurst, you'll be grateful for the 'technical fault' without which this incomparable garden would never have come into being.

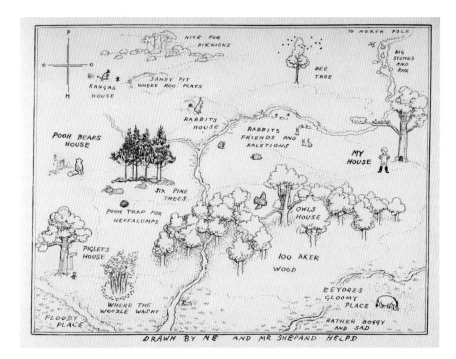

Map labels: P · TO NORTH POLE · NICE FOR PIKNICKS · BIG STONES AND ROX · BEE TREE · KANGAS HOUSE · SANDY PIT WHERE ROO PLAYS · RABBITS HOUSE · POOH BEARS HOUSE · RABBITS FRIENDS AND RALETIONS · MY HOUSE · SIX PINE TREES · POOH TRAP FOR HEFFALUMPS · OWLS HOUSE · PIGLETS HOUSE · 100 AKER WOOD · EEYORES GLOOMY PLACE · WHERE THE WOOZLE WASNT · FLOODY PLACE · RATHER BOGGY AND SAD · DRAWN BY ME AND MR SHEPARD HELPD

Ashdown Forest

A. A. MILNE

ashdownforest.org

T he country house in Hartfield, East Sussex, where Alan Alexander Milne (1882–1956) lived for many years, and where he wrote *Winnie-the-Pooh*, is in private hands, but there is nothing to stop you wandering through Pooh's Hundred Acre Wood and playing Poohsticks from the very bridge that Pooh and his friends used. The first ever game was actually played with fir cones, because that's what Pooh dropped into the river when he tripped going over the bridge. He then lay down and watched the river slipping away beneath him:

> *and suddenly, there was his fir-cone slipping away too.*
> *'That's funny,' said Pooh. 'I dropped it on the other side,' said Pooh, 'and it came out on this side! I wonder if it would do it again?' And he went back for some more fir-cones.*
> *It did. It kept on doing it. Then he dropped two in at once, and leant over the bridge to see which of them would come out first; and one of them did.*

And so the game was born, except that when Pooh and Piglet and Rabbit and the others played it together, they chose sticks rather than fir cones, because sticks were easier to mark so you could tell whose stick had won.

The bridge in Ashdown Forest where all this took place is officially called Poohsticks

Bridge these days; it can be found in Posingford Wood, at the northern end of the forest. Although it was rebuilt, modernised and health-and-safetified in the 1970s and again in 2000, it retains the look of the original: a traditional wooden bridge with slatted sides, ideal for dropping sticks through. Bring your own, though – previous visitors have more or less denuded the area of suitable twigs.

For more Pooh-related adventures and a walk linking them, you can pay the princely sum (at the time of writing) of 50p to download a map from the website given above. It will guide you not only to a memorial to A. A. Milne and his illustrator, E. H. Shepard, but also to the Sandy Pit where Roo played, the place where Piglet dug the Cunning Trap to catch a Heffalump and the site of the North Pole, which Pooh used to save Roo from drowning. Ashdown Forest is, in fact, about 640 acres (or Akers) in area, so there is plenty of scope for Expotitions.

Bateman's, Burwash
RUDYARD KIPLING
www.nationaltrust.org.uk/batemans

If you're ever walking through the tunnel leading on to the Centre Court at Wimbledon, you'll pass under two lines of the nation's favourite poem, 'If–', the work that more than any other has ensured Rudyard Kipling's enduring place in posterity:

If you can meet with Triumph and Disaster
And treat those two impostors just the same.

However, that is only likely to happen if you're a top-flight tennis player. A commentator may well point it out to you if you're watching the tournament on television. But for the fifty weeks of the year when Wimbledon isn't on, Kipling's country home in Sussex may be rewarding.

Most of us probably think of Kipling (1865–1936) in association with India, but despite *The Jungle Book*, *Just So Stories* and 'You're a better man than I am, Gunga Din', he spent a large part of his adult life in England and in 1902 bought a handsome Jacobean house, Bateman's, in what is now the High Weald Area of Outstanding Natural Beauty. At that time he was an international celebrity, having published, among other things, *The Jungle Book* and some of his most popular poetry, *The Barrack-Room Ballads*; five years later he became the first writer in English to be awarded the recently founded Nobel Prize in Literature – 'in consideration', the citation read, 'of the power of observation, originality of imagination, virility of ideas and remarkable talent for narration which characterize the creations of this world-famous author'.

Built in a mellow sandstone, with gables and mullioned windows, Bateman's looks like lots of people's ideal of an English country residence. Kipling and his wife fell in love with it at first sight and shortly after moving in he wrote this rapturous description to a friend:

> *Behold us, lawful owners of a grey stone lichened house – A.D. 1634 over the door – beamed, panelled, with old oak staircase, and all untouched and unfaked ... It is a good and peaceable place standing in terraced lawns nigh to a walled garden of old red brick and two fat-headed old oasthouses with red brick stomachs and an aged silver grey oak dovecot on top ... It hasn't a lodge or any nonsense of that kind. You walk up to the porch over a stone-paved path laid down in the turf ... The rest is all fields and farms and to the southward one glorious sweep of woods.*

Describing the inside of the house he mentioned 'a black and white tiled hall all panelled to the naked beamed ceiling' and a 'stone arched fireplace' in which the Kiplings burned huge logs. Both of these features are still there, and you can see at a glance why he also wrote that 'the worst of the place is that it simply will not endure modern furniture'.

Although the centuries-old Englishness of Bateman's appealed to the romantic in Kipling, he was also concerned with practicalities that would keep his servants happy. That meant, he decided, installing electricity – no mean feat in a secluded country house in 1902. He did it by removing the waterwheel from the mill at the end of the garden and turning it into a turbine, taking expert advice from no less a person than Sir William Willcocks, the prominent civil engineer who had designed the first Aswan Dam on the Nile a few years previously.

Despite being glad of the privacy that Bateman's offered, Kipling enjoyed touring the country by car: his Rolls-Royce is still to be seen in the garage. And he drew inspiration for his fantasy stories for children, *Puck of Pook's Hill* and *Rewards and Fairies*, from the glorious country walks and splendid views to be had on the surrounding estate. Many of the poems that are interwoven with these stories show his love of the local landscape:

There was once a road through the woods
Before they planted the trees.
It is underneath the coppice and heath
And the thin anemones.

Kipling had in many respects a tragic life, losing his elder daughter to pneumonia when she was only six and his only son in the First World War. Once peace was restored, the empire-building style of his early poems rather went out of fashion and has been much decried since. He died almost forgotten: his last brief illness coincided with that of King George V, who outlived him by two days, so that the nation's attention was elsewhere. Even so, he was granted a niche in Poets' Corner in Westminster Abbey (see page 14), where he lies close to Charles Dickens and Thomas Hardy. And, of course, his words are still over the entrance to Centre Court.

Lamb House, Rye
HENRY JAMES, E. F. BENSON AND OTHERS
www.nationaltrust.org.uk/lamb-house
www.mermaidinn.com

In some parts of the country, you can travel around a handful of sites in order to pay tribute to one author. In Rye, it's the other way round: go to one house and knock three very different novelists off your list in a single visit. In the course of the twentieth century Lamb House was home to – among others – Henry James (1843–1916), Edward Frederick Benson (1867–1940) and Rumer Godden (1907–1998), perhaps best remembered now for *Black Narcissus*, filmed in 1947 with Deborah Kerr as a nun in the Himalayas, and brought to a new audience by a 2020 television version.

Given all that, it's rather a shame to learn that Lamb House has nothing to do with Charles and Mary Lamb of *Lamb's Tales from Shakespeare* fame. It was built for a local wine merchant called James Lamb in 1722 and it's a handsome, red-brick Georgian mansion tucked away between the parish church and the historic Mermaid Inn. The Mermaid is one of Britain's most haunted pubs, once the stamping ground of smugglers – both the real-life eighteenth-century Hawkhurst Gang and the fictional Dr Syn in a series of novels by Russell Thorndike (1885–1972), set largely on the nearby Romney Marsh. The room known as Dr Syn's Bedchamber is reputed to be the Mermaid's most haunted, but there are opportunities for an eerie experience wherever you sleep.

Anyway, back to Lamb House. American by birth, Europhile by education and temperament, Henry James settled in Rye in 1897, having lived in London for over twenty years and become part of the literary scene there. Despite his success as a novelist – he had *The Portrait of a Lady, Washington Square, The Bostonians* and many others under his belt by this time – he had had no success as a playwright and had been booed off the stage when taking a bow at the première of his largely forgotten *Guy Donville*. (After the shortest of runs, the play was pulled in favour of another new work, *The Importance of Being Earnest,* which, it is fair to say, has stood the test of time rather better.) Deeply embarrassed by the experience, James fled to the country, intending to stay away for a few months. But then he fell in love with Lamb House and snapped up a twenty-one-year lease when it unexpectedly became available. It clearly suited him, because he produced almost a novel a year for the next seven years, including *The Wings of the Dove, The Ambassadors* and *The Golden Bowl*, none of which is a lightweight.

E. F. Benson is remembered today for the 'Mapp and Lucia' books, comedies of 1920s manners set in a seaside town called Tilling that is clearly modelled on Rye. Benson moved here in 1918 and stayed for the rest of his life, becoming mayor in 1934. In the early novels in the series, Miss Mapp lives in a house called Mallards, recognisably inspired by Lamb House. Sadly, the garden room – a self-contained wing conceived as a ballroom and added to the original house in 1743 – was destroyed by a German bomber in 1940. It had been both James's and Benson's writing room, and as we can no longer see it for ourselves we must be grateful to Benson for this gently vicious description of it. At the start of *Miss Mapp*, the protagonist is keeping an eye on her gardener and his family, lest they steal her vegetables:

> *She sat, on this hot July morning, like a large bird of prey at the very convenient window of her garden-room, the ample bow of which formed a strategical point of high value. This garden-room, solid and spacious, was built at right angles to the front of her house, and looked straight down the very interesting street which debouched at its lower end into the High Street of Tilling ... A side window of the garden-room ... commanded the strawberry beds; she could sit quite close to that, for it was screened by the large-leaved branches of a fig-tree and she could spy unseen.*

The main body of the house is intact, happily, and what you see in it is mostly James memorabilia, from his writing desk in the Green Room to the graves of his pet dogs in the walled garden. There's a fine collection of sketches by William Rothenstein of James himself and many of his distinguished friends: Joseph Conrad, G. K. Chesterton and the artist John Singer Sargent, to name but three. And, lest you fear that the destruction of the garden room means you've lost the chance of spying on the neighbours, there's a cosy nook at the top of the stairs with a window overlooking the street, a comfy chair and a pair of binoculars thoughtfully left on the table beside it.

When you've checked out the comings and goings in the street, take time to enjoy the garden. It was designed by James's friend Alfred Parsons (1847–1920), who was a book illustrator as well as a garden designer and of whom James wrote that he understood perfectly how Americans liked England to appear:

> *The England of his pencil ... is exactly the England that the American imagination, restricted to itself, constructs from the poets, the novelists, from all the delightful testimony it inherits.*

There are roses, a lily pond, herbaceous borders and someone selling tea and cake at a particularly delightful tea shop in the courtyard – you can't get more English than that.

One final literary connection: the great children's writer Joan Aiken (1924–2004), best known for novels of alternative history such as *The Wolves of Willoughby Chase*, was born in Rye. In her novel for adults *The Haunting of Lamb House*, the spirit of Toby Lamb, son of the original builder, makes its presence felt in the lives of both James and Benson. It is widely rumoured that Lamb House inspired James's very creepy *The Turn of the Screw*, and in the run-up to Christmas there are candlelit ghost tours following in Aiken's footsteps. So if you don't fancy sleeping in a haunted inn, you can have a hair-raising experience (with a mince pie and some mulled wine thrown in) and then go home to the safety of your own bed.

Literary Wining and Dining

thackerays-restaurant.co.uk

www.dukeshotel.com

In addition to Shakespeare-associated pubs (see page 134), tea shops connected with Charles Dickens (page 35) and Anna Sewell (page 152) and Oscar Wilde's Café Royal (page 24), it's worth checking out Thackeray's in Tunbridge Wells, which offers 'relaxed fine dining' in a house once owned by William Makepeace Thackeray (1811–1863), author of *Vanity Fair*. More than three hundred years old, and festooned with odd angles and staircases best negotiated when sober, it's just the place to remember the ambitious social climber Becky Sharp's discontent with the idle social life of Paris:

Opera-boxes and restaurateur dinners palled upon her: nosegays could not be laid by as a provision for future years: and she could not live upon knick-knacks, laced handkerchiefs, and kid gloves. She felt the frivolity of pleasure and longed for more substantial benefits.

Diamonds are a girl's best friend, as a later, more succinct writer put it.

If a cocktail is more what you're after, try Dukes Hotel in St James's, London. Ian Fleming (1908–1964) drank here during the Second World War, when he was working nearby for Naval Intelligence, and Dukes's long-established cocktail bar is, according to 007 tradition, the inspiration for James Bond's famous preference for 'shaken, not stirred'. A trolley laden with bottles of spirits is wheeled to your table, where, the head bartender has been quoted as saying, 'It's all about the theatre of the occasion.' You can even go for afternoon tea where each course is paired with its own martini. 'I must be dreaming,' as the movie Bond said in a different context.

Canterbury
GEOFFREY CHAUCER AND CHRISTOPHER MARLOWE
www.canterbury-cathedral.org

The Tabard Inn, like much of medieval Southwark, was destroyed by fire in 1676; like the nearby George (see page 135), it was promptly rebuilt and reopened. Unlike the George, however, it didn't survive the advent of the railways and is now commemorated only by a plaque in Talbot Yard and in the *Canterbury Tales*.

This great work of Geoffrey Chaucer (1340–1400) is one of the earliest to be written in English. Its background is the martyrdom of Thomas Becket, Archbishop of Canterbury in the time of Henry II (1154–89). Becket fell out with his royal friend when he (Becket) insisted on serving God in preference to the king. After Henry uttered the famous words, 'Who will rid me of this turbulent priest?' (or something along those lines), some of his knights took him literally, rushed to Canterbury and murdered Becket in the cathedral there. He was made a saint shortly afterwards and his tomb became England's most popular place of pilgrimage. The characters in *The Canterbury Tales* are a random cross-section of society, from a knight to a miller and including a number of priests and nuns, who find themselves travelling from Southwark to Canterbury together and agree to pass the time by telling each other stories; the one who tells the best will win a sumptuous dinner at the Tabard on their return.

The Tabard was conveniently situated at the point where the roads from Sussex, Surrey and Hampshire converged on the so-called 'Pilgrims' Way' (roughly today's A2 and M2), so it was common for pilgrims from the south and west of the country to spend the night there before setting off on their journey. A nineteenth-century popular history of London gives us this description of it:

> *The original 'Tabard' was in existence as late as the year 1602; it was an ancient timber house, accounted to be as old as Chaucer's time. No part of it, however, as it appeared at the time of its demolition in 1874, was of the age of Chaucer; but a good deal dated from the time of Queen Elizabeth ... The most interesting portion was a stone-coloured wooden gallery, in front of which was a picture of the Canterbury Pilgrimage ... Immediately behind was the chamber known as the pilgrims' room, but only a portion of the ancient hall. The gallery formerly extended throughout the inn-buildings.*

It's safe to assume, then, that at least in Elizabeth I's time, the general layout of the Tabard resembled that of the George today.

Chaucer's pilgrims set out on foot or on horse- or donkey-back; you probably won't want to do that, as it is about 55 miles to Canterbury. When you get there, though, the most important thing is to do what they did: head to the cathedral – arguably the most magnificent and most moving in England – and pay homage to Becket. A plaque on the floor of the northwest transept, in a section of the church known as the Martyrdom, marks the spot where he died, and a single candle burns in the Trinity Chapel, where his tomb used to be. Just round the corner, in the wonderfully named Beer Cart Lane, the Chaucer Bookshop keeps the literary connection alive.

While you're here, it's worth fast-forwarding a couple of hundred years from Chaucer and checking out the Christopher Marlowe Memorial. Marlowe (1564–1593?), a contemporary of Shakespeare's and also a playwright, was famously murdered, traditionally in a tavern in Deptford, southeast London, perhaps because he was a spy. Or a blasphemer. Or a homosexual. Or all three. Conspiracy theories abound. What is not in doubt, however, is that he was born in Canterbury. The local theatre is named after him and outside it stands a beautiful bronze called the Muse of Poetry, a scantily clad female figure carrying a lyre. She is supported by a plinth with a niche on each side containing statuettes of actors playing title roles from Marlowe plays: *Tamburlaine the Great, Doctor Faustus, The Jew of Malta* and *Edward II*.

So why the Muse of Poetry and not a statue of Marlowe himself? Well, the memorial dates from 1891 and at that time no known portraits of Marlowe existed. In 1953, workmen moving rubble in the Master's Lodge at Corpus Christi College, Cambridge, where Marlowe had studied, uncovered a painting of a young man. Its Latin inscription dates it at 1585 and its subject at twenty-one years old. That fits with its being Marlowe, but expert opinion remains divided. Given the controversy overshadowing much of his life, that seems entirely appropriate – and perhaps makes it just as well that his Canterbury memorial hasn't committed itself either way.

Dickens's Kent

CHARLES DICKENS

www.theangel.co.uk

charlesdickensbirthplace.co.uk

www.visitmedway.org

www.visitgravesend.co.uk/whats-on/tours-gads-hill-place

Open occasionally for guided tours only; book in advance.

www.thanet.gov.uk/info-pages/dickens-house-museum

Nowhere in southern or eastern England are you far from a reminder of the life and works of Charles Dickens (1812–1870), though some of them are more tangible than others. Search as you may on Great Yarmouth beach, you're unlikely to find the 'black barge, or some other kind of superannuated boat ... with an iron funnel sticking out of it for a chimney and smoking very cosily' that the Peggottys call home in *David Copperfield;* nor does any known churchyard in the Kentish marshes contain the tomb of 'Philip Pirrip, late of this parish, and also Georgiana wife of the above', as it does in *Great Expectations.* In *The Pickwick Papers* the narrator goes so far as to explain that he has no idea where to find the constituency of Eatanswill, scene of a riotously corrupt election.

These minor disappointments aside, there is plenty to satisfy. Heading southwest from

F. W. Pailthorpe del.

Great Yarmouth, you could break your journey at the Angel Hotel in Bury St Edmunds. Not only is it mentioned in *The Pickwick Papers*, but it's also a place where Dickens himself stayed more than once and which still offers a Charles Dickens suite.

Continuing appreciably further south and west brings you to the author's birthplace in Portsmouth. The theatre where the Crummles performed in *Nicholas Nickleby* was demolished in 1856 and Portsmouth Grammar School now occupies the site. It's not hard to recreate the theatre in your imagination, though:

> *Nicholas found himself close to the first entrance on the prompt side, among bare walls, dusty scenes, mildewed clouds, heavily daubed draperies, and dirty floors. He looked about him; ceiling, pit, boxes, gallery, orchestra, fittings, and decorations of every kind,—all looked coarse, cold, gloomy, and wretched.*

> *'Is this a theatre?' whispered Smike, in amazement; 'I thought it was a blaze of light and finery.'*

> *'Why, so it is,' replied Nicholas, hardly less surprised; 'but not by day, Smike—not by day.'*

In the Birthplace Museum, though, you can admire a fine collection of illustrations from Dickens's work, not to mention the couch on which he died, moved here from Gad's Hill Place, the country home in Higham, Kent, where he spent his last years.

Kent came into Dickens's life quite early on: he was five when the family settled in Chatham, where he spent several happy years. The Guildhall in nearby Rochester has an exhibition on The Making of Mr Dickens, and a stroll down the historic High Street offers a number of plaques explaining how he later incorporated the buildings into his novels. The Guildhall itself is the 'queer place ... with higher pews in it than a church' that bemuses Pip in *Great Expectations,* while the restaurant at Number 60 claims to have been the home of Mr Tope, the verger of the cathedral in the unfinished *Mystery of Edwin Drood*. The last scene that Dickens ever wrote, in which Mrs Tope cooks breakfast for her lodger, the mysterious Mr Datchery, is set in this very house.

Dickens's work is, of course, most closely associated with London (see pages 33 and 35), but in 1856 he was wealthy enough to buy Gad's Hill Place, a house he had known as a boy and longed to live in. After decades as a school, it is now sometimes open to the public. Dickens loved the place – his 'little Kentish freehold' – and wrote his last four novels, including *A Tale of Two Cities* and *Great Expectations*, here. Strolling through the extensive gardens, you can imagine how much this confirmed workaholic – used to the filth and bustle of London and to exhausting reading tours of the United States – was attracted to its peace.

Between these two phases in the Medway area, Dickens often spent summer holidays further east, in Broadstairs. Here he stayed in a house that was then known as Fort House and stands high on the cliff, overlooking the town, and it was here that he wrote *David Copperfield*. Many years later, presumably as a PR wheeze on the part of some forgotten Broadstairs entrepreneur, it was renamed Bleak House and until recently operated as a hotel. Ever since the name change, people have been disputing or defending the claim that it was the inspiration for the house in the novel. (There are also those who point out that the fictional Bleak House is in St Albans, where another real-life building stakes a similar claim.)

There seems to be no argument over the provenance of the Dickens House Museum, though. A few minutes' walk along the cliff from the Broadstairs Bleak House, this is housed in the cottage on which Dickens based the home of David Copperfield's aunt, the formidable Betsey Trotwood, and it still bears a striking resemblance to David's first impression:

> *a very neat little cottage with cheerful bow-windows: in front of it, a small square gravelled court or garden full of flowers, carefully tended, and smelling deliciously.*

Dickens and his son made friends with the lady who lived there, often had tea with her and immortalised her aversion to donkeys: like Aunt Betsey, she was determined to stop them passing along the cliff top in front of her cottage. Once indoors, you might also recognise the cupboard in the corner of the parlour as the 'press' from which Aunt Betsey produces various remedies when the dishevelled David turns up unexpectedly on her doorstep:

> *Her first proceeding there was to unlock a tall press, bring out several bottles, and pour some of the contents of each into my mouth. I think they must have been taken out at random, for I am sure I tasted aniseed water, anchovy sauce, and salad dressing.*

Fear not: although the museum has a gift shop, none of these concoctions is for sale in it.

4

CHAPTER FOUR

CENTRAL
ENGLAND

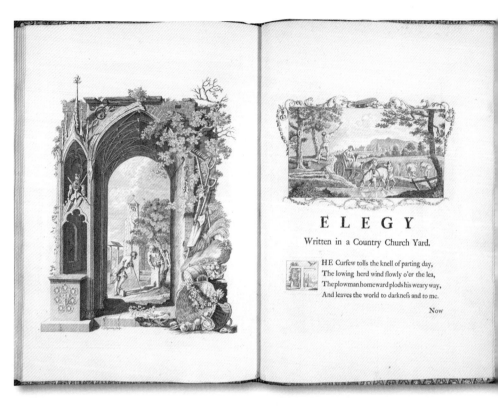

ELEGY

Written in a Country Church Yard.

HE Curfew tolls the knell of parting day,
The lowing herd wind flowly o'er the lea,
The plowman homeward plods his weary way,
And leaves the world to darknefs and to me.

Now

St Giles' Church, Stoke Poges
THOMAS GRAY
www.stokepogeschurch.org

If you're a James Bond fan, you may be familiar with the churchyard of St Giles' in Stoke Poges: Bond visits his wife's grave here at the start of *For Your Eyes Only*. (For added trivia appeal, the golf game between Bond and Goldfinger in *Goldfinger* was filmed on the local course.) But its real literary claim to fame is as the setting for 'Elegy Written in a Country Churchyard' by Thomas Gray (1716–1771), the poem that every-one of a certain generation learned at school and that begins 'The curfew tolls the knell of parting day.'

It's not 100 per cent certain that St Giles' was Gray's inspiration, but it is immensely likely. His mother and aunt, to both of whom he was devoted, lived in Stoke Poges and he was a frequent visitor. Although he wrote the poem over a number of years, he was with his mother in Stoke Poges at the time he finished it, shortly after his aunt's death, and he would certainly have visited her grave. Mrs Gray was buried alongside her sister a few years later and, although the poet spent most of his adult life in Cambridge, after he died his ashes were, at his own request, laid in the same vault.

It's an unassuming-looking tomb near the southeast window of the church, with an eloquent epitaph to the two women in Gray's own words; a modest tablet bearing his name is embedded into the brick wall nearby. To see a more imposing monument to the poet, you have to walk across an adjacent field to where it stands against the backdrop of a copse – desolate in winter; glorious at sunset on a sunny evening when the light strikes it just right. Some twenty years after Gray's death the prominent architect James Wyatt designed a mansion at nearby Stoke Park for John Penn, wealthy grandson of the founder of the state of Pennsylvania. Penn commissioned the monument to form part of a vista from the mansion: some 5 metres high, faced with Portland stone and surrounded by a ha-ha, it takes the form of a large pedestal topped by a decorative sarcophagus. Stoke Park is today a luxurious hotel and country club, but you can still admire the monument from a distance if you book in there for a spa break or a glass of fizz.

As you'd expect, the sides of the pedestal are inscribed with verses from Gray's most famous work. He would probably have been embarrassed by the fuss: a modest man who turned down the offer of becoming Poet Laureate, he might have been happier among the 'mute inglorious Miltons' of whom he wrote.

Roald Dahl Museum and Story Centre, Great Missenden
ROALD DAHL

www.roalddahl.com/museum *Open Thursday to Sunday.*
www.buckscountymuseum.org/roalddahl

The Roald Dahl Museum and Story Centre must be one of the few museums to offer an Automatic Grammatizator, encouraging children (and not only children – why should they have all the fun?) to build strange words and phrases into a story, BFG style: *hopscotchy, frobscottle, squibbling* – it's an interactive working model of Dahl's view that words are there to be played with.

Not only that, but you enter the museum through chocolate doors.

Well, no, of course you don't really (think what a mess they'd make on a hot day), but they're Dairy Milk coloured, marked out into squares like a slab of chocolate and you are greeted by a guide dressed as Willy Wonka.

In other words, the place is whoopsy whiffling, perhaps a bit frothbuggling, and all the more enjoyable for that.

Once you're through the chocolate doors, you can learn more about Dahl himself (1916–1990). The museum downplays the less pleasant aspects of his personality, but you can follow his creative process through his ideas books, an illuminated dream-catcher that creates BFG-like dreams, the reason he decided not to write *James and the Giant Cherry,* and examples of the way, in pre-computer days, he would literally 'cut and paste' – using scissors and glue – as he revised his work. You can find out about his childhood and his time in the Royal Air Force (memorably described in his autobiographies *Boy* and *Going Solo*). And if you happen to go to the loo, you can be assailed with Dahl-like noises such as *whizzpop.*

The museum is housed in an old coaching inn and in the courtyard is a replica of Dahl's writing hut. Here, his laptop writing desk sits across an armchair, with his glasses and writing pad at the ready. The table is covered with a random collection of bits and pieces: photos, a tub of yellow pencils, odd scribbled notes held down by chunks of fossil serving as paperweights. The ashtray by the phone hasn't been emptied lately; nor has the wastepaper basket. Authentic it may well be; tidy it certainly isn't. Dahl had the original hut built in the grounds of his home, Gipsy House, on the outskirts of Great Missenden, having been inspired by Dylan Thomas's boathouse at Laugharne (see page 187). Unlike Thomas, though, or Virginia Woolf at Monk's House (see page 98), he wasn't interested in the view: he kept the curtains drawn 'so I don't see the squirrels up in the apple trees in the orchard'.

Dahl is on record as having detested museums (not to mention beards, committees and speeches), but this one – described by his daughter Ophelia as a place where children's imaginations can roam and take flight – might have won him round. He might even have admitted he'd been crodsquinkled.

While you're in the area, nip up the road to Aylesbury and the Roald Dahl's Children's Gallery in Bucks County Museum. Crawl through the Fantastic Mr Fox tunnel, meet James's mini-beast friends inside the Giant Peach and travel in the Great Glass Elevator. Take some children with you to get the best out of the experience, but don't make the mistake of thinking any of this is beneath you. As Willy Wonka said:

A little nonsense now and then, is cherished by the wisest men.

CHAPTER FOUR: CENTRAL ENGLAND

Adlestrop
EDWARD THOMAS

adlestrop.org.uk

Few anthologies contain more than one poem by Edward Thomas (1878–1917), but even if you think you've never heard of him, you probably know that poem's opening line:

> *Yes, I remember Adlestrop –*

Thomas was on a train on Midsummer's Day in 1914 when it stopped unexpectedly at an abandoned station:

> *No one left and no one came*
> *On the bare platform.*

The platform was overgrown with willow-herb and meadowsweet, and a blackbird sang. It's a truly beautiful evocation of a rural English summer's day – the sort of peaceful idyll that Thomas, killed in the First World War less than three years later, would never experience again.

Adlestrop today is a village of around a hundred people and remains everyone's image of picture-postcard Cotswolds: cottages in that famous honey-coloured stone with roses clambering round doors and windows, a medieval church, even a thatched post office. But no railway station. It closed in 1966 and the old station sign and the bench that once sat on that lonely platform were moved to the bus shelter in the village. A plaque on the bench reminds you of the rest of Thomas's poem and you can, if the mood takes you, sit there and watch the buses go by, perhaps two of them a day.

Or you can seek another, earlier literary connection: just outside the village stands Adlestrop House, the former rectory of the parish. In the early nineteenth century the rector was one Thomas Leigh, a relation of Jane Austen's mother (born Cassandra Leigh), whose family lived here for more than four hundred years. Jane is known to have visited on several occasions, and may have used the house as the inspiration for Sotherton Court, Mr Rushworth's residence in *Mansfield Park*. Certainly the grounds at Adlestrop were reimagined in Leigh's time by Humphry Repton (1752–1818), the foremost landscape designer of the day, and in the novel Mr Rushworth, determining to improve the grounds of his own home, decides that no one but Repton will do for him, despite the fact that 'his terms are five guineas a day'. Adlestrop House remains in private hands, though you can get into the grounds on days when the local cricket club is playing there.

If you aren't a cricket fan, the best time to visit Adlestrop is the weekend in June when the village holds an Open Day: private gardens are opened, children's games organised and talks about Edward Thomas and Jane Austen given. Or you can just stroll around it any time and listen, as Thomas did, not only for the blackbird, but also for:

Farther and farther, all the birds
Of Oxfordshire and Gloucestershire.

Christ Church College, Oxford

LEWIS CARROLL

www.chch.ox.ac.uk
aliceinwonderlandshop.com

Christ Church, Oxford, where Charles Lutwidge Dodgson (better known as Lewis Carroll, 1832–1898) was first a student, then for twenty-six years Mathematical Lecturer, is perhaps Oxford's most magnificent college. It was conceived by Cardinal Wolsey and finished by Henry VIII, which is enough to suggest that it was always intended to be grandiose; add to that the fact that its chapel is actually the cathedral for the diocese of Oxford and you'll begin to get an impression. For most of Carroll's time here Henry Liddell was Dean of the college, living in the adjacent deanery; it was for Liddell's daughter Alice that Carroll wrote his famous books.

Apart from the cathedral itself, Christ Church's sixteenth-century hall is its most splendid feature, and it's a good place to start Alice-hunting. It boasts a series of modern stained-glass windows, one of which celebrates her and her creator. Among the many portraits of past dignitaries of the college is one of Carroll himself, and there is also a vast fireplace whose brass andirons are moulded into the form of women with enormously long necks. They look remarkably similar to the illustrator John Tenniel's drawing of Alice as she was 'opening out like the largest telescope that ever was' after eating the cake 'on which the words "EAT ME" were beautifully marked in currants'.

Outside, in the cathedral garden, a wooden door in an old stone wall leads into the deanery garden. Or it would, if it weren't kept locked and the deanery weren't private property. It's easy to imagine the real little Alice behind that door, peering longingly into 'the loveliest garden you ever saw', as her fictional counterpart did when she first fell down the rabbit hole and found herself unable to get through a door that was 'about 15 inches high'.

Once you've had your fill of Christ Church's grandeur, you may like to step out into St Aldate's Street and visit the nearby Alice's Shop. Today it describes itself as 'a treasure trove of Alice in Wonderland gifts and memorabilia' but in Alice's day it was a grocery, where she and her sisters bought sweets. It was also Carroll's model for the shop that is run by a sheep in *Through the Looking-Glass*:

The shop seemed to be full of all manner of curious things – but the oddest part of it all was, that whenever she looked hard at any shelf, to make out exactly what it had on it, that particular shelf was always quite empty: though the others round it were crowded as full as they could hold.

Tenniel's illustration depicts the shop exactly as it was, but with the details in reverse, because we are seeing it in a looking-glass. Even the proprietor was part of Carroll's inspiration: she may not have been a sheep wearing spectacles and a mob cap but she was, allegedly, an elderly lady with a bleating voice. In the story she is knitting with innumerable needles, a pair of which she hands to Alice; they promptly turn into oars and she finds herself 'in a little boat, gliding along between banks'. Rowing yourself up the Thames on a summer's day may be a fitting way to end this journey: it was in a boat on the river in 1862 that Carroll first told Alice Liddell and her sisters the story of that other Alice and her adventures in lands of make-believe.

Philip Pullman's Oxford
PHILIP PULLMAN
www.exeter.ox.ac.uk
www.obga.ox.ac.uk

Fans of Philip Pullman (born 1946) can be forgiven for being confused. In *Northern Lights* Lyra's home, Jordan College, is based on Pullman's own alma mater Exeter College, but when the book was filmed as *The Golden Compass,* both Exeter and Christ Church (which has also featured in the Harry Potter films) were used as locations; when the *His Dark Materials* trilogy (of which *Northern Lights* is volume one) was televised it was set in New College. But for lovers of the books, Exeter is the real deal.

Unlike Exeter – so far as we know – Jordan is as complicated underground as it is above:

> *Like some enormous fungus whose root-system extended over acres, Jordan ... had begun, sometime in the Middle Age, to spread below the surface. Tunnels, shafts, vaults, cellars, staircases had so hollowed out the earth below Jordan and for several hundred yards around it that there was almost as much air below ground as above.*

The college is also immensely wealthy: you're said to be able to walk to Bristol in one direction and London in another without leaving Jordan land.

That's in a parallel universe, of course. The Exeter College that exists in our universe isn't quite as rich as that, but it is one of Oxford's most beautiful colleges. It's been on

CHAPTER FOUR: CENTRAL ENGLAND

its city-centre site since 1315, has a seventeenth-century dining hall and a breathtaking neo-Gothic chapel; from its gardens you look up at the Radcliffe Camera, that iconic dome that features in any aerial photograph of the city. It's the archetype of what an Oxford college should be like and as its alumni include not only J. R. R. Tolkien (see page 137), Alan Bennett and many other writers, but also the designer William Morris and the artist Edward Burne-Jones, it's safe to assume that Exeter has done its fair share of inspiring over the years.

Plenty of other places in Oxford feature in Philip Pullman's work, although they are obviously in a parallel universe too. Lady Margaret Hall is the model for St Sophia's, where Lyra studies in *The Secret Commonwealth* and which, like its real-life equivalent, pioneers the education of women. (Happily, in our universe, visitors who have stayed at Lady Margaret Hall for conferences or open days report that the breakfasts are better than the cold toast, dry scrambled eggs and porridge with which Lyra starts the day.) The once industrial, now trendy residential suburb of Jericho is home to the water-dwelling Gyptians, and a walk along the Oxford Canal towpath, which marks Jericho's western boundary, may reward you with sightings. The Eagle Ironworks that feature in *Lyra's Oxford* have been pulled down and replaced by flats, but the statue of an eagle that still stands on a gatepost on the site could easily be a daemon.

No *His Dark Materials* pilgrimage would be complete without a visit to Oxford's Botanic Garden; founded in 1621, it's the oldest of its kind in Britain. When Lyra and Will have to separate at the end of *The Amber Spyglass*, they agree to return to sit there – each in their own world, of course – every year at noon on 24 June. Following Pullman's instructions, you can find their bench easily enough:

> *She led him past a pool with a fountain under a wide-spreading tree, and then struck off to the left between beds of plants towards a huge many-trunked pine. There was a massive stone wall with a doorway in it, and in the further part of the garden the trees were younger and the planting less formal. Lyra led him almost to the end of the garden, over a little bridge, to a wooden seat under a spreading low-branched tree.*

A truly romantic spot – in this universe or any other.

Holy Trinity Church, Headington Quarry

C. S. LEWIS

www.hthq.uk

www.headington.org.uk/history/pubs/ampleforth_arms.html

For the last thirty-plus years of his life, Clive Staples Lewis (1898–1963) lived at The Kilns in Headington, Oxford, a rambling, rose-covered cottage that is now a Christian study centre. You can visit it, but only by guided tour on certain days and you are advised to book well in advance. If you haven't got your act together to do that, try Holy Trinity Church in Headington Quarry, where Lewis worshipped throughout those years.

Christianity plays a huge part in Lewis's writings, so it's rather endearing to learn that

he disliked organ music: his Sunday ritual included attending the 8 a.m. Communion service, in which the organ didn't feature. He always sat in the same pew, as close to the pillar as possible, so he was hidden from the view of the rest of the congregation. It's said that, having let his attention wander during a dull sermon in 1940, he arrived home with an outline of *The Screwtape Letters* – surely the most hilarious work of theology ever written, taking the form of instructive letters from a senior demon to his novice nephew on the subject of luring a human soul to damnation – fully worked out in his mind.

Adjacent to the Lewis Pew is the beautiful Narnia Window, a memorial not to Lewis but to a brother and sister associated with the church who both died tragically young. Installed in the 1990s, it's a tasteful, understated piece – predominantly white and including many an image drawn from the Narnia chronicles, notably a majestic close-up of Aslan in one panel and in the other the flying horse Fledge soaring gracefully over the deserted citadel of Cair Paravel. You can feel yourself shivering in Narnia's perpetual winter as you gaze at it.

The rest of the church is worth a visit, even for non-Lewis fans. It was designed by Sir George Gilbert Scott (1811–1878), that master of nineteenth-century Gothic Revival, who also worked on the Midland Grand Hotel at St Pancras and the Albert Memorial in South Kensington. In addition to the Narnia window, Holy Trinity has a more conventionally coloured stained-glass memorial to the fallen of the Second World War, and an organ which dates only from the 1990s but whose pipes are adorned by art nouveau angels playing golden trumpets. Lewis might not have approved, but this organ was designed to fit neatly under an arch behind the choir and is much less obtrusive than the one that was there in his day.

In the churchyard, Lewis's tombstone bears a quotation from *King Lear*, chosen by his devoted brother Warnie (who was later buried in the same grave) as something that had always been significant in their family: 'Men must endure their going hence.' It seems particularly poignant on the tomb of a man who died on the very day that President Kennedy was shot in Dallas, 22 November 1963, and perhaps didn't receive the column inches of obituary that he deserved.

When you're done, nip (carefully) across the bypass to the Ampleforth, the cosy local pub where Lewis often had a drink or two with J. R. R. Tolkien (see page 137). It was reported by a friend – and it's not hard to believe – that these two great Oxford academics 'were often engrossed in conversation that was way above the heads of us locals'.

Madresfield Court, Malvern

EVELYN WAUGH

www.madresfieldestate.co.uk *Guided tours only, on specified days April to July.*

www.castlehoward.co.uk *Opening times for house and gardens differ – check in advance.*

'Great barrack of a place. I've just had a snoop round. Very ornate, I'd call it. And a queer thing, there's a sort of R.C. Church attached ... There's a frightful great fountain, too, in front of the steps, all rocks and sort of carved animals. You never saw such a thing.'

'Yes, Hooper, I did. I've been here before.'

That's part of the prologue of Evelyn Waugh's 1945 novel *Brideshead Revisited*, in which the disillusioned narrator, Charles Ryder, finds himself, during the Second World War, billeted back at the great house where he spent much of his golden youth. And a very great house it is, both in fiction and in fact. In the novel, Brideshead is the home of the aristocratic Flyte family who captivate the less sophisticated Ryder; in real life, Waugh (1903–1966) based it on Madresfield Court in Worcestershire, which he visited frequently during the 1930s. Madresfield was the home of the Earl of Beauchamp, whose younger son, Hugh Lygon, was Waugh's friend at Oxford and the inspiration for *Brideshead*'s other central character, Lord Sebastian Flyte. The house's origins can be traced back to the eleventh century, but what you see today is a moated, red-brick Tudor mansion with gables galore, intricate stonework and a rather fine bell tower. It was much revamped in Victorian times and the interiors owe a great deal to the Arts and Crafts movement.

To describe Madresfield as 'very ornate', as young Lieutenant Hooper does in the extract above, is grossly to understate its magnificence. The chapel, redecorated in the Pre-Raphaelite style in the late nineteenth century, is perhaps the grandest room of all. Charles Ryder's first impression of it gives the spirit:

The whole interior had been gutted, elaborately refurnished and redecorated in the arts-and-crafts style of the last decade of the nineteenth century. Angels in printed cotton smocks, rambler-roses, flower-spangled meadows, frisking lambs, texts in Celtic script, saints in armour, covered the walls in an intricate pattern of clear, bright colours. There was a triptych of pale oak, carved so as to give it the peculiar property of seeming to have been moulded in Plasticine.

Understated it is not. Catholicism and the stand it takes against adultery and divorce are key themes of the novel, and this rather oppressive space is a perfect backdrop to them. The library (eight thousand books) and the dramatic staircase hall (two storeys high and topped by domed skylights that illuminate dozens of portraits of Lygon ancestors) head a longish list of other jaw-dropping features.

Faithful readers of Waugh's novels would have been familiar with Madresfield well before *Brideshead* was published. Eleven years earlier he had based the Gothic pile Hetton Hall in *A Handful of Dust* on it:

the general aspect and atmosphere of the place; the line of its battlements against the sky; the central clock tower where quarterly chimes disturbed all but the heaviest sleepers; the ecclesiastical gloom of the great hall ... the dining-hall with its hammer-beam roof and pitch-pine minstrels' gallery ... his own dressing-room ... from whose bay window one could count, on days of exceptional clearness, the spires of six churches – all these things with which he had grown up were a source of constant delight and exultation to Tony.

Waugh's debt to Madresfield is well established, but to the many millions who watched the 1981 Granada television adaptation, Brideshead will always be Castle Howard, where both that landmark series and the 2008 remake were filmed. It's a stunning example of the flamboyant but short-lived style called English Baroque. Again, the chapel is perhaps the grandest room of all, boasting a painted ceiling, a substantial organ, and murals by Edward Burne-Jones and Dante Gabriel Rossetti. There are also echoing halls lined with marble statues, a staircase that must rank among the finest in England and a Great Hall topped by a painted dome that on the outside is covered in gold leaf and makes a spectacular background for firework displays. In the grounds Waugh describes three lakes, woods of beech and oak and, 'lest the eye wander aimlessly', a Doric temple by the water's edge. Castle Howard's 9,000 acres provide all of these, as well as formal gardens dotted with temples and follies.

Charles Ryder's exclamation when he first sees Brideshead could apply equally to Madresfield (with its one hundred and sixty rooms) and to Castle Howard (one hundred and forty-five):

'What a place to live in!'

The Cowper and Newton Museum, Olney
WILLIAM COWPER AND JOHN NEWTON
cowperandnewtonmuseum.org.uk

...and neatly tied
Are wedded this like beauty to old age,
For int'rest sake, the living to the dead.

You may think you've never heard of William Cowper (pronounced Cooper, 1731–1800) or his friend and neighbour John Newton (1725–1807), but you almost certainly know something of their works. Cowper, one of the most famous and influential poets of his day, is perhaps best known for a long poem called 'The Task', which he wrote in response to a challenge from a friend to produce a work in blank verse on the subject of a sofa.

Yes, really. It runs to six books, almost 40,000 words and some 5,000 lines, which makes it about half the length of Milton's epic *Paradise Lost* and appreciably longer than *Hamlet*. It was wildly successful in its day, is recognised as having inspired Wordsworth and Jane Austen, and was a favourite of Robert Burns.

And it's about a sofa. Well, to be fair, once you get into it, it's about rather more than that: despite its mock-heroic style, it has serious things to say about nature, religion, the church and contemporary English life. 'God made the country and man made the town,' Cowper writes, before going on to condemn the ludicrous emphasis city people put on new, fashionable clothes. Because, as he puts it (and now we're getting to the bit you know about) these people believe that 'Variety's the very spice of life'. We tend now to use that famous line approvingly, but Cowper meant quite the opposite: it's absurd, he says, to bankrupt ourselves by spending so much money on clothes:

> *We sacrifice to dress, till household joys*
> *And comforts cease. Dress drains our cellar dry,*
> *And keeps our larder lean; puts out our fires,*
> *And introduces hunger, frost, and woe,*
> *Where peace and hospitality might reign.*

Cowper suffered from depression and retired from London to the peaceful Buckinghamshire village of Olney when he was in his thirties. Here, he sought a cure for his melancholy by adopting three young hares, a present from neighbours, 'perceiving that, in the management of such an animal, and in the attempt to tame it, I should find just that sort of employment which my case required'. The leverets were so important a part of his life and he wrote at such length about them that they became almost as famous as he was.

In Olney, too, Cowper became friendly with Newton, a poet and the local curate, and the two collaborated on a collection called *The Olney Hymns*, for use in their parish. Newton had previously been a sea captain, working in the slave trade and becoming converted to Christianity (and abolitionism) during a storm at sea – an experience that inspired him to write the most famous of the Olney hymns, 'Amazing Grace':

Amazing grace! (how sweet the sound)
That sav'd a wretch like me!

and so on.

You can find out more about both men at the museum housed in Cowper's former home. It's a comfortable Georgian house kitted up to reflect domestic life of the period and including a room devoted to lace-making, the industry from which Olney drew its livelihood. Lace, the slave trade and hares: it's an unusual mix of subject matter.

Outside, the walled flower garden has been restored to grow flowers that would have been there when Cowper – a keen and inventive gardener – was in residence, and beyond it is his 'verse manufactory', the summer house where he did his writing. After his death, it became a place of pilgrimage for his admirers, many of whom inscribed their names on the walls and ceiling. You're discouraged from doing this now, but it's a touching tribute to the fame of a man who was so unconfident of his own success that he once wrote, 'Gardening was of all employments that in which I succeeded best.'

As for Newton, he moved to London in 1780 and spent the rest of his life as rector of the Hawksmoor church St Mary Woolnoth (see page 44) and became an active campaigner for the abolition of the slave trade. A plaque in St Mary's reminds us – in his own words – that he was 'once an infidel, and libertine, a servant of slaves in Africa' but was 'preserved, restored, pardoned and appointed to preach the faith he had long laboured to destroy'. The same words appear on his tomb in the churchyard in Olney.

Bedford and Surrounds

JOHN BUNYAN

www.english-heritage.org.uk/visit/places/houghton-house

In addition to being an author, John Bunyan (1628–1688) was a Nonconformist preacher. No big deal, you might have thought, but this was in the 1660s, just after the restoration of Charles II, when being a Nonconformist preacher was, to say the least of it, frowned upon. Born and bred near Bedford, Bunyan was arrested there in November 1660, indicted of having 'devilishly and perniciously abstained from coming to church to hear divine service' and having held 'several unlawful meetings and conventicles, to the great disturbance and distraction of the good subjects of this kingdom'. He was never going to be acquitted of charges like that, but the sentence would have been three months if Bunyan had agreed to give up preaching. He refused, and subsequently spent twelve years in Bedford jail. It's widely believed that, inspired by a dream, he started writing his best known work, *The Pilgrim's Progress*, during the period.

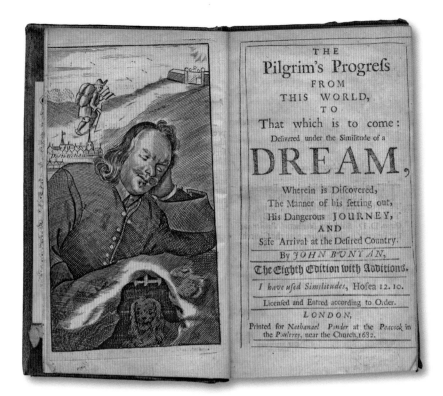

There's a plaque commemorating him in the pavement on the corner of the High Street and Silver Street, where the jail once stood (there is still an HM Prison, Bedford, but it's of a later date and on a different site). A few minutes' walk to the north, on the edge of St Peter's Green, is a bronze statue dating from Victorian times; it shows Bunyan in preacher mode with a Bible in his hand, while the plinth depicts scenes from *The Pilgrim's Progress* in which the eponymous pilgrim Christian overcomes temptation and the burden of sin.

Before he turned to preaching and writing, Bunyan had followed in his father's footsteps as a tinker – an itinerant mender of pots and pans. This is said to be how he met the ladies who owned Houghton House, a few miles to the south of Bedford. Perhaps because they were kind to a poor traveller, he used the house as inspiration for the Palace called Beautiful in *The Pilgrim's Progress*, the place where the weary Christian is welcomed in by Discretion, Piety, Prudence and Charity. Today, the Jacobean house (which was built as a grand hunting lodge for the wealthy and influential Countess of Pembroke and may in part have been designed by Inigo Jones) is a ruin, but a very sumptuous one. The two-storey covered loggias with decorative friezes still stand, you can make out the house's H-shaped floor plan and there are spectacular views over what was once the hunting park. It's missing its staircase, though: this elaborately carved feature can now be seen in the Swan Inn in Bedford.

Caught in a storm on his way to London, Bunyan died of a fever at the age of fifty-nine and was buried in Bunhill Fields (see page 37), the most appropriate place for a man of his religious views. As with the statue in Bedford, his tomb celebrates him as the author of *The Pilgrim's Progress* and makes no mention of his having served eleven and three-quarter years more than he needed to in prison for refusing to toe the Establishment line.

Shaw's Corner, Ayot St Lawrence
GEORGE BERNARD SHAW
www.nationaltrust.org.uk/shaws-corner

Perhaps best remembered now as the author of *Pygmalion*, the play that inspired the musical *My Fair Lady*, George Bernard Shaw (1856–1950) was much more than a prolific playwright. He was a journalist, an essayist and, as a young man, a committed socialist. Among the pamphlets he wrote for the socialist Fabian Society is one called *Socialism for Millionaires*, which begins:

> *The millionaire class, a small but growing one into which any of us may be flung tomorrow by the accidents of commerce, is perhaps the most neglected in the community.*

Shaw was also a renowned critic of both music and drama and a passionate advocate for a system of reforming the English language's idiosyncratic spelling. He was the first person to win both a Nobel Prize (in Literature in 1925) and an Academy Award (for the screenplay of the 1938 film of *Pygmalion*). He disapproved of organised religion and was in favour of eugenics. He even published a book called *Maxims for Revolutionists* which is full of provocative opinions, most famously, 'He who can, does. He who cannot, teaches.' He was not, in short, a man who shied away from telling the world what he thought – or how clever he was.

So it's perhaps odd that – although he travelled widely (getting as far as New Zealand when he was well into his seventies) and retained a flat in London – he should have been based for the last forty-four years of his life in a quiet country village, Ayot St Lawrence in Hertfordshire.

This was largely for health reasons. In a state of collapse through overwork, he had been nursed by a fellow political activist, Charlotte Payne-Townshend. When she insisted on their moving out of London for the sake of his health, they decided to marry to avoid the scandal that would have resulted from their living together. Scholars believe that the marriage was probably never consummated, but was nevertheless happy. Certainly it lasted until her death in 1943.

It's the house in Ayot St Lawrence, which the couple renamed 'Shaw's Corner', that you should visit today if you want to find out more about this extraordinary man. It's a former rectory, designed in 1902 in the Arts and Crafts style, which can still be seen in the stained-glass windows, the heart shapes cut into the banisters and the textiles designed by Morris & Co., under the auspices of Shaw's friend William Morris. Shaw's Academy Award, which he claimed to despise, is prominently displayed in his study; there is a bust of him sculpted by Auguste Rodin and, as you might expect, no shortage

of his books. It's also worth penetrating to the bottom of the garden to see the shed in which he worked and wrote many of his plays: a simple wooden structure that looks much like any other garden shed, it was mounted on a revolving mechanism so that Shaw could follow the sun in the course of the day without moving from his desk.

With his battered typewriter and spectacles still sitting on the simple wooden workbench, the shed seems a pleasantly modest place. But before you accuse Shaw of humility, you might stop to consider another of his controversial opinions: his deep-rooted dislike of Shakespeare. As he wrote in *Dramatic Opinions and Essays* in 1907:

With the single exception of Homer, there is no eminent writer, not even Sir Walter
Scott, whom I can despise so entirely as I despise Shakespeare when I measure my
mind against his. ... It would positively be a relief to me to dig him up and throw
stones at him.

It's tempting to mutter – as his acquaintances must have done most of his life – 'Don't
be shy, Bernard. Tell us what you *really* think.'

Shakespeare's Stratford
WILLIAM SHAKESPEARE
www.shakespeare.org.uk

There's no denying that Stratford-upon-Avon is touristy, but as the place where
William Shakespeare (1564–1616) was born, died and spent a good bit of time in
between, it can't be ignored. There are several places scattered around the town where
you can get to grips with various stages of Shakespeare's life. You might even take in a
halfway-decent play.

If you're of a logical, 'begin at the beginning' turn of mind, start at the Shakespeare
Centre, a purpose-built library, archive and exhibition space with an imposing statue of
the Bard in – of all places – the café area. It's a 3-metre bronze that was commissioned
for the original entrance hall in the 1960s. The building has since been reconfigured,
but as the statue weighs a good ton and a half, it was allowed to remain where it was
and the reconfiguring went on around it. The details on the back of Shakespeare's cloak
are worth a second look: the flower motif and fox's face pay tribute to the Chairman of
the Shakespeare Birthplace Trust, Sir Fordham Flower, and its director, Levi Fox, who
commissioned the statue.

It's easy to be cynical when you go into a twentieth-century complex, but Shakespeare's
Birthplace is genuinely what it claims to be: the sixteenth-century half-timbered cottage
where the Bard was born. You can walk on the very floor on which he learned to crawl,
explore the rooms in which he grew up and listen to recitations of some of his greatest
speeches in the garden.

Just along the street is another bronze worth taking a look at: it's called *The Jester* and
portrays a jester in traditional dress, with bells on his shoes and cap; he's balanced on
one foot on a plinth that looks far too small for this sort of capering. The inscription at
the front reads 'O noble fool! A worthy fool!' – a description of Touchstone in *As You Like
It* – but round the sides and back are references to Feste in *Twelfth Night* and Yorick in
Hamlet, so you can probably interpret the statue as representing whichever of Shakespeare's fools you choose.

Your next stop could be Shakespeare's New Place, which he bought in 1597 and
which was the family home until he died. The house has long since been demolished,
but modern technology gives a surprisingly lifelike impression of what it must have
been like: it's designed as an inspirational space where you're encouraged to let your

CHAPTER FOUR: CENTRAL ENGLAND

imagination run riot. No pressure, though: if you haven't written *King Lear* by the time you're ready to go home, that's absolutely fine, as long as you've had a good time.

Then, a mile or so out of town, there's Anne Hathaway's cottage – the place where the wife to whom he famously left 'my second best bed' was born and raised. She was the daughter of a successful sheep farmer and the family had lived in the cottage for several generations: the kitchen and parlour you can see today were part of the original house, built a hundred years before Anne was born. The so-called Hathaway bed, still on display, is an impressive four-poster with ornately carved oak. The gardens here are particularly lovely. The path to the front door winds through lush cottage-garden planting, while round the back there are Shakespeare-inspired sculptures, a tree garden planted with species mentioned in his works and a woven willow circle with a seat that positively invites you to loll in it. *This* might be the place for you to write *King Lear*.

The final stop has to be back in Stratford itself, at Holy Trinity Church, where Shakespeare and other members of his family are buried. It's probably prudent to be *particularly* respectful at the Bard's grave – not just because it's a grave, or even because of whose grave it is, but because of the curse attached to it. When you think of how many writers' graves are inscribed with lines from their work, and how easy it would have been for Shakespeare to choose 'This little life is rounded with a sleep' or 'The rest is silence', you've got to love a man who goes for:

> *Good friend for Jesus sake forbear,*
> *To dig the dust enclosed here.*
> *Blessed be the man that spares these stones,*
> *And cursed be he that moves my bones.*

It's believed that Shakespeare wrote these words himself, and the question as to why he should have done so has puzzled a lot of scholars over the centuries. It became even more intriguing when in 2016, the four hundredth anniversary of his death, ground-penetrating scans of the grave found no trace of a skull and seemed to confirm long-standing rumours that the Bard's bones *had* once been tampered with. Alas, poor William.

A Shakespearean Pub Crawl

William Shakespeare

thebellwelford.co.uk
www.greeneking-pubs.co.uk/pubs/warwickshire/windmill
www.greeneking-pubs.co.uk/pubs/greater-london/george-southwark
www.harteandgarterhotel.com

As good an excuse for a pub crawl as any, there are several hostelries scattered across the country which can claim (with greater or lesser credibility) that 'William Shakespeare drank here'. In Welford-on-Avon in Warwickshire, local legend has it that in 1616 he stopped at the Bell Inn for a drink with fellow playwrights Ben Jonson and Michael Drayton. He was on his way home to Stratford, about 4 miles away, but was caught in the rain and died of pneumonia as a result. An alternative version has it that he 'drank too hard' and died of a fever. Either way, he did die unexpectedly, on or about his fifty-second birthday, having been in good health a month before. A cheerless connection for a pub to claim, perhaps, but the Bell offers all the exposed beams, oak furniture and open fires you'd hope for in a seventeenth-century village inn. Welford also boasts one of the tallest maypoles in England (some 20 metres, about the height of a six-storey building), so if you time your visit for 1 May you'll be able to witness the traditional ceremony that has been going on since well before the Bard's time.

In Stratford itself, the Windmill was built in 1599 and became an alehouse a year later. It's a very short walk from New Place, the house Shakespeare bought in 1597 (see page 132), so there's a fighting chance that it was his local when he was in Warwickshire. A plaque inside doesn't claim that in so many words, but it does say, 'While Will Shakespeare was writing his immortal plays some of his fellow townsmen were enjoying their favourite drink here. They must have enjoyed his company, too, for he lived only a hundred yards away.' ▶

Assuming that Shakespeare also had a local in London, near the Globe (see page 48), it could easily have been the George in Borough High Street, the last surviving galleried pub in the capital. Before permanent theatres became established towards the end of the sixteenth century, the large yards of coaching inns, surrounded by galleries in which the audience stood or sat, were a popular venue for dramatic performances. There's no suggestion that any of Shakespeare's works appeared at the George, but the theatrical link would still have been there when he moved to London some time before 1592. The current building is a seventeenth-century replica of the one that existed in Shakespeare's day, the medieval version having been destroyed by fire in 1677. Whether or not the Bard actually drank here, we know that Charles Dickens did and he mentions the pub in *Little Dorrit* as a place someone might pop into to write a letter. (And perhaps have a drink while they were at it.)

Getting back to Shakespeare, what about the pubs he wrote about? In *The Merry Wives of Windsor*, Sir John Falstaff and his friends drink at the Garter Inn; the other medieval inn in the town was called the White Harte and in Shakespeare's time both were frequented by actors performing for royalty in the castle. Both inns burned down in 1681 and were rebuilt; in the nineteenth century they were rebuilt again to form the current Harte and Garter Hotel. The hotel's website confesses that the current building is 'in the "Jacobethan" style, much loved by Victorians and reflecting the Shakespearean connections'. It's been beautifully restored with many authentic touches – don't miss the ornate wooden carving in the hotel bar – though the sauna and jacuzzi are probably more upmarket than they were when Falstaff was here.

Most famously, though, Falstaff drank with the reprobate Prince Hal (the future King Henry V) in the Boar's Head in Eastcheap, in the City of London. That pub certainly existed in Shakespeare's day, though probably not in Henry V's, almost two centuries earlier; it was destroyed in the Great Fire of 1666, rebuilt and continued as a pub for another hundred years. The site is now buried under the approach to London Bridge, but just round the corner, in Eastcheap, is a nineteenth-century neo-Gothic building featuring a boar's head in its decoration: it's an eye-catching edifice that looks as if someone had started to design a cathedral and then changed their mind. In fact it was originally a vinegar warehouse and is now offices, but the boar can clearly be seen at the top of an archway above the main entrance. The boar's head pub sign was salvaged in the early years of this century and now sits in a display case in the foyer of Shakespeare's Globe Theatre. It's a rather ferocious-looking beast; you can't help thinking it would have disapproved of Falstaff getting 'fat-witted with drinking of old sack' and taking all morning to sleep it off. In its current location, though, it probably won't be too hard on anyone wanting a quick gin and tonic at the interval.

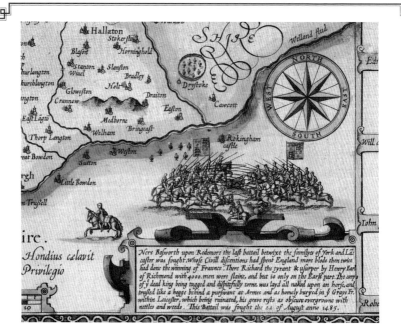

Nere Bosworth upon Redemors the last battail betwixt the familyes of York and Lancaster was fought: whose Civill dissentions had spent England more blode then twice had done the winning of Fraunce. There Richard the tyrant & usurper by Henry Earl of Richmond with 4000. men were slaine, and but is only on the Earls part. The corps of y dead king being tugged and dispitsfully torne. was layd all naked upon an horse, and trussed like a hogge behind a pursuant at Armes and as homely buryed in y Grays Fr. within Leicester, which being ruinated, his grave rests as obscure overgrowne with nettles and weeds. This Battail was fought the 22 of August anno 1485.

Some Shakespearean Locations

bosworthbattlefield.org.uk

leicestercathedral.org

www.heartofenglandforest.com

Shakespeare wrote ten plays about English kings, stretching chronologically from King John (r. 1199–1216) to Henry VIII (r. 1509–1547), with all of the Hundred Years War and the Wars of the Roses in between. Chunks of some of them, notably *Henry V*, are set in France, but inevitably much of the action takes place in England, with a smattering of *Richard II* in Wales.

Undoubtedly the best place to relive a Shakespearean battle is Bosworth, where, according to Shakespeare, Richard III (r. 1483–1485) famously offered his kingdom for a horse. Its Battlefield Heritage Centre and Country Park, just outside Leicester, has a war memorial in the form of a sundial, which talks you through what happened on 22 August 1485, the day when Richard's forces came face to face with those of the Earl of Richmond, soon to be Henry VII. 'Early in the morning men prepare their souls and their equipment for the forthcoming battle,' it tells you, at the point where the sun would have fallen at 8 a.m. By noon, 'Bodies strew the field, blood soaks the ground' and by three in the afternoon a thousand men are dead, including Richard, flung naked (or probably just armourless) over a horse to be taken into Leicester and buried under that much-publicised future car park. Shakespeare wasn't kind to Richard III, but both the battlefield and the new memorial to him at a place of honour in Leicester Cathedral are surprisingly moving. ▶

> In the Bard's day, large swathes of central England were covered by woodland, with the part nearest to Stratford being known as the Forest of Arden. Much of the action of *As You Like It* takes place here, though the play is supposed to be set in France and there may be confusion with the Forest of Ardennes. There's a lot of confusion in *As You Like It* – girls disguised as boys, mistaken identities and goodness knows who is really in love with whom – so getting the name of the forest wrong was probably the least of Shakespeare's worries. Most of Arden has disappeared over the centuries, but there's now a project to replant a huge broadleaf forest across the area it once covered and beyond. The new Heart of England Forest covers 4,000 acres, with waymarked paths to help you explore. Wander along them and you'll see what the exiled Duke, living in the Forest of Arden, meant when he said:
>
> *And this our life, exempt from public haunt,*
> *Finds tongues in trees, books in the running brooks,*
> *Sermons in stones, and good in everything.*
> *I would not change it.*

Tolkien's Birmingham

J. R. R. TOLKIEN

www.birminghammuseums.org.uk/sarehole *Sarehole Mill is open April to October, Wednesday to Sunday and Bank Holiday Mondays, guided tours only.*

www.birminghamconservationtrust.org/2015/10/23/friday-photo-perrotts-folly *Pre-booked guided tours only.*

John Ronald Reuel Tolkien (1892–1973) spent most of his adult life in Oxford (where he did some of his drinking with C. S. Lewis, see page 123), but the seeds of Middle Earth were sown during his childhood on the outskirts of Birmingham. From the ages of about four to nine he lived opposite Sarehole Mill, an eighteenth-century watermill on the River Cole. Unusually for a watermill, it was partly driven by steam and has a chimney that gives it a distinctive silhouette. The mill and its pool fascinated the young Tolkien, as did the surrounding countryside. Just 5 miles from the city centre, in those days it was in rural Worcestershire. In later years he described it as 'a kind of lost paradise', and also recalled that the smoky image of industrial Birmingham on the horizon inspired the hellish depiction of Mordor in *The Lord of the Rings*.

Today the mill is a museum with a permanent exhibition called 'Signposts to Middle Earth', reflecting on Tolkien's early life in the area. Until recently one of its two wheels was still functioning and helped produce the flour for the on-site bakery. (Repairs were underway at the time of writing, and it's hoped that the wheel can be restored to working order.)

The hamlet of Sarehole itself is widely believed to have been the inspiration for Hobbiton. It's even been suggested that the local people were the inspiration for the hobbits, though whether this is because they had hairy feet or lived in comfortable

holes in the ground is unclear. Perhaps, to quote Tolkien's own description of how he envisaged a hobbit, they were:

fattish in the stomach, shortish in the leg. A round, jovial face; ears only slightly pointed and 'elvish'.

There's also a local legend that a nearby hill covers a labyrinth of secret tunnels, a good place for a hobbit-hole to be situated. Whatever the truth of this may be, it is a fact that Tolkien's aunt lived in a farmhouse called Bag End, in the Worcestershire village of Dormston, and her nephew presumably decided that this would be a good name for Bilbo's residence.

Sarehole is less of a hamlet and more of a suburb now, but Moseley Bog Nature Reserve, a short walk from the mill, has (after an undignified period as a landfill site) been allowed to revert to the natural woodland that informed the ancient forests of Tolkien's Shire.

Head a little bit north and west from Sarehole and you'll come upon one of Tolkien's scarier inspirations: the tower of Perrott's Folly, overlooking Edgbaston Reservoir. This and the nearby Edgbaston Waterworks Tower are said to be the models for the 'Two Towers' from which volume two of *The Lord of the Rings* takes its name. Tolkien said that he was happy for the title to be ambiguous, but whichever towers he meant – Isengard,

Barad-Dûr or whatever – the folly is a suitably ominous model for one of them. As befits a folly, its origins are mysterious. It's known to have been built in 1758 by a local landowner called John Perrott, but was it to spy on his unfaithful wife, to watch over her grave, or just to show off to the neighbours? No one knows. Visit and let your imagination draw its own conclusions.

D. H. Lawrence Birthplace Museum, Eastwood

D. H. LAWRENCE

www.lleisure.co.uk/d-h-lawrence-birthplace-museum

thebreachhouse.co.uk

David Herbert Lawrence (1885–1930) led an erratic life, becoming involved with a married German woman called Frieda just two years before the outbreak of the First World War, marrying her in Germany and being accused of spying both there and, once hostilities broke out, in England. After the war he and Frieda left England and for the rest of his life divided their time between Italy, France, Mexico, the United States, Australia and what is now Sri Lanka, until he succumbed to the lung problems that had dogged him since childhood and died of tuberculosis in France at the age of forty-four. In the midst of all this he wrote prolifically, publishing poems, short stories and travel essays as well as novels, and spending much of his time dealing with accusations of obscenity and having his works either banned or severely censored.

He had started all this in a humble coal-miner's cottage in Eastwood, Nottinghamshire, which is today the D. H. Lawrence Birthplace Museum. It's built in severe-looking red brick; the rooms are small, the steps uneven and gas lighting does little to relieve the melancholy on a dull day. But that is all part of the charm. As anyone who has read the near-autobiographical *Sons and Lovers* knows, times were tough in Lawrence's childhood. There's an element of comfort in the sitting room, with an inviting armchair beside the fireplace and a piano begging to be played, but the bedrooms are spartan and the pump, the mangle and the tin tub designed for laundry show that domestic chores were never far away. You can see why Lawrence's mother – the model for the hero's mother Mrs Morel in *Sons and Lovers*, who came from a more comfortable background – resented the change in her circumstances and turned her affections away from her coarse, hard-drinking husband towards a smothering relationship with her son.

It's not his birthplace that Lawrence used as the basis for the Morels' home, though; that's The Breach House, a few minutes' walk away in Garden Road, where the family moved when Lawrence was two. It was supposed to be a step up in the world. From the outside, Lawrence tells us, 'the houses themselves were substantial and very decent', but inside:

> *The dwelling-room, the kitchen, was at the back of the house, facing inward between the blocks, looking at a scrubby back garden, and then at the ash-pits. And between the rows, between the long lines of ash-pits, went the alley, where the children played and the women gossiped and the men smoked. So, the actual conditions of living in the Bottoms, that was so well built and that looked so nice, were quite unsavoury because people must live in the kitchen, and the kitchens opened on to that nasty alley of ash-pits.*

Today The Breach House is much nicer than that description makes it sound and there's a fragrant garden trail inspired by the plants mentioned in the novel – 'little front gardens with auriculas and saxifrage in the shadow of the bottom block, sweet-williams and pinks in the sunny top block'. Lawrence emphasises the depressing aspects, however: he goes on to say that having an end-of-terrace house meant that Mrs Morel enjoyed 'a kind of aristocracy' among the other women (and paid an extra sixpence a week in rent), but that 'this superiority in station was not much consolation' to her. Small wonder that the young Lawrence escaped whenever he could, and fell in love with the countryside round about – what he described as 'the country of my heart'.

The museum is small and The Breach House open on only a few days a year, so if you want to make a day of it you can take a walk in Lawrence's footsteps. Heading northwest out of the village you soon reach Colliers Wood Nature Reserve, whose reservoir features as Nethermere in *The White Peacock* and as Willey Water in *Women in Love*:

> *the lake lay all grey and visionary, stretching into the moist, translucent vista of trees and meadow. Fine electric activity in sound came from the dumbles below the road, the birds piping one against the other, and water mysteriously plashing, issuing from the lake.*

So if Eastwood itself gives you an insight into the turmoil of the young Lawrence's home life, the countryside he grew up in helps you see the world through the eyes of this most sensual of writers. Try for a fine autumn day, like this one in *The Rainbow*:

> *To Ursula, it was as if the world had opened its softest purest flower, its chicory flower, its meadow saffron. The sky was blue and sweet, the yellow leaves down the lane seemed like free, wandering flowers as they chittered round the feet, making a keen, poignant, almost unbearable music to her heart.*

A Disenchanted Village

If the mining village where D. H. Lawrence spent his childhood was gloomy, at least it still had mining. By the time Meera Syal (born 1961) was growing up in Essington in Staffordshire, that village's coal mines were closed, meaning that it had lost the principal reason for its existence.

Essington, thinly disguised as the fictional Tollington, is the setting for Syal's semi-autobiographical novel *Anita and Me*. In it, the youthful heroine, Meena, longs to be tall and blonde like her rebellious friend Anita, and soon discovers the disadvantages of being part of the only Punjabi family in the village. In times of severe economic hardship, the racism she experiences is paralleled by the violence and frustration that infiltrate the whole community.

Despite Syal's bleak depiction, there are some handsome old farmhouses on the edges of Essington and a pretty walk of 2.5 miles to be had towards the Elizabethan Moseley Old Hall, one of the many places in the area said to have housed Charles II after his defeat at the Battle of Worcester in 1651. The picturesque views may be appreciated all the more when contrasted with the misery in Meena's description of her home:

No one wanted to think about the gangs of no-hope teenagers who already took over the nearby park all day, drinking lager and waiting for something to happen to them, trapped in a forgotten village in no-man's land between a ten-shop town and an amorphous industrial sprawl.

Newstead Abbey

LORD BYRON

www.newsteadabbey.org.uk *Grounds open daily; house open Saturdays, Sundays and Bank Holidays only.*

One of the many medieval abbeys that ceased to be religious houses around the time of Henry VIII and subsequently came into private hands, Newstead can trace its origins back to the twelfth century. Despite the best efforts of the Byron family to bring the place to rack and ruin, the west front survives from the façade of the thirteenth-century priory church.

The poet, born George Gordon Byron (1788–1824), inherited Newstead from his great-uncle when he was only ten and thus became the sixth Baron Byron. That great-uncle, by the way, has a claim to being even more 'mad, bad and dangerous to know' than his notorious great-nephew: he not only murdered a cousin in a drunken brawl, but also squandered the family fortunes on such extravagances as mock naval battles at Newstead for the entertainment of his guests. The result was that the future

poet inherited an estate in an advanced state of disrepair and very little money with which to put it to rights.

Over the next twenty years the time he spent there amounted to little more than summer holidays from school and university, and the occasional visit to his mother. Nevertheless it inspired a lengthy lyrical description in his satirical poem of 1819, *Don Juan*:

> *An old, old monastery once, and now*
> *Still older mansion; of a rich and rare*
>   *Mix'd Gothic, such as artists all allow*
> *Few specimens yet left us can compare*
>   *Withal: it lies perhaps a little low,*
> *Because the monks prefer'd a hill behind,*
> *To shelter their devotion from the wind*

... and much more in the same vein.

Byron achieved great success as a poet: describing the furore that greeted the publication of the first part of *Childe Harold's Pilgrimage* in 1812, he wrote that 'I awoke one morning and found myself famous'. Handsome, aristocratic and arrogant, he has also been described as the first modern-style celebrity, with adoring fans indulging in what his long-suffering wife Annabella described as 'Byronomania'. His personal life – rumours of incest, a scandalous affair with Lady Caroline Lamb (see page 26) and many other affairs with less prominent figures – and constant battles with debt led him to leave England in 1816, never to return. He sold Newstead in 1818, and much of the décor you see today is Victorian, the legacy of subsequent owners. Byron's writing desk is still there, as is his canopied bed, framed with gilt and hung with golden drapery, and a portrait of the man himself by Thomas Phillips, dressed rather less pretentiously than he is in the famous painting of him in Albanian costume (with an extravagant orange robe and turban) on display in the National Portrait Gallery.

In the grounds you can see an imposing monument to Byron's beloved dog, Boatswain, whose inscription begins:

> *Near this spot are deposited the Remains of one who possessed Beauty without Vanity, Strength without Insolence, Courage without Ferocity, and all the Virtues of Man without his Vices.*

The poet himself died of a fever in Greece after taking part in the Greek uprising against the Turks and becoming a national hero there. He was brought back to England for burial and lies in the family vault in St Mary Magdalene's Church in Hucknall, 5 miles from his ancestral home.

5

CHAPTER FIVE

EASTERN
ENGLAND

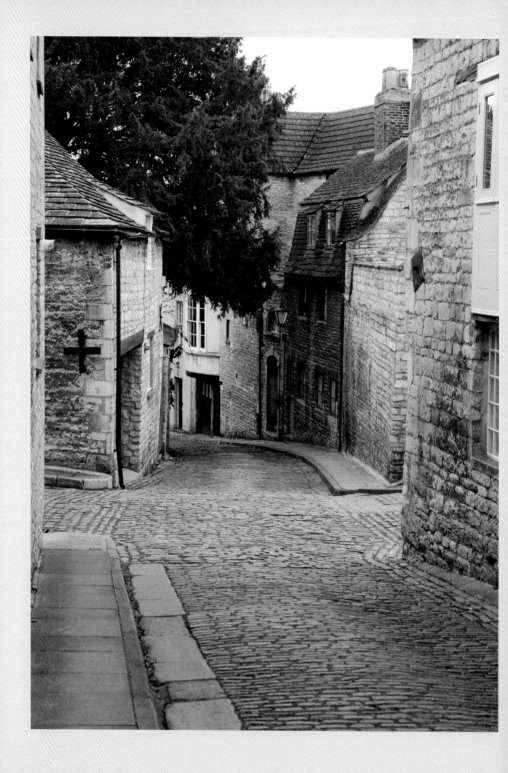

Stamford

GEORGE ELIOT

www.georgehotelofstamford.com

www.stamfordartscentre.com

The 1994 BBC television adaptation of George Eliot's *Middlemarch* was a landmark for two reasons: it made a bestseller out of what many people consider to be the great English novel and many others think they must get around to reading someday; and it made a tourist destination out of the Lincolnshire town of Stamford, where much of the series was filmed.

Middlemarch isn't the only classic to have been filmed in Stamford. Its unspoiled seventeenth- and eighteenth-century architecture also featured in the 1985 television adaptation of *Bleak House* and in the 2005 film version of *Pride and Prejudice*, where it served as the village of Meryton and looked just the thing as the militia marched down the High Street and turned the Bennet girls' heads. Still, it was *Middlemarch* that really put it on the map. St George's Church appeared as St Botolph's, where Dr Lydgate and Rosamond Vincy were married; buildings in St George's Square served as Mawmsey the grocer's, Spooner the jeweller's and various private houses; and the medieval alms-houses known as Browne's Hospital turned into the Old Infirmary.

Just strolling around Stamford makes you feel as if you are in a classic novel, the local limestone giving the buildings the soft, weathered feel that goes so well with bonnets and intricately tied neckcloths. In fact, the whole of the old town (north of the River Welland) and St Martin's (south of it) is designated 'an outstanding area of architec-tural or historic interest that is of national importance'. That said, there are two main places to visit. The first is the George Hotel – for refreshment, obviously, but also for its thousand-year-plus history. Stamford is on the A1, the Great North Road of ancient times, and as long ago as AD 947 there may have been an inn on this site catering for the needs of travellers heading south to London or north to Lincoln and York. The original building was flanked by two religious houses, which since about the fifteenth century have been incorporated into the present hotel. Nothing to do with George Eliot, but it isn't every hostelry that has a crypt under the Champagne Bar, nor a West Wing with a minstrels' gallery above the ceilings of some of the bedrooms.

The other indispensable port of call is the Stamford Arts Centre. It traces its origins back to 1727, when the Assembly Rooms – the eighteenth-century version of a dance hall-cum-social club – were built; the surviving ballroom is the oldest of its kind in England. The theatre opened in 1768, when it was described as 'wonderfully grand', and for the next hundred years all the great names of the acting profession, including Edmund Kean and Sarah Siddons, appeared here. Having fallen on hard times and closed in 1871, it then reopened as part of the new Arts Centre in the 1970s – in plenty of time to feature as Bulstrode's Bank and the White Hart Inn in *Middlemarch*. Its website also proudly boasts that:

> *actors were recruited from Stamford Operatic, Pantomime Players, Shoestring Theatre and Stamford Shakespeare Company to jeer, howl and laugh in a political rally as Robert Hardy made a fool of himself on a political platform pre-built for the day.*

Hardy was playing Arthur Brooke, uncle of the heroine Dorothea; he is described as a man of 'acquiescent temper, miscellaneous opinions, and uncertain vote' who 'would act with benevolent intentions, and ... would spend as little money as possible in carrying them out'. Just the sort of man you want to jeer, howl and laugh at in a political rally.

Purists will point out that George Eliot (real name Mary Ann Evans, 1819–1880) probably modelled the town of Middlemarch on Coventry. Even in the 1830s (when the novel is set), Coventry was a larger and more industrial place than Stamford is now. Non-purists won't care: no disrespect to Coventry, but Stamford is the one that feels like the setting for a Victorian novel.

Grantchester
RUPERT BROOKE
www.theorchardteagarden.co.uk *Closed on Mondays October to March.*

Grantchester is an easy walk from Cambridge, partly along the banks of the River Cam; or you can take the traditional route and arrive by punt. The Old Vicarage, where the poet Rupert Brooke (1887–1915) was a lodger before the First World War, isn't open to the public (it's a private residence, owned by Jeffrey and Mary Archer). It's a fine seventeenth-century building and you can see why Brooke waxed sentimental about it and its surroundings: the local tea shop in particular is something special, offering deck chairs where you can enjoy your scones under the dappled shade of fruit trees, being careful to stay alert enough to protect them from the depredations of the resident pheasants.

It's a bit dismissive to describe the Orchard Tea Garden as 'the local tea shop', because the orchard after which it's named has been there since 1868 and the tradition of Cambridge students (and nowadays other customers too) being served tea under the trees dates from 1897. Brooke, who lodged at the Orchard before moving into the Old Vicarage, isn't the only famous Cambridge student to have taken tea there: the guest list includes Virginia Woolf (see page 98), the philosopher Bertrand Russell, the computer pioneer Alan Turing, and James Watson and Francis Crick of DNA fame, among many others. In fact Woolf and Brooke were students together: she later boasted of having gone skinny-dipping with him in a moonlit pool.

That last bit isn't surprising: Brooke was stunningly good-looking – the Irish poet W. B. Yeats described him as 'the handsomest young man in England' and he attracted numerous admirers of both sexes. At Cambridge he was active in politics and drama, as well as leading a hectic social life. In addition to Woolf, he became friendly with other members of the Bloomsbury Group and associated with many literary figures of the day, including D. H. Lawrence (see page 139) and fellow 'war poets' Siegfried Sassoon and Edward Thomas (pages 211 and 119). But in 1912 he appears to have suffered a breakdown, and went to Berlin to recuperate. It was there, inspired by a homesick longing for a place he loved, that he wrote 'The Old Vicarage, Grantchester':

RUPERT BROOKE STUDYING IN GARDEN OF THE
OLD VICARAGE, GRANTCHESTER.

Just now the lilac is in bloom,
All before my little room;
And in my flower-beds, I think,
Smile the carnation and the pink

and, at the end, those quintessentially English lines:

oh! yet
Stands the Church clock at ten to three?
And is there honey still for tea?

When the First World War broke out, Brooke promptly volunteered. He soon achieved fame as a war poet, acclaimed particularly for 'The Soldier', with its elegiac:

If I should die, think only this of me:
That there's some corner of a foreign field
That is for ever England.

By April the following year he was dead, aged only twenty-seven, having succumbed to sepsis as the result of a mosquito bite while on his way to Gallipoli. He remains a symbol of the tragic loss of a generation of young men – one of the most interesting, most talented and most beautiful of them. He is also one of sixteen First World War poets commemorated by a plaque at Poets' Corner in Westminster Abbey (see page 14). The words inscribed on it are by Wilfred Owen (see page 211), but they express a sentiment that Brooke would have endorsed:

My subject is War, and the pity of War. The Poetry is in the pity.

Over a century on, you can still have tea under the same trees as he did. You can also look nostalgically across the road towards the Old Vicarage and the church of St Andrew and St Mary, whose clock, sadly, is no longer stopped at ten to three.

Literary North Norfolk
W. H. AUDEN, STEPHEN SPENDER AND OTHERS
www.greshams.com

You don't have to spend long on the gorgeous North Norfolk coast to find a surprising number of literary connections. Start at the pretty market town of Holt, or rather at Gresham's School, just outside it, where the poets Wystan Hugh Auden (1907–1973) and Stephen Spender (1909–1995) were near-contemporaries. Spender quickly moved on, but Auden stayed to make his mark, publishing poems in the school magazine and playing Katharina and Caliban in productions of *The Taming of the Shrew* and *The Tempest*. The school's theatre – which also hosts professional productions and is one of the venues for the Holt Festival in July – is named after him, and there is a memorial to him in the grounds, to the south of the chapel. It's a broken-topped pillar inscribed with Auden's words: 'Art should speak to us across centuries; it is the means by which we break bread with the dead.' On the other side of the chapel, a matching pillar by the same sculptor commemorates the composer Benjamin Britten, a later pupil at Gresham's; his 'Hymn to St Cecilia' was written to accompany words by Auden, and the inscription on this pillar is taken from that work.

Heading east from Holt, stop off at Cley, a birdwatcher's paradise today, just as it was when Rupert Brooke (see page 148) holidayed here in 1914. His poem 'Ornithologist' describes a scene that hasn't changed much in a hundred years:

Over the roof of the hide the seed plumes dance.
The hinged flap is up and he focuses
On the pool under the reed expanse.

From Cley it's a short hop to Sheringham, where Stephen Spender – despite not staying long at school here – spent childhood holidays. He clearly loved it, later writing that in the pastures were to be found:

heartsease (the small pansies which are the colour of the iris in a golden eye),
speedwell of a blue as intense as a bead of sky. There were scabious and cornflower
and waving grasses and bracken which came as high as my shoulders.

Finally, head just a little further east, to Cromer – an eerie place if you visit on a misty autumn day. Arthur Conan Doyle (see pages 18 and 73) must have thought so: he came here for a golfing holiday in 1901 and was struck by the appearance of Cromer Hall, a privately owned Gothic Revival pile just outside the town. You get a good view of it from the road between Cromer and Felbrigg. Or, if you aren't heading that way, turn to chapter 6 of *The Hound of the Baskervilles* for a remarkably accurate description:

> *The avenue opened into a broad expanse of turf, and the house lay before us. In the fading light I could see that the centre was a heavy block of building from which a porch projected ... From this central block rose the twin towers, ancient, crenellated, and pierced with many loopholes ... A dull light shone through heavy mullioned windows, and from the high chimneys which rose from the steep, high-angled roof there sprang a single black column of smoke.*

It's said that the legend of the 'gigantic hound' also had its origins in Norfolk's ghostly Black Shuck, even though Conan Doyle then relocated his story to Dartmoor.

Cromer may be eerie in the autumn, but it's delightful in the summer. A theatre critic and journalist called Clement Scott (1841–1904) visited in the 1880s and obviously experienced something similar to what Spender would see some thirty years later. He wrote in the *Daily Telegraph* extolling its 'blue sky without a cloud across it, a sea sparkling under a haze of heat, wild flowers in profusion' and many Victorian literati (presumably all *Telegraph* readers) flocked to witness these delights for themselves. A series of stone rings set into the town's promenade features quotations from some of them, including Oscar Wilde (see page 24; he stayed at the Hotel de Paris on the High Street in 1892, probably working on *A Woman of No Importance* while he was there) and the poet Algernon Swinburne (1837–1909). The quotation that most people photograph, though, contains the dejected words 'I am not enjoying myself very much', attributed to a youthful Winston Churchill, who holidayed here in 1888. He presumably hadn't read Swinburne's poem 'A Haven', written only a few years before, which is rather more enthusiastic. In it, Cromer features as 'where the small town smiles, a warm still sea-side nest'. Catch it on a fine day – when there are no gigantic hounds around – and you'll probably agree.

Black Beauty Country
ANNA SEWELL

kirstyscakery.co.uk *Closed on Mondays, and on Sundays except in summer.*
www.literarynorfolk.co.uk/old_catton.htm

Without straying from Norfolk – indeed, without travelling more than about 20 miles – you can see two 'Anna Sewell Houses'. The first is the early seventeenth-century home in Great Yarmouth where Sewell (1820–1878) was born and which is now a tea room; the second is a handsome Georgian house in Old Catton, just outside Norwich,

where she was living when she wrote *Black Beauty* and where she died a few months after it was published. It's a private residence, but if you stand in the street you can make out the coach house, now a mews-style flat, where Anna, unable to walk easily after a childhood accident, kept the pony and trap that allowed her to get around. If you turn and face the other way you can see horses grazing on the Deer Park opposite, much as they did in her day.

Black Beauty is regarded as the forerunner of the 'pony book', a genre that has been entrancing little girls for almost a century and a half; narrated by the horse Black Beauty himself, it's also one of the first books to advocate treating animals humanely. To see the place that really inspired it, you need to go a few miles further north from Old Catton, to the village of Buxton where Anna stayed as a child with her grandparents, and where she learned to ride. In the novel, Black Beauty's home is called Birtwick Park; in real life it's Dudwick Park, and although the house has been demolished (there's a new one in its place) you can still walk through the estate. Beauty's description of the park rings true to this day:

> *It was entered by a large iron gate, at which stood the first lodge, and then you trotted along on a smooth road between clumps of large old trees; then another lodge and another gate, which brought you to the house and the gardens. Beyond this lay the home paddock, the old orchard, and the stables. There was accommodation for many horses and carriages; but I need only describe the stable into which I was taken; this was very roomy, with four good stalls; a large swinging window opened into the yard, which made it pleasant and airy.*

Sewell moved around quite a lot in the course of her life: childhood in London, then to the south coast and later to Bath in the hope of improving her delicate health. In 1866, family circumstances brought her back to Norfolk and when she died she was buried at the Quaker chapel in Lamas, a village in the same parish as Buxton. The chapel has since been converted into a house and the graveyard controversially destroyed, but Anna's gravestone and those of other members of her family can be seen mounted into a wall by the roadside.

The family – particularly Anna's brother Philip, who owned a considerable estate nearby – has also left its mark in Norwich itself, donating to the city the land that became Sewell Park. At the entrance to the park is a former horse trough, now planted with flowers, dedicated to Anna by her niece; and the so-called Centennial Sign, erected to mark the park's centennial in 2009, bears an image of a certain black horse.

Anyone who dismisses *Black Beauty* as 'just another pony book' needs to think again. Although it was originally written for adults, it now ranks as one of the bestselling children's books of all time and working animals everywhere owe a debt of gratitude to the humanity of Anna Sewell.

6

CHAPTER SIX

NORTHERN
ENGLAND

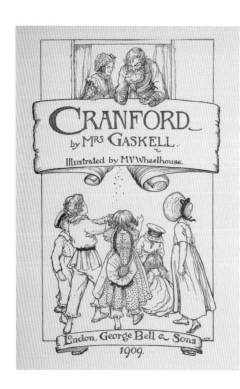

Knutsford

ELIZABETH GASKELL

tattonpark.org.uk *Opening times for house, gardens and farm differ – check in advance.*

www.knutsfordcheshire.co.uk/visiting

elizabethgaskellhouse.co.uk *Open Wednesdays, Thursdays and Sundays only.*

If you've only seen *Cranford* on television, you'll have watched Dame Eileen, Dame Judi et al. walking down the streets of Lacock in Wiltshire, a quaint little village that also featured as Meryton in the BBC's 1995 version of *Pride and Prejudice* (the Colin Firth one, see page 158) and appeared in a couple of Harry Potter films too. The real Cranford is Knutsford in Cheshire, childhood home of the book's author, Elizabeth Gaskell (1810–1865).

The word most often used to describe the fictional Cranford is 'genteel'. It's a small town dominated by women who pay scrupulous attention to slightly outdated etiquette and consider it vulgar to offer guests expensive refreshments. In modern Knutsford, King Street and Princess Street are still lined with the Georgian houses in which Mrs Gaskell's characters lived, although at street level you may see familiar twenty-first-century shops. Here and there a plaque reminds you that this building inspired Miss Matty's tea shop or that this one used to be the Royal George Hotel, where the ladies of Cranford met for evenings of formal entertainment in the Assembly Rooms:

> *Many a county beauty had first swung through the minuet that she afterwards danced before Queen Charlotte in this very room. ... Now, no beauty blushed and dimpled along the sides of the Cranford Assembly Room; no handsome artist won hearts by his bow,* chapeau bras *in hand; the old room was dingy; the salmon-coloured paint had faded into a drab; great pieces of plaster had chipped off from the fine wreaths and festoons on its walls; but still a mouldy odour of aristocracy lingered about the place...*

Sadly even the mouldy odour eventually faded away: what remains of the Royal George is now part of a restaurant chain with no immediate prospect of its being restored even to its former dilapidated glory. The Angel, also mentioned in the novel, still operates as a pub at its original nineteenth-century location, opposite the site of an earlier coaching inn. The latter is now an office block, but the cobbled lane that runs under the so-called Marble Arch to its courtyard still offers a stone mounting block, in case you aren't tall enough to get on your horse unaided.

Heathwaite, the house where Elizabeth grew up, can also be seen, at what is now 17

Gaskell Avenue. A large red-brick house facing the heath, it's in private hands, but a plaque by the door tells you you're looking at the right place.

Just outside the town is Tatton Park, whose elegant neoclassical mansion features in another Gaskell novel, *Wives and Daughters*. When the young heroine Molly first visits, she is dumbstruck by the beautiful grounds:

> *the like of which she had never even imagined. Green velvet lawns, bathed in sunshine, stretched away on every side into the finely wooded park ... Near the house there were walls and fences; but they were covered with climbing roses, and rare honeysuckles and other creepers just bursting into bloom. There were flower-beds, too, scarlet, crimson, blue, orange; masses of blossom lying on the greensward.*

Tatton is now the venue for an annual Royal Horticultural Society flower show, but even on the 360 days of the year when this event isn't taking place the grounds remain as beautiful as when Molly first saw them. *Wives and Daughters* is renowned for its portrayal of many different strata of society and Tatton is a great place to consider this theme: it has extensive and well-preserved servants' quarters which give an unusually clear impression of life 'below stairs'.

Elizabeth left Knutsford when she married the Reverend William Gaskell in 1832 and they spent much of the rest of their lives in Manchester: you can visit their house there, at 84 Plymouth Grove. But she never lost her fondness for the town where she had grown up and chose to be buried in Knutsford, in the grounds of Brook Street Chapel.

The town retained its fondness for her, too, and constructed the Gaskell Memorial Tower in King Street in the early years of the twentieth century. This contains two images of Elizabeth: on one side, beneath a list of her works, is a bronze relief; around the corner, tucked into a niche facing the street, is a elegant stone bust which shows her with hair neatly tied back and wearing a modest, high-necked gown. It's a look that's appropriate not only for a minister's wife, but also for a Cranford lady who, following the code of conduct that Mrs Gaskell so affectionately lampooned, would never let more than three days elapse before returning a call, nor stay longer than a quarter of an hour.

Lyme Park and Chatsworth House

JANE AUSTEN

www.nationaltrust.org.uk/lyme *Grounds open daily; house closed on Wednesdays and Thursdays.*

www.chatsworth.org *Open daily.*

Remember Colin Firth diving into the lake? The famous scene where he (as Mr Darcy in the 1995 BBC television adaptation of Jane Austen's *Pride and Prejudice*, in case you were on another planet or not born at the time) bumped into Jennifer Ehle as Elizabeth while still half-dressed and damp from his swim?

Filmed at Lyme Park.

It's a house that positively oozes history, having begun life as a hunting lodge in the fifteenth century, been transformed into a mansion in Elizabethan times and much altered in the Palladian and/or baroque styles (expert opinion differs) in the eighteenth century. Owned by the same family, the Leghs, from the very beginning until it was given to the National Trust in 1946, it offers the visitor an extraordinarily ornate drawing room with a carved overmantel (over one of the largest fireplaces you'll ever see in a

private house) bearing the arms of Elizabeth I; a bedroom where Mary Queen of Scots is said to have slept; a parlour where the Cheshire Club met to discuss restoring the ousted James II to the throne in the 1690s; some fifty antique clocks; and a fascinating collection of other *objets*, notably the Lyme Missal, an early printed version of a religious text that has been in the family's possession for more than five hundred years.

But it's the exterior that commands the literary pilgrim's attention. Colin Firth's famous dive was made into a secluded pool, but the façade of the house and its magnificent reflecting lake were filmed as Pemberley, Mr Darcy's home. Jane Austen (1775–1817) doesn't bother with details of the architecture, but she gives us this description of Elizabeth's first impression of the house and grounds:

> *They gradually ascended for half a mile, and then found themselves at the top of a considerable eminence, where the wood ceased, and the eye was instantly caught by Pemberley House, situated on the opposite side of a valley, into which the road with some abruptness wound. It was a large, handsome, stone building, standing well on rising ground, and backed by a ridge of high woody hills;—and in front, a stream of some natural importance was swelled into greater, but without any*

artificial appearance. Its banks were neither formal, nor falsely adorned. Elizabeth was delighted. She had never seen a place for which nature had done more, or where natural beauty had been so little counteracted by an awkward taste.

There's a strong school of thought (particularly in Derbyshire) that this description is based on Chatsworth House, which gets a passing mention in the novel, and which Austen visited in 1811, when *Sense and Sensibility* had just been published and she was revising *Pride and Prejudice*. If you go to Chatsworth today, you'll be forgiven for believing that you are indeed at Pemberley, as parts of the 2005 Keira Knightley and Matthew Macfadyen version were filmed here. The grand staircase and the painted hall in particular may look familiar.

There's a caveat to be entered, though. Chatsworth is undeniably magnificent, its gardens some of the most gorgeous in the country and its accumulation of art, silverware, jewellery and furniture rivalling the Royal Collection. But Jane Austen couldn't have seen the house or grounds as they are today – the house was extended and the gardens completely redesigned (by the great Joseph Paxton, who later created the Crystal Palace) a decade after her death.

What it boils down to is this: if you want to go to Pemberley, you have a choice. Visit either. Better yet, visit both. You won't regret it.

Manchester's Landmark Poetry
LEMN SISSAY

If you visit the University of Huddersfield you'll see a poem displayed on an outside wall of the Creative Arts building. It's some 13 metres high and nearly 10 metres wide, so hard to miss. If your travels take you to the University of Manchester's University Place, you'll see the same poem painted on the wall of the atrium space, overlooked by tall windows so that you can also read it from the corridor above. It's called 'Let There Be Peace' and it's by Lemn Sissay (born 1967), who has, since the 1990s, made a project of installing 'landmark poems' across Manchester and other parts of the country. This idea of poetry-as-artwork has taken flight lately, with the 2020 exhibition Everyday Heroes on London's South Bank involving, among others, the Poet Laureate Simon Armitage (see page 169). But it was Sissay who kick-started it.

His first landmark piece, 'Hardy's Well', was painted onto the wall of the pub of the same name, at the end of Manchester's famous Curry Mile, in 1994. A poetic invitation to visit the pub, it's also a masterpiece of alliteration, opening with the injunction 'Wait Waterless Wanderer' and going on to celebrate the pub's wand whirling 'a warm-hearted wackiness into a weary week'. When the poem first appeared it attracted so much attention and caused so many accidents that traffic-calming measures had to be introduced as a result.

At the time of writing the Hardy's Well had closed down and was likely to be demolished in the name of 'development', though enthusiasts were hoping to find a wall nearby to which the poem could be transferred. In the meantime, you can check out

Sissay's 'Rain' on the corner of Oxford Road and Dilworth Street, 'Flags', laid into the pavement of Tib Street in the Northern Quarter, and one of his 'morning poems' as part of a truly beautiful mural, decorated with a kingfisher, a peacock, a hummingbird and other exotica, at the end of a red-brick terrace in Old Trafford. Other Sissay landmarks can be found in the Children's Hospital at the Royal London, at the Olympic Park in London, at the Turner Contemporary in Margate and as far afield as Addis Ababa in Ethiopia and Durban in South Africa.

'Let There Be Peace' is an impassioned plea to put an end to war and there are plans to display it in many more locations. When it was unveiled in Huddersfield in 2014, coinciding with the centenary of the outbreak of the First World War, Sissay said, 'My ambition is to have the peace poem tattooed into the skin of the world. Why have small ambitions?' Why indeed?

Mexborough
TED HUGHES
tedhughesproject.com/the-trail
www.legendarydartmoor.co.uk/ted_hughes.htm

Ted Hughes (1930–1998, Poet Laureate from 1984 until his death) was born in Mytholm-royd, West Yorkshire, but when he was seven his family moved 40 miles southeast to Mexborough, near Doncaster. Although this was a much more industrial landscape than the one in which he had spent his early years, it was here that he developed the fascination with the hardships of rural life and farming that coloured much of his poetry – the poetry that described a tractor failing to start as 'an agony to think of' and thistles getting in the way of hoeing as 'every one a revengeful burst of resurrection'.

Hughes' birthplace – which you can rent as a writer's retreat – is in the care of the Elmet Trust, established in 2006 to celebrate his life and work. But it's Mexborough, and specifically the Ted Hughes Project based there, that has really gone out of its way to demonstrate its pride in its most famous son. An annual Ted Hughes Poetry Festival (over a weekend in September) is only one of several literary events throughout the year; in 2017 a statue of the poet sitting reading on a bench was unveiled outside the former grammar school (now the local business centre) that Hughes attended in the 1940s; and there's a 2-mile walking trail for those wanting to discover local places that were import-ant to him. These include two pubs in which he's known to have drunk, various ports of call along his teenaged paper round and the piece of land across which he was once chased by a horse, an experience that inspired the early short story 'The Rain Horse':

> *From the high point on which he stood the hill dipped slightly and rose to another crested point fringed with the tops of trees, three hundred yards to his right. As he watched it, the horse ran up to that crest, showed against the sky – for a moment like a nightmarish leopard – and disappeared over the other side.*

It's a bleak landscape: go there on a bleak day and shiver.

If you're a committed writer or an aspiring one, you can also head back closer to Hughes's birthplace and enrol in a residential creative writing course at the Ted Hughes Arvon Centre, near Hebden Bridge. Based at his former home at Lumb Bank, this is an eighteenth-century millowner's house, set in 20 acres of woodland and offering views to make any would-be poets reach for their quills.

At the other end of the country, there's another Hughes memorial, somewhat more remote than the one in downtown Mexborough. From 1961 onwards, when he moved to Devon with his first wife, the American poet and novelist Sylvia Plath (1932–1963), Hughes owned a house in the village of North Tawton. He loved walking on nearby

Dartmoor and before he died he asked that a granite stone engraved with his name be placed at his favourite spot. Thanks to special permission from the Duchy of Cornwall and other interested parties, a stone was airlifted there in 2001. It reads simply 'Ted Hughes OM 1930–1998', in recognition of the Order of Merit (recognising a distinguished contribution to literature) with which he had been invested just days before his death. The stone's location was originally secret, but word inevitably leaked out: even so, from a distance it looks for all the world like any other stone lying around in open country. It's on a grassy mound above the Taw River, reachable only after a stiff walk across military firing ranges from the village of Belstone. Hughes recorded the moor's bleakness and notoriously ferocious weather in his 1981 poem 'Snipe', which refers to 'the downpour helmet' that 'tightens on your skull'. Prudent visitors may choose to go on a more clement day.

Hull

PHILIP LARKIN AND WINIFRED HOLTBY

www.thelarkintrail.co.uk

I n a scene from Alan Bennett's 2004 play *The History Boys,* the headmaster discusses his background with Irwin, the new teacher:

> HEADMASTER: *I was a geographer. I went to Hull.*
> IRWIN: *Oh. Larkin.*
> HEADMASTER: *Everybody says that. 'Hull? Oh, Larkin.' I don't know about the poetry ... as I say, I was a geographer ... but as a librarian he was pitiless.*

We needn't go into what this says about geographers, but it says a lot about what most people know about Hull. Which is unfair, really. Because although, yes, Philip Larkin (1922–1985) was university librarian there for thirty years, from 1955 until his death, he's a rather more interesting poet than this makes him sound. Plus he's not the town's only claim to literary fame.

There's also Winifred Holtby (1898–1935). Born in the rural East Riding of Yorkshire, of which Hull is by far the largest conurbation, she's best known now as the author of the novel *South Riding.* This is set in a fictional place based on the East Riding – there has never been a South Riding of Yorkshire (South Yorkshire came into being when the counties of England and Wales were reorganised in the 1970s, but it's not the same thing).

South Riding was published in 1936, after Holtby's premature death; in her lifetime she was known for her journalism and for other novels, notably *The Land of Green Ginger* (1927). Like *South Riding,* its background is rural and small-town Yorkshire, but its title is drawn from a little lane in Hull's old town. No one seems to be sure where this peculiar name came from: it may have been something to do with the ginger trade (Hull has been an important port since medieval times, and spices were big business back then); or it may have evolved from the name of some local dignitary. The City Council has even put up a plaque acknowledging that the name's origin 'remains a mystery'. Whatever the truth may be, Holtby fans can derive joy from strolling down this quirkily named street, which so captivated the youthful heroine of her novel, and admiring what is said to be Britain's smallest window: it's little more than a slit between two blocks in the wall of the George Hotel, through which a porter apparently kept a lookout for the arrival of coaches so that these could receive immediate attention.

To go back to Larkin, though, a short walk from the Land of Green Ginger will bring you to Hull's railway station, the Paragon Interchange. Here you can admire a larger-than-life statue of the poet, unveiled on 2 December 2010, the twenty-fifth anniversary of his death. It's the work of Martin Jennings, who also created John Betjeman's statue at St Pancras (see page 60), and it shows Larkin in similarly informal style: hatless, raincoat open, posed one foot in front of the other, as if he were coming out of the station hotel and turning hastily towards the platforms, anxious not to miss his train. Appropriately, the base is inscribed with a line from his poem 'The Whitsun Weddings': 'That Whitsun I was late getting away'. Whether the notoriously curmudgeonly and publicity-shy poet would have approved is open to question.

From the statue you can – if you are not bothered about missing your train – set out on the Larkin Trail. In three sections (Larkin's Here: City Centre; Larkin's Here: Beyond the City Centre; and Larkin's Elsewhere), it covers twenty-five key points in the poet's life, work and landscape. These range from his favourite pubs to the local Marks & Spencer (described in the poem 'The Large Cool Store' as 'selling cheap clothes / Set out in simple sizes plainly'); further afield are the fields 'too thin and thistled to be called meadows' past which he used to cycle, and the suspended 'giant step' of the Humber Bridge. As you follow in his footsteps, or perhaps his bicycle tracks, you can see why the stark beauty of the area he described as his 'dear landscape' appealed to him. You might also begin to understand how it helped him to explore what one critic described as 'the failures and remorse of age, about stunted lives and spoiled desires' – the themes that most of us associate with the man who famously wrote that sexual intercourse began 'rather late for me'.

The Brontë Parsonage Museum, Haworth
CHARLOTTE, EMILY AND ANNE BRONTË
www.bronte.org.uk *Closed Mondays and Tuesdays.*
www.haworthchurch.co.uk

If you have the choice, go to Haworth on a miserable day. Visiting the Brontës' parsonage when there is precious little light in some of the smaller rooms and the wind is, yes, wuthering around outside gives you a real insight into how the three sisters – Charlotte (1816–1855), Emily (1818–1848) and Anne (1820–1849) – came to write as they did. As Emily explained in the opening chapter of *Wuthering Heights*:

> *Wuthering Heights is the name of Mr. Heathcliff's dwelling. 'Wuthering' being a significant provincial adjective, descriptive of the atmospheric tumult to which its station is exposed in stormy weather. Pure, bracing ventilation they must have up there at all times, indeed: one may guess the power of the north wind, blowing over the edge, by the excessive slant of a few stunted firs at the end of the house.*

Anne's description of the hall in *The Tenant of Wildfell Hall* could almost be of the same place:

> *built of dark grey stone, venerable and picturesque to look at, but doubtless, cold and gloomy enough to inhabit, with its thick stone mullions and little latticed panes, its time-eaten air-holes, and its too lonely, too unsheltered situation, - only shielded from the war of wind and weather by a group of Scotch firs, themselves half blighted with storms, and looking as stern and gloomy as the Hall itself.*

The famous opening of Charlotte's *Jane Eyre* may be less wild but it still focuses our attention on the effect that the weather had on the characters' daily lives:

There was no possibility of taking a walk that day ... the cold winter wind had brought with it clouds so sombre, and a rain so penetrating, that further out-door exercise was now out of the question.

That said, we know that when the Reverend Patrick Brontë and his family lived in the parsonage it was cosy, comfortable and always immaculately clean. When Charlotte's friend Mrs Gaskell (see page 156) visited in 1853, she described the dining room as 'the perfection of warmth, snugness and comfort' and Charlotte wrote of her bedroom, 'My room was really beautiful in some lights, moonlight especially.' But the overwhelming impression you gain from what is now the Brontë Parsonage Museum is of how small it is, given how many people it had to house. When the Reverend Patrick moved here in 1820, he had six children under the age of twelve (including a three-month-old baby, Anne) and a dying wife. His sister-in-law subsequently joined them to act as nurse, nanny and housekeeper, and there were two servants as well. The four children who survived to adulthood spent most of their lives here; Charlotte, the only one to marry, continued here for the few remaining months of her life, because her husband was her father's curate. Who shared with whom in the few bedrooms available seems to have changed continually depending on the ages and needs of all concerned.

The other thing that can't help striking you is the extent to which the Brontës were dogged by tragedy. Having lost their mother when her first child was eight, the two eldest sisters died of tuberculosis before they were twelve; Emily and Anne fell victim to the same disease at thirty and twenty-nine respectively, and their only brother, Branwell, succumbed to his addictions at thirty-one. Charlotte outlived all her siblings and became successful enough to make extensions and improvements to the parsonage, but even so died before her thirty-ninth birthday; their father outlived them all. Perhaps the

most pitiful story is the one told about Charlotte after Emily and Anne had died. The three sisters had done most of their writing together, in the dining room, walking round the table in the evening, reading and discussing whatever they were working on. Left on her own, Charlotte carried on the ritual; one of the servants recorded that 'My heart aches to hear Miss Brontë walking, walking on alone.'

The local church, St Michael and All Angels, isn't the same building in which the Reverend Patrick preached; it's a late nineteenth-century rebuild, although the Brontës would have recognised the surviving eighteenth-century tower. Inside, the Brontë Memorial Chapel is built over the family vault, near where the family pew used to be. All except Anne are buried here; she died at Scarborough, where she had gone to see if sea air would improve her health, and her grave is there, in the churchyard of St Mary's, high above the old town, near the castle. It was Charlotte's decision to 'lay the flower where it had fallen', at least in part to spare her father the pain of conducting the third funeral service within eight months for one of his own children.

Charlotte, Emily and Anne are also commemorated by a tablet in Westminster Abbey which bears the fitting inscription 'With courage to endure'. They had, indeed, had much to endure, and not just the weather.

Literature Out of Doors

Some years before he became Poet Laureate, Simon Armitage (born 1963) took it into his head to walk the Pennine Way in the guise of a modern troubadour, with not a penny in his pocket and 'singing for his supper' by giving poetry readings at various pubs, village halls and churches along the way.

He also chose to do it backwards. Most hikers attack the Pennine Way from the south, walking its gruelling 268 miles with the sun and wind behind them. Not Armitage. He started in Kirk Yetholm, just on the Scottish side of the border, and headed south for Marsden, the West Yorkshire village where he grew up. The advantages were: first, that he'd be going downhill for most of the way and, second, that he was heading home, which meant he could hardly give up en route. Plus, as a poet, he wrote, he's naturally contrary. He recorded his journey in the memoir *Walking Home*.

Rachel Joyce (born 1962) describes an even longer – and perhaps even more contrary – trek in her novel *The Unlikely Pilgrimage of Harold Fry*. Sixty-five-year-old Harold, having learned that his former colleague Queenie Hennessy (who takes centre stage in a later book) is dying, goes out to post a letter to her. Somehow he walks past the post box and carries on walking – all the way from South Devon to a hospice in Berwick-on-Tweed. Some 627 miles. 'So you put yourself at the mercy of strangers?' a stranger asks. 'No, I'm careful,' Harold replies:

There have been one or two moments when I was afraid. I thought a man on the A439 was going to mug me, but he was actually about to offer me an embrace. He had lost his wife to cancer. I misjudged him because he was missing his front teeth.

There are shorter literary walks to be done if these sound too energetic for you. Try Frenchman's Creek (see page 71), the Coleridge Way (page 80) or the Ted Hughes Trail (page 162). Or head down to Dorset's Jurassic Coast and walk along the amazing 18 miles of shingle known as Chesil Beach. Ian McEwan (born 1948) sets the all-too-brief honeymoon with which his *On Chesil Beach* begins in a (fictitious) hotel here, and the beach is a symbol of the difficulties Florence and Edward signally fail to overcome. It begins well enough:

A shift or a strengthening of the wind brought them the sound of waves breaking, like a distant shattering of glasses. The mist was lifting to reveal in part the contours of the low hills, curving away above the shoreline to the east. They could see a luminous grey smoothness that may have been the silky surface of the sea itself.

But that's before the couple so disastrously fail to consummate their marriage. After that hideous experience, the shingle becomes 'exhausting', fit only for the frustrated bridegroom to stand on, 'hurling stones at the sea and shouting obscenities'. You can't even really walk on McEwan's beach, you have to 'trudge'.

Cheer yourself up by looking at the view southeast towards Portland Bill – it features in the Top Ten of Simon Jenkins's *England's 100 Best Views* – and by remembering that not everyone's honeymoon is as catastrophic as this one.

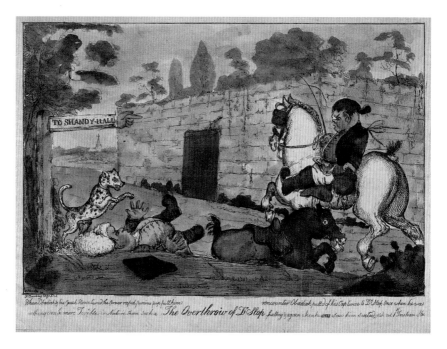

When Obadiah his peach Horse-Lived the former rapid furious pop-full-him) — nonencenter Oladiak puled of his Cap lance to D'Slop Once when he was nothing can be more Terrible in Nature than Sen ha · *The Overthrow of D'Slop* falling again; he who was draw him limited; sich ned l'Gentlean Ste

Shandy Hall, Coxwold

LAURENCE STERNE

www.laurencesternetrust.org.uk/shandy-hall.php *Opening times for house and gardens differ – check in advance.*

*T*he Life and Opinions of Tristram Shandy, Gentleman by Laurence Sterne (1713–1768)
is notorious for its long-windedness and rambling style: although it's ostensibly a
biography, the narrator isn't born until volume four (of nine), tells us little about his life
or opinions and disappears from the story in volume six. The book is full of comic characters, such as Tristram's Uncle Toby, who studies the art of attacking fortified towns
by laying out plans on a bowling green. Some of it is hilarious, some of it learned; you
could even argue that, given its rambling, non-linear approach, it was postmodern, two
centuries before that term became familiar. An early twentieth-century critic, including
Tristram Shandy in a series of the world's greatest books, acknowledged that it had its
imperfections but referred to 'the many passages of genuine humour and wit ensuring
an immortality for the wayward genius of Laurence Sterne'. Whatever your views, it was
hugely successful when it was first published between 1759 and 1767: by the time two
volumes had appeared the humble clergyman had become a celebrity .
  The Shandy family's fictional home is Shandy Hall, so when Sterne was appointed
perpetual curate of the village of Coxwold, North Yorkshire, in 1760, his friends
promptly gave this name to his new residence. It was here that he wrote the later volumes of *Tristram Shandy* and – after extensive travels in Europe as part of his battle
against tuberculosis – his only other novel, *A Sentimental Journey Through France and Italy*.
Coxwold remained his home for the rest of his life, though he made annual pilgrimages
to London, enjoying the fame and even notoriety that *Tristram Shandy* brought him: he
was happy for people to abuse his work, he said, as long as that meant they bought it.

Visiting Shandy Hall today, you take a guided tour that, thanks to the passion of the resident curator and volunteers, will enthuse even those who've never read a word Sterne wrote. It's not a large house – the man was only a curate when he moved here, after all – but it's based round a fine fifteenth-century hall with some original wall paintings dating back to 1430. The room in which Sterne wrote sits at the heart of a collection of more than two thousand items of memorabilia, from books and letters to the exquisite marbled pages that were a unique feature of first editions of his work.

There are gardens, too, both formal and wild – at their best in June, when beautifully scented old roses scramble over the front of the house. There's also the remains of a sweet chestnut tree that was probably there in Sterne's time, but was struck by lightning in 1911 and now serves as support for a spectacular climbing clematis.

You can see why Sterne, a keen gardener, loved the place: 'I am as happy as a prince, at Coxwould,' he wrote, 'and I wish you could see in how princely a manner I live – 'tis a land of plenty.' You also have to warm to the man who wrote, as part of the dedication to *Tristram Shandy*, that he was:

firmly persuaded that every time a man smiles, - but much more so, when he laughs, that it adds something to this Fragment of Life.

Walney Island
THE REVEREND W. AWDRY
www.watermill.co.uk *Closed Mondays and Tuesdays.*
www.walney-island.com
www.norfolkchurches.co.uk
www.visit-gloucestershire.co.uk/directory/listing/rodborough-parish-church

If you cross the Jubilee Bridge from Barrow-in-Furness to Walney Island – it's about 320 metres long – you find yourself in an enchanted land. Eleven miles long, just under a mile at its widest point, Walney is one of the largest islands off the coast of Britain to have direct road access to the mainland. Half its area is given over to nature reserves – one at the northern tip, the other at the south – and at different times of the year you may be lucky enough to spot everything from grey seals to eider ducks or a substantial population of natterjack toads.

One thing you won't find, though, is a railway and if you were brought up on *The Railway Series*, written by the Reverend Wilbert Awdry (1911–1997) and later by his son Christopher (born 1940), this may come as a disappointment. That's because Walney is the model for Sodor Island, home of the Reverend's most famous creations, Thomas the Tank Engine and his friends.

In the stories, Sodor is rather larger than Walney and is linked to the mainland by two bridges rather than one – the second one is, conveniently, a railway bridge, allowing Thomas and the others to take their adventures further afield. The books contain various harbours and docks for which you will have to use your imagination, but Walney's lighthouse, at the southern end of the island, is real enough and, until it was

fully automated in 2003, had the distinction of being the last manned lighthouse in England. Walney's principal settlement is called Vickerstown, which Awdry (himself a vicar during part of his career) changed to Vicarstown. The name Sodor has a clerical origin, too: the official name of the local diocese, covering the Isle of Man and other nearby islands, is Sodor and Man. Awdry, realising that there was no Isle of Sodor (the name means 'southern islands', so there wouldn't be), decided to create one.

Away from the island itself, the Reverend drew inspiration from various places and incidents in the Furness area. Just outside the village of Rampside is an even smaller village called Roa Island. It was indeed once an island, accessible in the nineteenth century by a constructed causeway along which a railway ran until 1936 (there's a road there now, but some of the sleepers can still be seen, reinforcing the sides of the causeway).

The original water mill which appears near Elsbridge on Thomas's branch line (and where he once heard strange noises that led him to believe there was a troll under the bridge) can be found a few miles north, close to the ruined Gleaston Castle: it has a fully functional water wheel, an impressive 5.5 metres in diameter, housed in a building that dates back to 1774.

While you're in the area, look in at the former mining hub of Lindal-in-Furness, now a pretty little commuter village with more than its share of listed buildings. It features in *The Railway Series*' annals because it was once the scene of a real-life accident that the Reverend turned to good account. In September 1892 a goods train was crossing the embankment near Lindal when the ground simply opened up in front of it. The driver and fireman jumped clear and watched in horror as a substantial part of their train disappeared into a vast hole. In 'Down the Mine', one of the stories in *Gordon the Big Engine,* it is Thomas who falls into just such a hole, with Gordon coming to the rescue. A railway line still passes through Lindal, linking Lancaster to Barrow, but the station closed in 1951 and no trace of it remains. The last mine in the area is also long gone, but the underground workings can still make their presence felt: in 2015, a large sinkhole, believed to be the site of a former mine, opened up in the course of a wet weekend and, according to the *Westmorland Gazette*, 'swallowed a 20ft cabin, a wagon and a Nissan Micra'. Sadly, Gordon seems not to have been on hand to help.

If all this is too frivolous for you, or you aren't of an age to care about the Awdrys' railway stories, head back to Rampside and stare out to sea, to the tiny island of Piel with its ruined castle. This is what William Wordsworth (see page 176) did in the summer of 1805, when Rampside was a popular bathing resort and he was inspired to write:

> *I was thy neighbour once, thou rugged Pile!*
> *Four summer weeks I dwelt in sight of thee:*
> *I saw thee every day; and all the while,*
> *Thy Form was sleeping on a glassy sea.*

The view hasn't changed much since Wordsworth's time and if you pick the right day the sea can still be every bit as glassy as it was then.

Although his works were largely inspired by this part of the northwest, the Reverend Awdry wrote many of them while he was vicar of Emneth in Norfolk from 1953 to 1965. There aren't many churches where a stained-glass window is devoted to an 0-6-0 tank locomotive, but St Edmund's in Emneth is an exception: a memorial to the Reverend features Thomas, with his familiar blue and red paintwork and the number 1 on his side. Come to that, there aren't many trains of any description that merit two stained-glass windows, but Thomas does. When the Reverend retired he moved to Rodborough in Gloucestershire and spent his last years there. Its parish church, St Mary Magdalene, contains a window he designed himself: in the bottom right-hand corner he is shown shutting the doors on Thomas and friends for the last time.

Hill Top, Near Sawrey
BEATRIX POTTER
www.nationaltrust.org.uk/hill-top

Hill Top is small and tickets can't be bought in advance: arrive early in the day and be prepared to queue. Opening times for house and gardens differ – check in advance.

www.nationaltrust.org.uk/beatrix-potter-gallery-and-hawkshead

armitt.com/armitt_website

thelingholmkitchen.co.uk

The publication of *The Tale of Peter Rabbit* in 1902 put Beatrix Potter (1866–1943) on the road to becoming a wealthy woman. Three years later she was able to buy a seventeenth-century farmhouse called Hill Top in Near Sawrey, in what was then Lancashire but is now Cumbria, in the Lake District; it was to be her home for the next seven years. During that time, she wrote most of the rest of her twenty-three hugely successful 'little books', including the tales of Squirrel Nutkin, Benjamin Bunny, Mrs Tiggy-Winkle and Jemima Puddle-Duck, using her garden, the village and the surrounding country-side as inspiration. The local pub, the Tower Bank Arms, is illustrated in *The Tale of Jemima Puddle-Duck*; a traditional whitewashed farmhouse (now a B&B) is clearly identifiable as the building past which the ducks waddle in *The Tale of Tom Kitten*; recognisable views over the nearby lakes feature in *Squirrel Nutkin*; and Potter's own kitchen garden can be discerned any time one of her rabbit characters fancies a snack.

In 1913, when she was forty-seven, Potter married a local solicitor and moved to a larger home nearby. She had by this time developed a love of sheep farming in general and the local Herdwick breed in particular; she owned Hill Top for the rest of her life and constantly extended her property by buying adjacent land. Having taken an early interest in the fledgling National Trust, on her death she bequeathed to it 4,000 acres: the largest bequest the Trust had received up to that time and a significant factor in establishing the Lake District National Park, which came into being in 1951.

The Trust also owns Hill Top and has maintained it as it would have been when Potter lived there. There's plenty to see in the little house: artwork, photographs and other memorabilia, including a letter to the invalid child of a friend in which Peter Rabbit and his sisters made their first appearance. There's a brass statuette of Jeremy Fisher and a collection of miniature china rabbits, one of which must have been the model for Peter. There's even a doll's house in which you can spot the metal fireplace, the tiny plates and spoons and the baby's cradle that feature in the illustrations for *The Tale of Two Bad Mice.* A copy of the book has been thoughtfully placed on the window seat so that you can check if you've missed anything.

The garden, as you'd expect from someone who loved nature as much as Potter did, is both lush and productive; as you approach the house you see that it's almost as rampant as it was when she wrote:

The flowers love the house, they try to come in! House leek grows on the window sills and ledges; wisteria climbs the wall, clematis chokes the spout casings ... But nothing more sweet than the old pink cabbage rose that peeps in at the small paned windows.

Though Hill Top and its surrounds were Potter's inspiration, you'll see more of her original artwork if you take a short drive down the hill to Hawkshead, to the Beatrix Potter Gallery. This is housed in another quirky seventeenth-century building, the former office of Beatrix's husband, William Heelis. It is, as its guidebook tells you, 'the only place you can step into the pages of your favourite Beatrix Potter titles, as you get up close to her original artwork'. You can indeed get very close to Mrs Tiggy-Winkle and her laundry, or to Tom Kitten and his sisters leaning over the wall to talk to the Puddle-Ducks.

Having done this, continue on a few more miles to the Armitt Museum and Library to discover a less well-known aspect of this extraordinary woman's talent. Before she became famous, Potter had studied botany, fossils, insects and fungi and could have become a respected and successful mycologist if she hadn't been female: as it was, the scientific establishment didn't take her seriously. Even so, she learned to draw botanical subjects with great detail and accuracy. She bequeathed to Armitt a collection of 450 exquisite drawings and watercolours, as well as her personal first editions of her 'little books'.

Finally, head north towards Keswick and the Kitchen and Walled Garden on the Lingholm Estate, a favourite holiday home of the Potter family in Beatrix's young days. The octagonal walled kitchen garden, recently restored, was the basis for Mr McGregor's garden in *Peter Rabbit*, though today it is a terracotta Squirrel Nutkin who guards the grand entrance. Where better to stop for tea, as long as you don't overindulge in the soporific lettuces or get caught in a gooseberry net and end up in a pie?

Dove Cottage, Grasmere
WILLIAM WORDSWORTH

wordsworth.org.uk Closed Thursdays and Fridays.

It's chocolate-box pretty at any time of year; William Wordsworth (1770–1850) called it 'the loveliest spot that man hath ever found' and a century and a half of tourism following his death have done surprisingly little to discredit that claim. To appreciate the full Wordsworth vibe, you really should go in daffodil season. Just up the road from the churchyard where William, his sister Dorothy and his wife Mary are buried is the Wordsworth Daffodil Garden where you are invited to plant a daffodil for yourself or a loved one. Pick the right day and, with daffodils abundant in the churchyard and along the roadside as well as in the garden, you could almost claim – as he did in his most quoted work – 'ten thousand saw I at a glance'.

We're talking, of course, about the Lake District village of Grasmere, where Wordsworth lived from 1799 to 1808 (and where he wrote many of his best-known poems). Less than half a mile from the church, his former home, Dove Cottage, has recently benefited from substantial lottery funding and, in celebration of the 250th anniversary of his birth, 2020 saw the opening of something that the Wordsworth Trust has had the good taste not to call the Wordsworth Experience. They've gone for 'Reimagining Wordsworth' and are aiming to tell the story of his life and poetry in new ways. They've stripped away centuries of paint to restore an authentic look, leaving rooms where you can read by candlelight and where a tall person has to duck to avoid bashing their head against the beams. If you consider that William was 5 feet 10 inches tall (1.78 metres, which was not short by the standards of his day, and, according to his friend and fellow writer Thomas De Quincey, he wasn't 'a slender man' either), it's hardly astonishing he did so much fell walking – he must have been uncomfortably cramped indoors. Not to mention the fact that the household was constantly expanding. Having originally been just William and Dorothy, after three years it took in not only his new wife, Mary Hutchinson, but her sister Sara as well; the first three of William and Mary's five children were born here; and at one time De Quincey was an apparently permanent guest. No wonder that by 1808 they were looking for larger lodgings; the only surprise is that they hadn't done so years before.

Nineteenth-century gloom and crowdedness may be all very authentic, but the Wordsworth Trust has also borne in mind that the landscape was a huge inspiration to him and has created galleries where you can just sit and look out of the window, as he once did.

Literary enthusiasts needn't worry about dumbing down, though. Wordsworth is known to have been an obsessive reviser of his own work, and the Trust owns twenty-three of the twenty-four known manuscripts of his master work, *The Prelude*. You can look at his scribbles and see how he agonised over words and phrases. He began work on this fourteen-volume, six-thousand-line epic in 1798, was still revising it in the 1830s and was never sufficiently satisfied with it to publish it (it appeared only after his death in 1850). If you are one of those who have an unfinished novel in the bottom drawer or folders of poems on the laptop that you've never dared show anyone, you'll probably, as you explore his old home, feel William's spirit patting you sympathetically on the shoulder and telling you he knows exactly what you are going through.

Step outside for a breath of air and you'll find another recent gesture towards the authentic: Dorothy's diaries contain constant reference to the orchard, where they often sat on mild days, where William wrote and where they grew apples and pears and cultivated scarlet runner beans. Now known as the Dove Cottage Garden, the space has been reimagined to include more of the features that William and Dorothy introduced: snowdrops, bluebells, daffodils (of course) and fruit trees.

The beauty of the fells certainly played a huge role in William's creative process, but the often-overlooked Dorothy was no mean writer or observer of nature either. Her diary for 15 April 1802 contains the remark:

I never saw daffodils so beautiful they grew among the mossy stones about & above them, some rested their heads upon these stones as on a pillow for very weariness & the rest tossed & reeled & danced & seemed as if they verily laughed with the wind that blew upon them over the Lake, they looked so gay ever glancing ever changing.

Anyone who knows 'I Wandered Lonely as a Cloud' will recognise a scene that Dorothy's brother later immortalised in verse.

A Harry Potter Odyssey

www.alnwickcastle.com

westcoastrailways.co.uk/jacobite/steam-train-trip *The Jacobite steam railway runs from July to October only.*

www.leadenhallmarket.co.uk

'All you've got to do is walk straight at the wall between Platforms Nine and Ten. Best do it at a bit of a run if you're nervous.'

That is Mrs Weasley's advice to Harry on how to get on to Platform 9¾ at London's King's Cross Station at the start of the film *Harry Potter and the Philosopher's Stone* (published in 1997, filmed in 2001). You probably don't need to be told that on Platform 9¾ you will find the Hogwarts Express, the magnificent old steam train that will transport you to the Hogwarts School of Witchcraft and Wizardry, according to the famous books by J. K. Rowling (born 1965).

If you really want to leave the Muggle world behind, an Edinburgh-bound train (not, sadly, from Platform 9¾) will take you to within a short distance of Alnwick, the Northumbrian castle in whose Outer Bailey Harry and Ron learned to ride a broomstick and play Quidditch; broomstick training classes are available to Muggles, too.

You may also recognise the castle's Lion Arch as the one through which Harry and friends walk to get to Hagrid's house and the Forbidden Forest. ▶

Alnwick, transformed from ruined Norman castle to High Gothic palace in the eighteenth century, is the ancestral home of the Percy family – the Earls of Northumberland in Shakespeare's Wars of the Roses plays. Unfortunately, Shakespeare has them living at Warkworth, another of their ancient properties a few miles away, but it is just possible that the rebellious Harry 'Hotspur' Percy — killed in single combat by Prince Hal in *Henry IV, Part I* – was born at Alnwick. So if Harry Potter isn't literary enough for you, you can salve your conscience by muttering 'this same child of honour and renown/ This gallant Hotspur, this all-praised knight' as you wander around.

From Alnwick to the Jacobite Steam Railway is a trek – you need to get to Fort William, in the Highlands of Scotland – but it's worth it. Once you're there, you can take an 84-mile round trip by steam train that passes both Ben Nevis and the monument marking the spot where Bonnie Prince Charlie landed in 1745 to begin the ill-fated Jacobite Rising that gives the route its name.

The train also travels over the truly spectacular twenty-one-arched Glenfinnan Viaduct, just as the Hogwarts Express does on its way to Hogsmeade Station. Hogsmeade scenes were, confusingly, filmed at the picturesque Goathland Station on the North Yorkshire Moors Heritage Railway, but any self-respecting wizard can overcome this sort of geographical hurdle with a mere flick of the wand.

Back at Kings Cross, Harry Potter nerds will be quick to point out that there's no wall between Platforms 9 and 10, so filming was done between Platforms 4 and 5. Today, a Harry Potter-themed gift shop sits adjacent to Platform 9, and you can have your photo taken next to the luggage trolley that appears to be vanishing into the wall, as if abandoned by a novice wizard.

Finish your visit with a short Tube journey from King's Cross that brings you to Diagon Alley, known in the Muggle world as Leadenhall Market. There's been a market on this City of London site since the fourteenth century, but it's the soaring Victorian roof with its ornate wrought-iron frame that gives the site its magic today. Not to mention the fact that, with enough imagination, you can nip into The Leaky Cauldron for a pint of butterbeer.

Whitby

BRAM STOKER

www.english-heritage.org.uk/visit/places/whitby-abbey

www.whitbygothweekend.co.uk

This is a lovely place. The little river, the Esk, runs through a deep valley, which broadens out as it comes near the harbour ... The houses of the old town ... are all red-roofed, and seem piled up one over the other anyhow ... Right over the town is the ruin of Whitby Abbey ... It is a most noble ruin, of immense size, and full of beautiful and romantic bits. There is a legend that a white lady is seen in one of the windows.

So runs Mina Murray's description of Whitby, taken from Bram Stoker's *Dracula*. Stoker (1847–1912) spent a summer holiday in Whitby in 1890; he was already working on a novel about an Eastern European vampire, but it was in Whitby Public

Library that he first read about a fifteenth-century Wallachian prince called Vlad Tepes, said to have impaled his enemies on wooden stakes. Like other Wallachians of the period who were renowned for evil or cruelty, he was nicknamed Dracula – 'son of the dragon'. Stoker's version of his story wasn't published for another seven years, but it began to take shape in Whitby, and the rest, as they say, is Gothic-novel and horror-film history.

Today, if you visit Whitby during a particular weekend in April or another later in the year, around Hallowe'en, you'll be struck by the number of Goths and Goth musicians who have congregated for the bi-annual Goth Weekend. In addition, there'll be people who have come to watch the Goths, photographers who want to photograph Goths posing in the ruins of the abbey, and people who aren't Goths at all but choose to parade the streets in Victorian costume. Entering into the spirit, the town's long-established bakery has been known to produce a Whitby Gothic Cake, richly chocolatey with just enough beetroot to make it look like something Dracula might like to get his fangs into, while a local ice-cream company offers a Whitby Gothic flavour – blackcurrant and liquorice – which is a suitably spine-chilling colour.

Even away from Goth weekends, you can visit the Dracula Experience, where, according to its website, 'The count's mysterious appearance and frightening warning will make you wonder if you should have come to Whitby ...' and you can encounter one of three voluptuous ladies, victims of Dracula who are now vampires themselves. You might think this was a modern and exploitative take on the story but in fact it's quite authentic. 'Voluptuous' was a favourite word of Stoker's and his description of one of the Count's victims is surprisingly, even shockingly, sensual:

> *She seemed like a nightmare of Lucy as she lay there; the pointed teeth, the bloodstained, voluptuous mouth – which it made one shudder to see – the whole carnal and unspiritual appearance, seeming like a devilish mockery of Lucy's sweet purity.*

As for the abbey, it's one of the finest and most photogenic ruins you are ever likely to meet, and the adjacent St Mary's Church, reached by a gruelling climb of 199 steps, is well worth the effort. In addition to offering amazing views, it boasts a bizarre three-tiered pulpit and eighteenth-century box pews, some of which bear the inscription – welcome after all those steps – 'For Strangers Only'. And, as you might expect, the churchyard has an atmosphere all its own. Here's Mina Murray again, exploring after Lucy's death:

> *Then as the cloud passed I could see the ruins of the abbey coming into view; and as the edge of a narrow band of light as sharp as a sword-cut moved along, the church and the churchyard became gradually visible. Whatever my expectation was, it was not disappointed, for there, on our favourite seat, the silver light of the moon struck a half-reclining figure, snowy white ... it seemed to me as though something dark stood behind the seat where the white figure shone, and bent over it. What it was, whether man or beast, I could not tell.*

Maybe she couldn't tell, but I think we can guess.

Sunderland

LEWIS CARROLL

lewiscarrollcentre.org.uk

www.atlasobscura.com/places/mowbray-park-walrus

www.guildford.gov.uk/museum

Charles Lutwidge Dodgson, better known as Lewis Carroll (1832–1898), covered a lot of the country in the course of his life and he and his two most famous works – *Alice's Adventures in Wonderland* and *Through the Looking-Glass* – seem to be commemorated anywhere that can possibly lay claim to him. He was born in Daresbury, Cheshire, where his father was the parson. The parsonage where he spent his early years was destroyed by fire a century ago and today the site is marked by little more than a commemorative stone, though the nearby well is covered by a dormouse design in wrought iron. However, there is a Lewis Carroll Centre telling the story of 'Daresbury's most famous villager'; and the local All Saints' church boasts a stained-glass window in the top part of which Carroll and Alice are devout-looking witnesses to an otherwise conventional nativity scene. Below them, though, are panels depicting the White Rabbit, the Dodo, the Hatter, the March Hare and Dormouse, the Fish Footman, the Mock Turtle and other *Alice* characters.

When Carroll was eleven the family moved to Croft-on-Tees in North Yorkshire and here, in St Peter's Church, the budding author may have found the inspiration for his Cheshire Cat: the church has many ancient carvings, most famous of which is a cat (or a lion – it's hard to be sure) that seems to be grinning. Or it does when you sit down and look at it. As you stand up, the grin seems to disappear. Fanciful perhaps? Well, go there with a copy of the book in your hand, hold Tenniel's original drawing up to the carving and you can just about trace a resemblance. The legend persists, as they say.

From Croft, you could nip up to Sunderland (it's only an hour's drive) and investigate another persistent legend. Two of Carroll's sisters lived in nearby Whitburn and he visited them frequently. It is said – repeatedly – that in the course of a walk on Whitburn beach he fell into conversation with a carpenter who worked in the Sunderland shipyards. At the same time, Sunderland Museum's collection included a stuffed walrus head that Carroll probably saw. It's tempting to imagine that the combination of the two was an irresistible basis for a poem. Whether there is any truth in all this is open to question ('I doubt it, said the Carpenter, / And shed a bitter tear' are lines that may pop into your head), but it inspired a fine bronze statue of a walrus that adorns the lakeside in Mowbray Park, just opposite the museum. The idea was for it to have a bronze carpenter to keep it company and fundraising is underway.

Carroll and his relationship with Alice Liddell are most closely associated with Oxford (see page 120) and you can follow their trail to the British Library, which holds Carroll's original manuscript – written in sepia ink and complete with his own illustrations – under its early title of *Alice's Adventures Under Ground*. It seems a shame to leave him, though, without heading to Guildford, where he spent the last months of his life, in a house that he had bought some years earlier for his unmarried sisters. Just across the lane from the house, in the grounds of the ruined Guildford Castle, is the tiny and tranquil Alice Garden, where you can see one of the most original of the many

Alice-related statues scattered round the country: a kneeling bronze of Alice, seemingly halfway through the glass that surrounds her. Her face is rather expressionless, as if crawling through a looking-glass was something that happened every day, and – given how many other celebrations of Alice verge on the twee – the effect is surprisingly eerie.

Take yourself 3 minutes' walk along the road to the Guildford Museum and you'll see a collection of domestic objects that once belonged to Carroll's family. Among the toys that were passed from generation to generation is a rather adorable small-scale wooden croquet set, suggesting that the children were able to play the game in the conventional way, rather than struggling with flamingos as mallets.

Finally, it was in Guildford that Carroll died: he's buried just across the river from his sisters' home, in Mount Cemetery. Here, his grave pays more attention to Charles Dodgson the clergyman than to Lewis Carroll, the creator of Alice. His memorial at Westminster Abbey, though, is a green stone with lettering designed in a circle meant to lure us down the rabbit hole, which is, of course, how Alice's adventures began.

7

CHAPTER SEVEN

WALES &
NORTHERN
IRELAND

Fourth East View

TINTERN ABBEY.

Tintern Abbey
WILLIAM AND DOROTHY WORDSWORTH

cadw.gov.wales/visit/places-to-visit/tintern-abbey *Opening days vary through the year – check in advance.*

For an introduction to Tintern Abbey, it's hard to beat what it says on the website of CADW, the historic environment service of the Welsh Government:

> *Tintern Abbey is a national icon – still standing in roofless splendour on the banks of the River Wye nearly 500 years since its tragic fall from grace.*

The 'fall from grace' was Henry VIII's Dissolution of the Monasteries in the 1530s – an act of vandalism and looting that left many great religious houses in ruins and bankrupted many more. Tintern had been founded by the Cistercian order of monks some four hundred years earlier, but expanded in the thirteenth century – about the same time as Henry III was turning Westminster Abbey into the English Gothic church we know today – to become one of the masterpieces of that style of architecture. Although Tintern is now little more than a skeleton, the walls of the nave and the west front with its seven narrow, pointed windows (known as lancets) are sufficiently intact to give an idea of how impressive it once was. Inside, you can see the delicate tracery that used to hold the windows in place and that now frames views of the green hills beyond. As abbey ruins go, you could argue that these were the most impressive in Britain.

Be careful, by the way, to say 'Britain' rather than 'England'. Although its style is English Gothic, geographically Tintern is in Wales. By a matter of metres: at this point the River Wye marks the boundary between England and Wales, and the abbey is on the Welsh bank.

The Wordsworths – William (1770–1850) and his sister Dorothy (1771–1855) – must have seen something akin to what we see now when they visited in 1798. By then Tintern had become a major tourist attraction, as travellers, unable to visit Europe because of the Napoleonic Wars, took to exploring wild places at home. You can see the allure of this particular wild place: a 1794 painting by J. M. W. Turner shows the same resplendent arches, although the almost-too-picturesque ivy he depicts clambering over them has been cleared away. William and Dorothy must have been impressed, though William's poem 'Lines Composed a Few Miles above Tintern Abbey, on Revisiting the Banks of the Wye during a Tour, July 13, 1798' – usually known simply as 'Tintern Abbey' – doesn't even mention the ruins. It focuses on his memory of a visit five years earlier and is more concerned with the surrounding landscape:

> *Once again*
> *Do I behold these steep and lofty cliffs,*
> *That on a wild secluded scene impress*
> *Thoughts of more deep seclusion; and connect*
> *The landscape with the quiet of the sky.*

Sadly, Dorothy, an extraordinarily observant diarist in her Grasmere years (see page 176), seems not to have kept a record of their time in the Wye Valley. Her evocation of the atmosphere of the ruins would certainly have been worth reading: not for nothing did William say of her, 'She gave me eyes, she gave me ears.'

The best way to admire Tintern is to climb up to the jutting limestone rock known as the Devil's Pulpit (because, legend has it, the Devil preached from it to the monks below, urging them to desert their order and turn to him). The Wordsworths – both energetic walkers – would almost certainly have done so, and you can see why he should have written that 'no poem of mine was composed under circumstances more pleasant for me to remember than this'.

Laugharne
DYLAN THOMAS

www.dylanthomasbirthplace.com
www.dylanthomasboathouse.com
www.dylanthomasbirthdaywalk.co.uk

Dylan Thomas's birthplace in the Uplands area of Swansea is an Edwardian semi-detached at Number 5 Cwmdonkin Drive. Thomas's parents, a schoolmaster

and a former seamstress aiming to move up in the world, bought the house new as an up-to-the-minute 'des res' with an extraordinarily luxurious feature for 1914 – an indoor, fully plumbed-in bathroom and separate WC. A few months after they moved in, Dylan (1914–1953) was born in the front bedroom, overlooking Cwmdonkin Park. Having degenerated to something akin to a run-down student bedsit in the intervening years, the house has been restored by the present owners to a condition that the Thomases would have recognised and approved of: in recognition of Dylan's father's habits, you're even allowed to smoke in his study.

It's a cosy, friendly family house and the enthusiastic owners will organise guided tours to local places that inspired the budding poet. But for a real Dylan Thomas pilgrimage you have to head further west.

You have to be pretty determined, too: Thomas's final home at Laugharne – roughly midway between Llanelli and Pembroke – isn't on a main road from anywhere to anywhere. But Thomas became fascinated by it on his first visit (by ferry, across the Taf estuary), at the age of nineteen; he lived there intermittently for much of his adult life

and settled there in 1949. Used to the Swansea lilt, he was struck by the fact that, for complicated historical reasons, the residents of this tiny seaside settlement spoke with English accents; he described it as 'the strangest town in Wales' and 'a timeless, mild, beguiling island of a town'. Although New Quay in Ceredigion, where Thomas also lived for a short while, stakes a claim to be the setting for his great 'play for voices' *Under Milk Wood*, Laugharne undoubtedly provided the inspiration for many of its characters. Brown's Hotel, where Thomas used to drink, has been refurbished as a boutique hotel, but there's still a certain thrill to be got from rubbing shoulders with locals who might have been citizens of Llareggub.

Perched somewhat precariously above the waterside, the boat-house where Thomas lived is now a museum dedicated to his memory. Entering it feels like stepping back in time to the 1950s. There's a tiled fireplace with china firedogs and an old-fashioned mantel clock above it, a dropleaf table, a table lamp with fringed lampshade – all the sorts of things your grandparents had in their living room. Except that your grandparents probably didn't have a recording of Dylan Thomas reading his own works playing in the background, nor a bust of him that used to be owned by Richard Burton and Elizabeth Taylor (two other former visitors to Brown's Hotel). The house is frankly a little shabby, but then it's probably meant to be – Thomas, for all his success, never had money to throw around. Just up the hill, the 'writing shed' – the converted garage where he did most of his work – has an air of studied dis-array. A jacket hangs over the back of the chair, the desk is strewn with papers, the wastepaper bin is two-thirds full. The poet, dissat-isfied with what he is trying to write, has clearly just thrown down his pen in frustration and gone to the pub. But the view! Stare out the window or, better still, head back to the boathouse, have tea on the terrace and gaze out to sea and you'll see why any artist would have sold his soul to live here.

When you've gazed enough – which may be some time later – you might go for a walk up Sir John's Hill, on the other side of the town. That's what Thomas did, early in the morning of his thirtieth birthday, 27 October 1944; he recalled it in 'Poem in October', celebrating the beauty of the shore, the diving heron he observed and the larks and the blackbirds he heard. Today, there's an app that encourages you to follow his path, reciting his magical words to yourself. Go on your own birthday, the organisers suggest. There can be few lovelier ways of making a day seem important.

As is well known, drink and overwork took their toll on Thomas and he collapsed and died during a poetry-reading tour of the United States at the age of thirty-nine. His body was brought home to Laugharne, where he was buried in St Martin's churchyard and a simple white cross marks his grave. It's a rather understated memorial to someone who dedicated his life to excess, but it's easy to imagine that he chose the spot so that he could spend eternity admiring that glorious view.

Plas Newydd, Llangollen
LADY ELEANOR BUTLER AND THE HONOURABLE SARAH PONSONBY

www.denbighshire.gov.uk/en/visitor/places-to-visit/museums-and-historic-houses/plas-newydd.aspx

In the collection of the British Museum (currently on display in Room 47, but these things change) is a pair of eighteenth-century porcelain cups and saucers. In the centre of each saucer is a monogram, one EB, the other SP. On one side of each cup a roundel shows a picture of a strange-looking Gothic house, tucked away at the end of a lane; on the other, two coats of arms are bound together.

There's a suggestion of intimacy about these cups, a hint of the cosy comfort to be found in starting the day with your partner and a cup of hot chocolate, which was the early-morning drink of choice for those who could afford it, in the days before tea and coffee became popular.

And intimacy is just what the cups ought to convey. They, and the monograms and coats of arms, belonged to Lady Eleanor Butler (1739–1829) and the Honourable Sarah Ponsonby (1755–1831), daughters of aristocratic Irish families who refused to knuckle down to their families' wishes that they make 'eligible' marriages and, one night in 1778, escaped out of their respective bedroom windows to run away together. They settled in Llangollen, in Denbighshire, and lived there – in something very close to perfect harmony, if Eleanor's minutely descriptive diaries are to be believed – for fifty years.

Their former home is called Plas Newydd ('New Hall') and is not to be confused with the house of the same name in Anglesey. 'The Ladies of Llangollen', as they became known, had intended to establish themselves in a quiet rural idyll, focusing on their garden, their reading and writing, their charitable works and improvements to what had originally been little more than a cottage. In that period, however, two ladies setting up house together in this way caused quite a scandal. They became something of a tourist attraction; indeed, towards the end of their lives they were so famous that there was a demand for prints of them: people who never met them could own a picture of them, just as a teenager of today might have a poster of a pop star on their bedroom wall. The Ladies found themselves entertaining the writers Anna Seward (1742–1809), William Wordsworth (see pages 176 and 186) and Sir Walter Scott (page 203), the potter Josiah Wedgwood, the Duke of Wellington and many others. The French novelist Madame de Genlis (1746–1830), travelling in England, heard them described as 'a model of perfect friendship' and set out immediately 'by the circuitous route of Brighton, Portsmouth, and the Isle of Wight' to visit these curiosities; the Ladies, having been forewarned by a letter from a mutual friend, received her and her companions with 'grace, cordiality and kindness'. On a more practical level, Queen Charlotte, consort of George III, wrote to ask about their garden and eventually persuaded her husband to grant them a pension.

It was the nature of the ladies' relationship that attracted most interest and, after the initial scandal died down, that interest seems mostly to have been admiring. Seward, who herself never married and was frank about preferring a friendship based on equality and mutual esteem to submitting herself to the will of a man, wrote approvingly:

Proof

The R.^t Honble Lady Eleanor Butler and Miss Ponsonby.
"The Ladies of Llangollen."

From a Drawing by LADY LEIGHTON, carefully taken from life.

Drawn on Stone by R.J.LANE A.R.A.

S. Ponsonby

Eleanor Butler

Printed by J. Graf.

Died Novr 8th 1831. Aged 74.

Died June 2nd 1829. Aged 90.

Now with a vestal lustre glows the VALE,
Thine, sacred FRIENDSHIP, permanent as pure;
In vain the stern Authorities assail,
In vain Persuasion spreads her silken lure,
High-born, and high-endow'd, the peerless Twain,
Pant for coy Nature's charms 'mid silent dale, and plain.

Wordsworth visited several times and in 1824 was inspired to write the sonnet 'To the Lady E. B. and the Hon. Miss P.', which ended with the lines:

Sisters in love, a love allowed to climb,
Even on this earth, above the reach of Time!

The feeling of contentment is still there when you visit Plas Newydd. The website calls the house 'a Gothic fantasy of projecting stained glass and elaborately carved oak' and, frankly, to describe the entrance hall as ornate is like describing the Atlantic Ocean as wet. Every surface, including the ceiling, is indeed heavily carved; there's even a carved lion sliding down the banister of the main staircase and looking as if he is thoroughly enjoying himself. The hall, however, is the only overpowering feature. By comparison, the library, with its piano, harp and the stained glass in its bay windows, is an oasis of calm, suggesting the quiet, comfortable evenings at home that Eleanor's diaries record. Outside, the formal front garden is all clipped parterres and topiary, but there is a more relaxed cottage garden and meadow with a riot of purples and pinks at the right time of year. You can, if you like, walk the 4 miles to Thomas Telford's extraordinary Pontcysyllte Aqueduct, completed in 1805, while the Ladies were at Plas Newydd. Or you can just stroll down through the garden to the Cyflymen River, as Wordsworth once did in the Ladies' company and as Eleanor and Sarah did, frequently and very contentedly, by themselves.

Lough Neagh
SEAMUS HEANEY
www.discoverloughneagh.com
seamusheaneyhome.com

The biggest lake in the British Isles, a unique landscape, steeped in heritage, folklore, flora and fauna – that's what the tourist brochures say, and you can't argue with them. About 20 miles west of Belfast and with a surface area of about 150 square miles, Lough Neagh dwarfs Loch Lomond (at 27 square miles the largest lake in Great Britain) and could swallow up all the waters of the Lake District about six times over. On an island in the lough you can visit the remains of a thousand-year-old Celtic monastic settlement; on the lough's shores are the ruins of Shane's Castle, ancient home of an influential branch of the O'Neill dynasty, burned down in 1816 and still haunted – according to tradition – by the family banshee, a ghostly old woman whose appearance

and keening cry herald the approach of death. Fortunately the black carving of a head, set into the castle's rock, survived the fire; otherwise – tradition again – the clan would have been doomed.

Thousands of waterfowl, notably the large and vocal whooper swan, spend the winter around the lough, but its literary reputation rests with a less glamorous member of the animal kingdom. Lough Neagh has one of the largest wild-eel fisheries in Western Europe, and it was this that inspired local boy and future Nobel laureate Seamus Heaney (1939–2013). One of his earliest published poems, seven individual pieces that make up *A Lough Neagh Sequence,* is dedicated 'For the fishermen' and begins with a spine-chilling vision of the fields that the eels cross at night, a 'jellied road' over which 'Phosphorescent, sinewed slime / Continued' at the feet of the man watching them. Even to the experienced fishermen the lough is quietly menacing: whatever they do, whatever they say to reassure those who never learned to swim, it will 'claim a victim every year'.

A little way to the north of the lough, at Bellaghy, close to Heaney's birthplace, is the literary and arts centre known as Seamus Heaney HomePlace. Here, you can learn about his life and influences, marvel at the vast amount of crossing out and rethinking that can be seen on his manuscripts, explore the sensory garden and, best of all, listen to his incomparable voice reciting his own work.

You can also visit his grave in the churchyard of nearby St Mary's: his headstone is inscribed with a line from his poem 'The Gravel Walks':

walk on air against your better judgement.

Having used the same line in his speech accepting the Nobel Prize, Heaney later explained that the poem focused on heavy work as well as the 'paradoxical sense of lightness' when lifting heavy things:

> *I like the in-betweenness of up and down, of being on the earth and of the heavens ... I think that's where poetry should dwell, between the dream world and the given world, because you don't just want photography, and you don't want fantasy either.*

When you come to think of it, you probably don't want eels moving across a field in front of you at night, but a combination of the atmosphere of this extraordinary lough

and the gentle, matter-of-fact tones of one of Ireland's greatest poets may reconcile you even to that.

Middle Sister's Belfast

ANNA BURNS

deadcentretours.com/a-history-of-terror-the-tour/

None of the main characters in *Milkman* has a name, not even the teenaged narrator ('middle sister' in a sprawling family) or her maybe-boyfriend. The city in which the novel is set isn't named either, nor is the street that divides it in two. Anna Burns (born 1962) makes no specific mention of Catholics and Protestants, of Northern Ireland or Great Britain, of the Irish Republican Army, the Provisional IRA or the Royal Ulster Constabulary. Instead there are 'our religion' and 'the opposite religion', countries 'over

the water' and 'over the border': terms laden with hidden meaning that middle sister clearly expects us to understand. There's also the 'interface road' – a 'sad and lonely road' that 'ran between the religions' – and 'the ten-minute area on the outskirts of downtown':

> *This ten-minute area wasn't officially called the ten-minute area. It was that it took ten minutes to walk through it. This would be hurrying, no dawdling, though no one in their right mind would think of dawdling here ... the ten-minute area was, and always had been, some bleak, eerie,* Mary Celeste *little place.*

It's all very clearly Belfast during the 1970s, at the height of the Troubles – the protracted and frequently violent conflict over whether or not Northern Ireland should remain part of the United Kingdom. Car bombs, informers, brothers on the run, surveillance cameras that photograph you when you go jogging in the park are part of daily life. This is a place where drawing attention to yourself is asking for trouble, putting yourself 'beyond the pale'. Middle sister, criticised for wandering the streets with her nose in a book, wonders: 'Are you saying it's okay for him to go around with Semtex but not okay for me to read *Jane Eyre* in public?' If you didn't know about the Troubles, you could be forgiven for thinking that *Milkman* was set in some nightmarish future dreamed up by George Orwell (see page 30) or Margaret Atwood.

But no. As a visitor to Belfast today you can do a walking tour based on the history of the Troubles, taking in the locations of bombings, the many murals representing both Catholic and Protestant/Republican and Unionist points of view, and the peace walls installed to keep warring communities apart. It's easy to pinpoint the 'ten-minute area' as Carlisle Circus, where the once notorious 'interface' Crumlin Road meets Antrim Road and where Luftwaffe bombs wiped out nearby Trinity Church long before the events of *Milkman*. The park where middle sister goes running is Waterworks Park, originally designed around a reservoir that supplied water to the city, now a wildlife haven that appeals to lovers of ducks and swans. It's hard to imagine it as the threatening place middle sister describes:

> *This was two conjoined large parks during the day, a sinister environment at night, though during the day also it was sinister. People didn't like to admit to the day section being sinister because everyone wanted at least one place where they could go.*

It's not easy to visit any part of middle sister's city without shuddering at the memory of the violence it conjures up. Perhaps most chilling of all is the matter-of-fact way in which she describes a friend's funeral, at the graveyard:

> *also known as 'the no-town cemetery', 'the no-time cemetery', 'the busy cemetery' or just simply, the usual place.*

8

CHAPTER EIGHT

SCOTLAND

Ecclefechan
THOMAS CARLYLE
www.nts.org.uk/visit/places/thomas-carlyles-birthplace
www.nationaltrust.org.uk/carlyles-house

If you happen to find yourself in Ecclefechan, in the Scottish Borders, you'll be struck by a statue, on the northern edge of the town, of an elderly man in a dressing gown. Bearded and rather wistful, he is the Victorian historian and man of letters Thomas Carlyle (1795–1881), who was born here and whose birthplace and grave you can also visit.

The birthplace, known as the Arched House because of the substantial whitewashed arch that leads through it to the yard behind, is considered a fine example of the local vernacular architecture and was built by Carlyle's father and uncle, both stonemasons. Inside, the rooms are much the same as they were when they were first opened to the public in 1881. Although small, the exhibition takes a fascinating 'cradle to the grave' approach – there's not only Carlyle's cradle, but also his writing desk, many of his books and a copy of the tribute given to him on his eightieth birthday in 1875 and signed by over a hundred Victorian luminaries, including Charles Darwin, Anthony Trollope and Alfred, Lord Tennyson (see page 92).

Carlyle left home at the age of thirteen and walked 84 miles to Edinburgh to attend the university. His work may not be much read except in scholarly circles nowadays, but the fact that he gained a place at university at that tender age gives you an inkling of how extraordinary he was. He studied first divinity and later mathematics, taught for a while, then took up journalism, learned German and translated a novel by Goethe, before turning to history and philosophy. He wrote what was at the time the definitive study of the French Revolution and an acclaimed biography of the Prussian king Frederick the Great, and became one of the great social critics and literary figures of his age.

In among all this, he married Jane Welsh (1801–1866), a doctor's daughter whose intellect was on a par with his own, and in 1834 moved to London, where they both lived for the rest of their lives. You can visit their home at 24 Cheyne Row, Chelsea, and if you approach from the Embankment you'll pass the original of the statue in Ecclefechan. Once inside the house you can again revel in the vast numbers of books, the extraordinary roll call of famous friends and the fact that Chopin played the very piano that still sits in a corner of the living room. As in Ecclefechan, you'll be struck by the fact that this isn't a luxurious home. In 1834, when the Carlyles moved there, Chelsea properties didn't command the prices they do today (far from it) and a young Virginia Woolf (see page 98), visiting after their death, remarked on the absence of indoor running water: 'Every drop ... had to be pumped by hand from a well in the kitchen' and there was a 'wide and wasteful old grate upon which all kettles had to be boiled if they wanted a hot bath'.

The exception to the general feeling of pokiness is the attic conversion that Carlyle used as a study. The official explanation was that he wouldn't be disturbed by noise from the street, but it also protected him from interruptions from visitors on the floors below. Jane was the hospitable one of the couple: her letters are lively, witty and gossipy, suggesting that she could have become a successful writer herself if she hadn't chosen to devote all her energies to supporting her husband's career and idiosyncrasies. Their relationship

was not entirely harmonious, however: Thomas was cantankerous, possibly depressive, and Jane was far from being a doormat. Their contemporary, the satirical novelist Samuel Butler, famously remarked that 'It was very good of God to let Carlyle and Mrs Carlyle marry one another, and so make only two people miserable and not four.'

That said, Carlyle's intellect and generous sharing of his knowledge brought him a host of admirers. That eightieth-birthday tribute, of which the original is in Cheyne Row, describes him as 'a teacher whose genius and achievements have lent radiance to his time'. Earlier Charles Dickens (see pages 33, 35 and 111) wrote that 'I would go at all times farther to see Carlyle than any man alive.' Dickens dedicated his 1854 novel *Hard Times* to the man who had become known as the Sage of Chelsea, and in his preface to *A Tale of Two Cities* five years later he wrote that, while he had hoped to contribute to the 'popular and picturesque' understanding of the French Revolution, 'no one can hope to add anything to the philosophy of Mr. CARLYLE's wonderful book'. (Carlyle, who had been the prime mover in the founding of the London Library in 1841, is said to have lent Dickens two cartloads of the library's books to help him with his research.)

To return to Ecclefechan, Carlyle's standing at the time of his death was such that he might have been granted a place in Westminster Abbey, but he had expressed a wish to be taken back to the churchyard of his birthplace and buried alongside his parents. Jane, who had predeceased him by fifteen years, can be found in the church of St Mary's in her own birthplace, Haddington, East Lothian, where she lies alongside her father. Presumably both Thomas and Jane are having a more peaceful time than if they had been forced to spend eternity side by side.

Alloway and Dumfries
ROBERT BURNS

www.nts.org.uk/visit/places/robert-burns-birthplace-museum
www.visitscotland.com/info/see-do/robert-burns-house-p250471 *Open all year, but closed Sundays and Mondays from October to March.*

The life of Robert Burns (1759–1796) – 'the Bard of Ayrshire', 'Scotland's national poet', call him what you will – is neatly encapsulated, cradle-to-grave style, in two small towns within 60 miles of each other in the southwest of Scotland. He was born in Alloway, now a suburb of Ayr, and died only thirty-seven years later, in Dumfries. The houses in which these two momentous events took place have both been converted into museums dedicated to his memory.

The obvious place to start is the Robert Burns Birthplace Museum in Alloway. In addition to displaying plenty of traditional memorabilia, the purpose-built museum will appeal to those who get a buzz out of choosing a song from a Burns playlist, but the real joys are to be found in the older features of the complex. The humble farm cottage where Burns was born is a mere four rooms and at one point Robert would have been sharing this tiny space with his parents, three younger siblings and their farm animals. Cosy.

Outside, though, there's room for the imagination to let rip. The landscaped gardens would be stunning even without the extraordinary Burns Monument that stands in

them: it's a 21-metre, Grecian-style temple raised by admirers in the early nineteenth century and offering well-worth-the-climb views from the top. Only slightly further afield are the ruined Auld Kirk and the medieval bridge known as the Brig o' Doon, both of which feature in the narrative poem 'Tam O'Shanter', inspired by local legends. If you fancy standing in the very spot where warlocks supposedly hung around 'Alloway's auld haunted kirk', this is your chance.

Born and raised in agricultural poverty which had a lifelong effect on his health, Burns achieved great success but little wealth in his short career. (The famous portrait of him by Alexander Nasmyth that hangs in the Scottish National Portrait Gallery in Edinburgh was commissioned by his publishers and the elegant clothes he wears were surely borrowed for the occasion.) The house in Dumfries where he spent his last three years is – in terms of size, style and location – an unremarkable, modest family home, kitted out in the way you'd expect of a house-turned-museum: the study furnished as he would have left it, iron pots and kettles above the kitchen fire, a wooden crib in which the various Burns babies slept, lots of his books and manuscripts. There are a couple of odd quirks that make it worth the trip, though: a pane of glass on which he scratched his name and – just the thing for the ghouls among you – a snuffbox, made from part of the bed on which the poet died ...

If you want something a bit more upbeat than a snuffbox made from a deathbed, cross the River Nith to the Robert Burns Centre, a recent installation in an eighteenth-century watermill. Like the Birthplace Museum, it doesn't disdain traditional memorabilia but it also offers more modern extras, in this case an intriguing scale model of the town in the 1790s, and what its website describes as a 'haunting audio-visual presentation'. Another one for the ghouls.

Between the mill and the house, you'll have passed St Michael's Church and the Burns Mausoleum. Burns was originally buried in the churchyard in such an insignificant grave that when William and Dorothy Wordsworth visited in 1803 they had difficulty finding it. At about the same time as Burns's friends in Alloway were raising money for his monument there, another well-wisher started fundraising in Dumfries and even received a donation from the future King George IV. Again, it's a classical-looking temple, less flamboyant than its Alloway counterpart, but it's eye-catchingly white in a churchyard where almost all the other monuments are in the local red sandstone. Inside is a white marble carving of Colia, a muse Burns created in his poem 'The Vision'; she is seen casting her mantle of inspiration over the poet as he labours with his plough.

You'd think the tomb might bring you to the end of your travels, but you haven't finished with Dumfries yet. Burns's birthday – 25 January – is an international excuse for revelry and has been since 1899, when the first ever Burns Night supper took place in the Globe pub in the High Street. As the local paper reported:

> *This famous hostelry was Burns's favourite resort during the closing years of his life in Dumfries, and he was the life and soul of many a merry meeting held within its walls. The chair which he occupied on these occasions is still pointed out to visitors.*

Scots the world over have been celebrating the Bard of Ayrshire's birthday ever since, and even if you aren't there in January you can still pop into the Globe for haggis fritters and an impressive array of whiskies. Just remember to precede them with the traditional 'Selkirk Grace', attributed to Burns himself:

> *Some hae meat and canna eat,*
> *And some wad eat that want it,*
> *But we hae meat and we can eat,*
> *Sae let the Lord be Thankit!*

Let the words roll round your mouth like a good single malt.

Abbotsford

SIR WALTER SCOTT

www.scottsabbotsford.com *Gardens open daily, house Thursdays to Sundays only.*

I t's been said that Sir Walter Scott (1771–1832) invented the Scottish Borders. To be a tiny bit less sweeping, if you visit the little museum in Selkirk that has been created from the courtroom where he sat as Sheriff Depute from 1804 until his death, you'll be told:

> *Through his literature Scott created a romantic heritage for the Borders. Although not always historically correct, this romantic view has endured and even in Scott's lifetime drew visitors to the area.*

Scott was actually born in Edinburgh, and you'd be hard put to miss the monument to him in Princes Street Gardens: it's in that supremely eye-catching style known as Victorian Gothic, and it's 61 metres tall. He spent significant parts of his childhood with his grandparents at their farm near Kelso in the Borders, and there he picked up both the language and the lore that permeated much of his writing. In a mouth-watering description of the preparations for a feast in *The Bride of Lammermoor* (1819), he even mentions the local delicacy, the Selkirk bannock, to be served alongside sweet scones and 'petticoat-tail' shortbread.

In addition to 'inventing' the Borders, Scott invented the historical novel; his works, ranging in subject matter from the Crusades (*Ivanhoe, The Talisman*) to an imagined third Jacobite rebellion (*Redgauntlet*), were stupendously popular. Their success enabled him in 1811 to buy a small farm on the banks of the Tweed which he renamed Abbotsford, in reference to the monks from nearby Melrose Abbey who had traditionally forded the river at this point. In the succeeding years he extended the estate so that at its peak it covered 1,400 acres. He also expanded the house into what he described as 'a sort of romance in Architecture', starting the fashion for Scots baronial architecture (a style that reached its apotheosis at Balmoral Castle and has a touch of Disney's Fantasyland about it). If you consider that his principal architect, William Atkinson (1774/5–1839), later remodelled what is now the Prime Minister's country residence at Chequers, and that the interiors at Abbotsford were designed by David Ramsay Hay (1798–1866), who later worked on Holyrood House in Edinburgh for Queen Victoria, you'll realise that this was not a modest undertaking.

Scott must have thought it was worth it. Abbotsford's position on the banks of the Tweed inspired more than one artist, most notably J. M. W. Turner, and if you look at the house from across the river (as Turner did), you'll be hard pushed to imagine a more romantic setting.

On top of all this, Scott amassed a vast collection of books, many sent to him by admirers: his library contains the first volume of the Grimms' fairy tales, a gift from the authors, and, as a present from the governor of New South Wales, the tale of an Australian bushranger, the first book ever to be published in Tasmania. He also amassed mementos of Scottish history and in particular arms and armour. When the future Poet Laureate Simon Armitage visited (at the start of the Pennine Way adventure he wrote about in *Walking Home,* see page 169), he noted 'swords, pistols, daggers, pikes, armour,

plus the heads, horns and hides of many an unfortunate beast'. Scott had suffered from polio as a child so couldn't fulfil any military ambitions he might have had, but, as Armitage continued, 'Like Lord Byron with his club foot, he clearly wasn't embarrassed by the concept of over-compensation.'

The book-lined gallery around Scott's study would gladden the heart of any biblio-phile, even if the heavily carved wood panelling in the armoury may be just a bit too Gothic for modern tastes. Taken all in all, though, it's glorious. It's obviously the work of a man of great passion, even obsession, and it becomes all the more poignant when you know that, despite all his success, he couldn't really afford it. Having survived one financial disaster and the collapse of his publishers in 1813, Scott in 1825 faced twin horrors: the consequences of his own extravagance and a nationwide banking crisis. He averted bankruptcy (and the loss of his beloved home) only by setting up a trust fund that, coupled with his extraordinary output over the last few years of his life, enabled him to pay off his debts and save Abbotsford for his family. Some of his descendants continued to live here until 2004, and if you visit today you'll be grateful that he was able to pull himself and his beloved home back from the brink.

Kirriemuir

J. M. BARRIE

www.nts.org.uk/visit/places/j-m-barries-birthplace

By 1904, James Matthew Barrie (1860–1937) was already an established playwright, with successes such as *Quality Street* and *The Admirable Crichton* under his belt. But it is the play first performed in that year that in various incarnations – stage play, novel, pantomime, film and more – has kept his reputation alive ever since and that dominates a visit to his birthplace in the Angus village of Kirriemuir.

The original version of *Peter Pan: The Boy Who Wouldn't Grow Up* or *Peter and Wendy* was a 'straight' play; Barrie subsequently turned it into a novel and also wrote an epilogue, giving the story a happier ending. In this version, Wendy's daughter and granddaughter continue to visit Neverland in a tradition that Barrie says will endure as long as children are 'gay and innocent and heartless'. Pantomimes ever since have taken liberties with the plot, adapting it to suit their audience or the talents of the big name playing the villainous pirate Captain Hook.

In the little house in Kirriemuir, you can read the smudged original typescript of the play, and its ending is terribly sad: a much older Wendy goes back to visit Peter, who hasn't aged at all. He neither remembers nor cares much about their adventures. The boy who refused to grow up has been left behind as others matured. This sadness seems to be a reflection of Barrie's own life: his close friendship with the Llewelyn Davies family (who inspired him to write the play) has led to latter-day suggestions that he might have had inappropriate relationships with one or more of the children, though as an adult the youngest of them denied this categorically: 'He was an innocent,' he said, 'which is why he could write *Peter Pan*.'

Nothing remotely sordid emerges from a visit to Kirriemuir. In addition to the *Peter Pan* typescript, you can see costumes from its first stage production and visit the wash-house in which the seven-year-old Barrie performed his first play. In the garden you can admire a life-size (and rather ferocious-looking) sculpture in driftwood of Captain Hook's nemesis, the crocodile that has swallowed a clock that ticks constantly inside it, alerting people to its presence. In the novel, Hook explains to his bosun Smee that he can 'hear the tick and bolt' before the crocodile (which bit off his arm and enjoyed it so much that it wants the rest of him) can reach him:

> *'Some day,' said Smee, 'the clock will run down, and then he'll get you.'*
> *Hook wetted his dry lips. 'Ay,' he said, 'that's the fear that haunts me.'*

Barrie didn't give his crocodile a name, but the 1953 Disney film repaired this omission by calling it Tick Tock, which is also the name of the sculpture.

A statue of Peter Pan, playing his characteristic pipe, stands in Kirriemuir High Street, just along from an art gallery called The Wendy House. Although Barrie lived most of his adult life in London, and died there, he was brought home to Kirriemuir to be buried. He lies in the local churchyard, next to his parents and two of his siblings.

Another Peter Pan statue can be found in Kensington Gardens in London, where Barrie first met the Llewelyn Davies boys. Commissioned by Barrie himself, this Peter

is also playing his pipe, while fairies and small animals scramble around his plinth. Six replicas exist around the world, the only one in Britain being in Sefton Park in Liverpool. The story continues to captivate: come Boxing Day, well over a hundred years after the play was first performed, you're never likely to be far from a pantomime featuring the boy who wouldn't grow up.

Some Scottish Villages

Coastal Scotland is dotted with fishing villages, some of which survive more as tourist attractions than as working harbours and others of which remain rather dour and remote. The one that Jackie Kay (born 1961) calls Torr in her novel *Trumpet* doesn't exist under that name, but it's a bus ride from Pittenweem, which gives you a choice of places along the coast of Fife. There's also a long-distance footpath, the Fife Coastal Path, if you want to do your exploring on foot.

The further from Pittenweem you go, whether north or south, the more remote and unchanged the village, so you can choose between picturesque Crail, bustling Anstruther and atmospheric St Monans with its dramatic ruined castle. Or go a little further south and savour the bleakness of Elie Ness Lighthouse.

Bleak is probably what you want, if you're trying to recapture the mood of Torr and of recently bereaved Millie:

So strong, the smell of the sea if you haven't been close to it for a while. I can taste the seaweed and the fish in my mouth. The salt in my hair, on my cheeks. The wind blows behind me, making a balloon of my coat, rushing me along faster than I want to go. The sea isn't so calm, close up. I can stare right into its heart. The waves leap over each other in a frenzy. Above the waves themselves are the shadows of ghost waves trying to speak. I can see them chasing the real waves, wanting their life back.

On the plus side:

The harbour has stayed the same since I was a girl and came up from England on holidays here with my family. The chippie is the same chippie.

Kay, the Scots Makar (national poet of Scotland) from 2016 to 2021, was writing *Trumpet* in the 1990s, but there's still no shortage of good fish and chips along the Fife coast. There's no shortage of atmosphere, either.

An Edinburgh Walk

ROBERT LOUIS STEVENSON AND OTHERS

www.edinburghmuseums.org.uk/venue/writers-museum

www.nationalgalleries.org

As the birthplace of and/or inspiration for many Scottish writers, Edinburgh is one of the most satisfying cities in which to do a literary ramble. It's frequently said (often by people from Glasgow) that the Scottish capital is a Jekyll-and-Hyde sort of place: the elegantly laid out New Town presenting a smiling façade to cover the evils of the foggy and higgledy-piggledy Old Town, literally on the other side of the tracks, once the home of graverobbers and site of public hangings. Never mind that Edinburgh-born Robert Louis Stevenson (1850–1894) chose to set *The Strange Tale of Dr Jekyll and Mr Hyde* in London, these commentators add – the inspiration clearly came from his home city.

Whatever you think of this analysis, that last bit is true: the idea for *Jekyll and Hyde* came to Stevenson from the real-life story of Deacon William Brodie, respectable cabinet-maker by day, housebreaker and gambler by night, who was publicly hanged – in the Old Town, obviously – in 1788. The Old Tolbooth, where the hanging took place, was demolished in 1817, but you can still see where it stood, adjacent to St Giles Cathedral. You can drink in the Deacon Brodie tavern, on the Royal Mile; its pub sign is suitably two-faced, with solid-citizen Brodie by daylight on one side and masked, furtive-looking thief on the other.

Of course, to make the most of all this you should visit the Old Town on a foggy night and the New Town on a sunny day; if you can't fix that, find out more about Stevenson's life and works in the Writers' Museum, just off Lawnmarket. A highlight of its collection is a wardrobe made by Brodie which was actually in the possession of the Stevenson family.

The museum is a celebration not only of Stevenson, but also of Robert Burns (see page 200) and Sir Walter Scott (page 203) too. It owns a rocking horse that Scott played with as a child and the press on which his Waverley novels were printed; a first edition of Stevenson's *A Child's Garden of Verses* and a ring given to him later in life by a Samoan chief; and Burns's writing desk and a cast of his skull. If you can't find something to amuse you among the Writers' Museum's treasures, you are prodigiously hard to please.

Deacon Brodie cast his shadow over another great Edinburgh work, too: in Muriel Spark's *The Prime of Miss Jean Brodie*, Miss Brodie claims him as one of her ancestors. As she boasts to her pupils:

> *I am a descendant, do not forget, of Willie Brodie, a man of substance, a cabinet maker and designer of gibbets, a member of the Town Council of Edinburgh and a keeper of two mistresses who bore him five children between them. Blood tells. ... Of course, he was arrested abroad and was brought back to the Tolbooth prison, but that was mere chance. He died cheerfully on a gibbet of his own devising in seventeen-eighty-eight. However all this may be, it is the stuff I am made of.*

She also takes them for a walk through the Old Town, an area of Edinburgh that is new to the girls:

> *because none of their parents was so historically minded as to be moved to conduct their young into the reeking network of slums which the Old Town constituted in those years. The Canongate, The Grassmarket, The Lawnmarket, were names which betokened a misty region of crime and desperation.*

That would be an unfair description of Edinburgh's historic sector nowadays – Spark (1918–2006) was writing about the 1930s – but you can still appreciate how the Brodie girls reacted to the castle, 'which was in any case everywhere, rearing between a big gap in the houses where the aristocracy used to live'.

Deacon Brodie's isn't the only literary pub in Edinburgh, either: you can do a literary pub crawl, of which the highlight is probably the Oxford Bar, in the New Town, favourite drinking place of Inspector John Rebus in Ian Rankin's novels. Rebus's address, Arden Street in Marchmont, is a real place, too; Rankin himself (born 1960) was living there when he wrote the first Rebus novel, *Knots and Crosses*, in the 1980s.

From Arden Street, a 40-minute walk through the New Town will take you to another real address, Scotland Street. The gallery that features in *44 Scotland Street* by Alexander McCall Smith (born 1948), where there is a painting that may or may not be by Samuel Peploe, is harder to track down. If you want to pursue your studies of the Scottish colourists you'll need to go to the National Gallery. Fear not: this is conveniently situated back in the centre of town, near Edinburgh's most famous literary landmark, the Scott Monument. Once you've dealt with Peploe, climb the 287 steps to the monument's highest viewing platform and marvel at the views that inspired so many writers. (Feel free to pause for breath in the Museum Room on the first floor and learn more about Scott himself.) Then clamber back down again and study the other statues that adorn the monument. These include sundry Scottish authors from Robert Burns to James Thomson (1700–1748), who wrote the words to 'Rule, Britannia', as well as various characters from Scott's novels. Some of these were crafted by a renowned nineteenth-century sculptor called William Brodie: not the same man, but you have to admit it's a glorious coincidence.

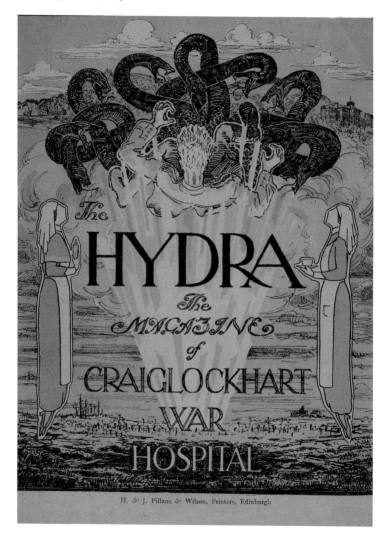

Pat Barker (born 1943) based her novel *Regeneration* on a genuine encounter between the First World War poets Siegfried Sassoon (1886–1967) and Wilfred Owen (1893–1918) at Craiglockhart War Hospital near Edinburgh. Opened as a Hydropathic Establishment in 1880, it had been requisitioned during the war for use as a hospital for the treatment of officers suffering from 'shell shock', the condition we'd now call post-traumatic stress disorder (PTSD).

Whatever its psychiatric merits, architecturally Craiglockhart could hardly be described as welcoming. As Barker puts it:

Nobody arriving at Craiglockhart for the first time could fail to be daunted by the sheer gloomy, cavernous bulk of the place. Sassoon ... took a deep breath, squared his shoulders, and ran up the steps.

He was there – in the novel and in life – because he had written to his commanding officer protesting against the continuation of the war:

I am making this statement as an act of wilful defiance of military authority because I believe that the war is being deliberately prolonged by those who have the power to end it.

At Craiglockhart, Sassoon, the older and more established poet, became a mentor to the traumatised Owen, encouraging him to persevere with his writing: the British Library and the Imperial War Museum in London both hold manuscript versions of Owen's 'Anthem for Doomed Youth' with handwritten amendments by Sassoon. We might never have read the impassioned 'What passing-bells for these who die as cattle?' if it hadn't been for Sassoon's rebelliousness and Owen's nervous collapse.

Craiglockhart is now part of Edinburgh Napier University and houses a War Poets Collection, offering a harrowing insight into personal experiences of war, not least from members of the medical profession. You don't come out without remembering the line from the Latin poet Horace that Owen quotes in another Sassoon-influenced poem: 'Dulce et decorum est pro patria mori' (It is sweet and honourable to die for one's country). Horace, writing during the glory days of the Roman Empire, may have meant it sincerely; Owen famously called it 'the old Lie'. You also can't help noticing that, although Sassoon lived to see the 1960s and his own eightieth birthday, Owen was killed only a week before the Armistice, at the age of twenty-five. Not for nothing is another of his best-known works called 'Futility'.

Away the Crow Road
IAIN BANKS

www.duntrunecastle.com

www.historicenvironment.scot

What most people seem to remember about Iain Banks's *The Crow Road* is the opening paragraph:

> *It was the day my grandmother exploded. I sat in the crematorium, listening to my Uncle Hamish quietly snoring in harmony to Bach's Mass in B Minor, and I reflected that it always seemed to be death that drew me back to Gallanach.*

Certainly there is a lot of death in the novel; the title reflects the Scottish expression 'they're away the Crow Road', meaning 'they're dead'. If you're more interested in the living, though, there's plenty of local detail to help you follow the young narrator Prentice McHoan's journey across western Scotland.

Don't be tempted to take that detail too literally. Yes, Banks (1954–2013) sets his story against a realistic landscape, much of which sounds like Oban. However, he once admitted:

> *I'd decided I wanted to locate the fictional town of Gallanach near Crinan on the mainland. I needed the place to have a deep-water port with easy access to the Atlantic and I didn't want to edit out the Corryvreckan [Strait, between the islands of Jura and Scarba], so I blithely cut Jura in two. You get to do this sort of thing when you are a writer.*

That said, there's plenty in the novel that is real. The Crow Road is a genuine street in Glasgow; another Crow Road, a few miles north in Lennoxtown, forms part of a popular and scenic cycle route. It's normally a circular ride that would take you back to central Glasgow, but you could easily make it the first leg of your journey to Crinan.

Heading on north towards Oban, you'll come to Dunadd, the hill fort known for its stone carvings, including a footprint that may have been part of a coronation ritual dating back to the seventh century. The fort dominates the otherwise flat landscape as it has done for perhaps two thousand years, and the whole area is riddled with prehistoric rock art.

Closer to Crinan are Duntrune Castle, said to be haunted by a handless piper whose music once warned his master of an approaching ambush, and Carnasserie, formerly a

fine Renaissance residence, now a ruin with spectacular views towards Kilmartin Glen. Either or both might be the model for Gaineamh Castle, home of Prentice's wealthy Uncle Fergus.

Carry on into Oban itself and you'll find the church where Prentice's father Kenneth came (like so many characters in *The Crow Road*) to a bizarre end, in his case being struck by lightning while climbing the steeple.

This is how Prentice sums up his childhood home:

The land around Gallanach is thick with ancient monuments; burial sites, henges, and strangely carved rocks. You can hardly put a foot down without stepping on something that had religious significance to somebody sometime. Verity had heard of all this ancient stoneware but she'd never really seen it properly ... And of course, because we'd lived here all our lives, none of the rest of us had bothered to visit half the places either.

The locals may not bother, but as a visitor you could take in all these sites, as well as some spectacular scenery. In case you're wondering, though: Prentice's grandmother exploded because her doctor had forgotten to warn the undertaker that she had a pacemaker. It's the sort of mishap to which the McHoan family is prone.

'Dunsinane' Hill and Birnam Wood
WILLIAM SHAKESPEARE
www.visitscotland.com/info/towns-villages/the-birnam-oak-p255851

There's a point in Shakespeare's Scottish play when Macbeth – beginning to lose his grip since Banquo's ghost upset his banquet a couple of scenes earlier – consults the three witches about what the future holds. The apparitions the witches produce egg him on, declaring, among other things, that:

> *Macbeth shall never vanquish'd be, until*
> *Great Birnam wood to high Dunsinane hill*
> *Shall come against him.*

I should be safe enough, then, Macbeth thinks. No one is going to 'bid the tree unfix his earth-bound root'. That's before Malcolm, son of the murdered King Duncan, instructs each of his ten thousand followers to hew down a bough and use it to camouflage their numbers. Macbeth, holed up in his castle at Dunsinane, receives the alarming news that his messenger 'look'd toward Birnam, and anon, methought / The wood began to move'.

Today's maps show a place called King's Seat on a winding back road between Perth and Dundee. It's a rather stark, forbidding peak at the base of which a useful signboard asks 'Dunsinnan Hill Fort – Macbeth's Castle?' Dunsinnan, with the stress on the second syllable, is the local pronunciation; there's a school of thought that says Shakespeare called it Dunsinane, stressing the first or the third, because that suited his verse better. However you pronounce it, there was once a powerful hilltop citadel here, and it would have commanded views over the surrounding countryside (including, some 12 miles away, Birnam Wood). It was probably occupied in Macbeth's time (the eleventh century) and it's not historically ridiculous to believe that it was Macbeth who occupied it. He did exist, after all. He had to be somewhere.

You're welcome to climb Dunsinnan and there's plenty of atmosphere on which to feed your imagination, but to be honest there isn't an enormous amount to see. Happily, that isn't true of what remains of Birnam Wood. It lies along the south bank of the Tay,

Siward.

What wood is this?

Menteith.

The wood of Birnam.

Malcolm.

Let every soldier hew him down a
bough,
And bear't before him : thereby shall
we shadow
The numbers of our host.

Act VI., Scene 3.

some of the loveliest country in Scotland, and contains an ancient tree known as the Birnam Oak. From the village of Birnam you can follow signs along Oak Road and very quickly arrive at an enormous tree. In front of it stands a gravestone-shaped slab on which are carved the words, 'It's not me – I'm a sycamore.' A little further on: 'Not me either. Keep going.' So you do, and there it is – the Birnam Oak, some 7 metres in girth and soaring skywards as far as the eye can see. It's been dated to at least five hundred years old, so if it wasn't there in Macbeth's day it certainly was in Shakespeare's (1564– 1616). Next to it is the Birnam Sycamore, with vast buttress roots, a girth of nearly 8 metres and massive horizontal branches not much above head height. Sadly, it's a mere three hundred years old, and not even a native species, but goodness it's impressive.

To have been part of Malcolm's strategy, these trees would need to be hundreds of years older than they are, but that is a minor disappointment. They are so magical, with such a life of their own, that it's easy to forget about the ten thousand men lopping off branches. Instead you can picture the trees uprooting themselves and advancing towards that sombre tor, where Macbeth – his wife dead, his conscience driving him mad – clings desperately to the witches' promises. From the moment he hears that the wood has moved, he knows it's all over.

And here you are, in the very same wood, nearly a thousand years later.

Gosh.

Pause.

Time for tea? There was a nice-looking place just over the bridge. What do you fancy? Eye of newt? Toe of frog? No? Well, I expect they have scones. And we don't have to talk to each other. We can just sit and read a book.

LIST OF ILLUSTRATIONS

p.2 Illustration of the sign for the Writers' Museum, Edinburgh © Joanna Lisowiec.

p.9 Illustration of Peter Rabbit © Joanna Lisowiec.

p.13 Illustration of Shakespeare's Globe © Joanna Lisowiec.

p.15 Entrance to Poets' Corner, Westminster Abbey. Coloured aquatint by J. Bluck after A. Pugin, 1811. Wellcome Collection.

p.17 Lord Chamberlain's copy of the script for *The Birthday Party* by Harold Pinter. British Library, LCP 1958 no.20.

p.19 The Sherlock Holmes pub. Photo: alenakr/123RF.

p.20 Sherlock Holmes by Frederic Dorr Steele, front cover of *Collier's* magazine, 31 October 1903. British Library, NEWS13401.

p.21 The Sherlock Holmes House and Museum, Baker Street. Photo: bloodua/123RF.

p.23 Illustration by Gilbert Wilkinson, 'Thank you Jeeves!', *The Strand*, August 1933. British Library, P.P.6004.glk.

p.25 Photo of Oscar Wilde and Lord Alfred Douglas, 1894. British Library, C.131.f.11.

p.26 The Albany, Piccadilly. Illustration by Harry Keen, *The Picture of Dorian Gray*, 1925. Mary Evans Picture Library.

p.28 *The Interesting Narrative of the Life of Olaudah Equiano, or Gustavus Vassa, the African*, 1789. British Library, 1489.g.50.

p.31 Senate House, University of London. Photo: victor10947/123RF.

p.32 Plaque to Mary Prince, Malet Street, London. Photo: Sally Nicholls.

p.33 Charles Dickens at his writing desk, 1872–74. British Library, Dex.316, f.129.

p.34 Title page, *Nicholas Nickleby*, 1838. British Library, 12276.f.1.

p.36 Illustration by F. W. Pailthorpe, *Oliver Twist*, 1885. British Library, Dex.312 (2).

p.37 Bunhill Fields. Photo GrindtXX/CC-BY-SA-4.0.

p.39 Dr Johnson's House. Illustration by E.W. Haslehust, *In London's By-ways* by Walter Jerrold, 1925. British Library, w60/3906.

p.41 'The Great Fire of London in the Year 1666', engraved and published by W. Birch, 1792. British Library, Maps K.Top.21.65.b.

p.43 Elevation of the west front of St George in the East, drawing by Nicholas Hawksmoor. British Library, Maps K.Top.23.21.k.

p.45 Brick Lane street sign. Photo: George Robertson/123RF.

p.47 Windows relating to John Bunyan, Geoffrey Chaucer, Oliver Goldsmith and Samuel Johnson, Southwark Cathedral. Photos courtesy of: Southwark Cathedral.

p.49 The Globe Theatre, detail from a panorama of London from the South Bank by C. I. Visscher, 1616. British Library, Maps C.5.a.6.

p.51 Brixton Market, Electric Avenue. Photo Loop Images Ltd/Alamy Stock Photo.

p.52 Linton Kwesi Johnson on Railton Road, 1979. Photo: © Adrian Boot/urbanimages.tv.

p.55 *The Lonely Londoners*, 1956. British Library, RF.2013.a.2.

p.56 Bronze statue of Paddington Bear, Paddington Station. Photo 53535434 © Aija Lehtonen/Dreamstime.com.

p.58 Endpapers designed by Janet and Anne Grahame-Johnstone, *The Hundred and One Dalmatians*, 1956. British Library, 07295.eee.110.

p.59 Frontispiece designed by Dante Gabriel Rossetti, 'Goblin Market', 1862. British Library, Cup.401.b.14.

p.60 Statue of John Betjeman, St Pancras Station. Photo: Edwardx/CC-BY-SA-3.0.

p.61 Shree Swaminarayan Temple , Willesden. Photo: Kevin Cole 44/Shutterstock.

p.63 'A view on Hampstead Heath looking towards London', 1804. British Library, Maps K.Top.29.13.d.

p.65 Circle of Lebanon, West Cemetery, Highgate. Photo 105153796 © Pjgibson/Dreamstime.com.

p.67 South front of Strawberry Hill. British Library, Maps C.18.d.6.(143.).

p.69 Illustration of Thomas Hardy's cottage © Joanna Lisowiec.

p.70 Daphne du Maurier at Menabilly. Photograph by Compton Collier, *The Tatler*, 4 July 1945. Photo © *Illustrated London News*/Mary Evans.

p.71 The cliffs at St Just, West Cornwall. Photo: margaretclavell/123RF.

p.72 Stained-glass window by Veronica Whall at King Arthur's Great Halls, Tintagel. Photo: md2399photos.

p.73 *The Hound of the Baskervilles*, 1902. British Library, RB.23.a.34655.

p.74 Dartmoor. Photo: Marcin Jucha/123RF.

p.75 Burgh Island Hotel, Devon. Photo: Peter Titmuss/123RF.

p.77 Illustration by William Sewell for *Lorna Doone*, 1920. British Library, 012618.i.13.

p.78 *Westward Ho!*, 1896. British Library, 12620.dd.22.

p.79 Coleridge's writing desk in the cottage at Nether Stowey. Photo: Daderot.

p.81 A view of Bath, *c.*1790-1810. British Library, Maps K.Top.37.25.h.

p.83 West front of the Abbey Church at Bath, 1788. British Library, Maps K.Top.37.26.c.3.

p.85 St Michael's Church, East Coker. Photo: John Snelling/Alamy Stock Photo.

p.88 Illustration by C. E. Brock, *Persuasion*, 1909. British Library, 012208.g.2/2.

p.89 Map of Wessex, *Under the Greenwood Tree*, 1925. British Library, W9/8284.

p.90 Thomas Hardy's cottage near Higher Bockhampton, Dorset. Photo 143472697 © Davidyoung11111 Dreamstime.

p.91 Illustration of Ashdown Forest © Joanna Lisowiec.

p.92 Farringford House. Photograph by Frank Mason Good, c. 1865. J. Paul Getty Museum, Malibu.

p.93 *Blandings Castle*, 1935. British Library, NN.15132.

p.95 Chawton from the garden. Photo: Dmitry Naumov/123RF.

p.96 Jane Austen's writing slope. British Library, Add. 86841.

p.97 Cover design by George Salter, *Brighton Rock*, 1935. Heritage Auctions, HA.com.

p.99 Virginia and Leonard Woolf, from the Monk's House Album. Houghton Library, Harvard University.

p.101 Charleston, West Firle. Photo: parkerphotography/ Alamy Stock Photo.

p.102 The garden at Sissinghurst. Photo: Mathieu van den Berk/123RF.

p.103 Endpaper map of 100 Acre Wood, *The House at Pooh Corner*, 1928. © E.H. Shepard estate/Curtis Brown. British Library, C.125.dd.14.

p.104 Bateman's, East Sussex. Photo © Defacto/CC-BY-SA-4.0.

p.106 Henry James in his library at Lamb House. Photo: Granger Historical Picture Archive/Alamy Stock Photo.

p.108 *Vanity Fair*, 1847. British Library, C.144.d.4.

p.109 Illustration to the prologue of the *Canterbury Tales*, 1485. British Library, G.11586.

p.111 Photograph of Gad's Hill by Adolph Naudin, 1864. British Library, 1758.a.19.

p.112 Frontispiece illustration by F.W. Pailthorpe, *Great Expectations*, 1885. British Library, K.T.C.28.b.20.

p.115 Illustration of Oxford © Joanna Lisowiec.

p.116 'Elegy Written in a Country Church Yard'. Illustrations by Richard Bentley, 1753. British Library, C.57.h.5.

p.118 The Roald Dahl Museum and Story Centre, Great Missenden. Photo: Loop Images Ltd/Alamy Stock Photo.

p.119 Adlestrop railway station sign. Photo: Tim Galney/ Alamy Stock Photo.

p.120 The Dining Hall, Christ Church College, Oxford. Photo 159553767 © Nonglak Bunkoet/Dreamstime.

p.121 Illustration by John Tenniel, 'Through the Looking Glass, and what Alice found there', 1927. British Library, 1280.r.11.

p.122 Exeter College from the tower of St Mary's Church, Oxford. Photo: Chon Kit Leong/123RF.

p.124 Narnia window, Holy Trinity Church, Headington Quarry. Photo: Martin Anderson/Alamy Stock Photo.

p.125 Madresfield Court. Photo © Historic England/ Mary Evans Picture Library.

p.127 Cowper and his hare. Illustration by Richard Westall, *The Task*, 1817. British Library, 1467.b.35.

p.129 'The Pilgrim's Progress from this world, to that which is to come', 1679. British Library, C.70.aa.3.

P.131 George Bernard Shaw on the doorstep of his writing shed, Ayot St Lawrence, 1950. Photo: Mary Evans/SZ Photo/Sherl.

p.133 A view, in Indian ink, of Shakespeare's House at Stratford-upon-Avon, 1788. British Library, Maps K.Top.42.86.c.

p.134 Illustration by Hugh Thompson, *The Merry Wives of Windsor*, 1910. British Library, Tab.538.a.13.

LIST OF ILLUSTRATIONS

INDEX